Oxford Studies in European Law

Series Editors: Paul Craig and Gráinne de Búrca

JUSTICE IN THE EU

OXFORD STUDIES IN EUROPEAN LAW

Series Editors: Paul Craig, Professor of English Law at St John's College, Oxford and Gráinne de Búrca, Professor of Law at New York University School of Law

The aim of this series is to publish important and original research on EU law. The focus is on scholarly monographs, with a particular emphasis on those which are interdisciplinary in nature. Edited collections of essays will also be included where they are appropriate. The series is wide in scope and aims to cover studies of particular areas of substantive and of institutional law, historical works, theoretical studies, and analyses of current debates, as well as questions of perennial interest such as the relationship between national and EU law and the novel forms of governance emerging in and beyond Europe. The fact that many of the works are interdisciplinary will make the series of interest to all those concerned with the governance and operation of the EU.

OTHER TITLES IN THIS SERIES

The European Fundamental Freedoms
A Contextual Approach
Pedro Caro de Sousa

National Identity in EU Law
Elke Cloots

The Constitutional Foundations of European Contract Law
A Comparative Analysis
Kathleen Gutman

The Criminalization of European Cartel Enforcement
Theoretical, Legal, and Practical Challenges
Peter Whelan

Fundamental Rights in Europe
Challenges and Transformations in Comparative Perspective
Federico Fabbrini

The Principle of Loyalty in EU Law
Marcus Klamert

Constitutional Pluralism in the EU
Klemen Jaklic

EU Consumer Law and Human Rights
Iris Benöhr

The Principle of Mutual Recognition in EU Law
Christine Janssens

The Coherence of EU Free Movement Law
Constitutional Responsibility and the Court of Justice
Niamh Nic Shuibhne

European Law and New Health Technologies
Edited by Mark L. Flear, Anne-Maree Farrell, Tamara K. Hervey, and Thérèse Murphy

European Agencies
Law and Practices of Accountability
Madalina Busuioc

The Legal Effect of EU Agreements
Mario Mendez

The Foundations of European Union Competition Law
The Objective and Principles of Article 102
Renato Nazzini

The Emergence of EU Contract Law
Exploring Europeanization
Lucinda Miller

Participation in EU Rule-making
A Rights-Based Approach
Joana Mendes

Regulating Cartels in Europe
Second Edition
Christopher Harding, Julian Joshua

Religion and the Public Order of the European Union
Ronan McCrea

Justice in the EU

The Emergence of Transnational Solidarity

FLORIS DE WITTE
Assistant Professor, London School of Economics and Political Science

OXFORD
UNIVERSITY PRESS

OXFORD
UNIVERSITY PRESS

Great Clarendon Street, Oxford, OX2 6DP,
United Kingdom

Oxford University Press is a department of the University of Oxford.
It furthers the University's objective of excellence in research, scholarship,
and education by publishing worldwide. Oxford is a registered trade mark of
Oxford University Press in the UK and in certain other countries

First Edition Published in 2015

Published in the United States of America by Oxford University Press
198 Madison Avenue, New York, NY 10016, United States of America

British Library Cataloguing in Publication Data
Data available

Library of Congress Control Number: Data available

ISBN 978–0–19–872434–6

SERIES EDITORS' PREFACE

This book tackles the timely and difficult question of justice in the EU, and examines the extent to which the process of European integration has given rise to forms of transnational solidarity, and hence to justice claims, which have not been adequately institutionalized either at EU or at national level.

The core argument of the author is that new claims of justice have arisen in the EU context due to cross-border interactions and relationships between citizens, but that these relational claims of justice have not been able to be translated into transnational legal and social norms due to the lack of an adequately sophisticated EU political and democratic system for undertaking such translation. The author suggests that the EU already recognizes and articulates many of these 'associative connections', and that it embodies the related (mainly functional) justice claims in its laws, in particular in its free movement laws and its equal citizenship laws. However, he argues that it does so without sufficient nuance and that the Court of Justice similarly has not contextualized existing transnational commitments in its case law with sufficient explicitness or precision. At the same time, the national legal systems do not take into account these transnational associative connections or the justice claims arising from them, nor do they translate them into legal norms. Hence there is a problematic gap: the existence of actual relations of transnational solidarity in Europe coupled with the absence of any political forum capable of converting these relations and claims into legal norms, and capable ultimately of 'producing' justice.

The book provides a helpful conceptual analysis of the actually-existing forms of transnational solidarity in the EU to which the process of European integration has given rise. The author identifies three such forms, and the central thesis of the book is that the possibilities and limits of each of these forms of transnational solidarity needs to be better understood if the EU is to contribute to rather than to impede or obstruct the pursuit of justice. The first form is 'market solidarity', which he describes as stemming from economic relations and from the interaction of labour and capital on the European market; the second he calls 'communitarian solidarity', stemming from the degree of social integration of migrants within EU states; and the third he refers to as 'aspirational solidarity', which he suggests flows from the political commitment of states (enforced by the EU) not to prevent their citizens from pursuing their aspiration to a good life, including by taking advantage of the right to trans-border movement and the instruments they need to achieve this.

On the positive side, the author's argument is that the EU's tiered institutional and normative structure which takes account of both EU and national levels is better able to reflect (to 'exhaust', as he expresses it) the various requirements of justice, even though the EU-level political process cannot adequately mediate them all. He concludes ultimately that in view of the EU's lack of capacity to translate its existing relational forms of solidarity and the justice claims arising from them into effective legal norms, the national legal systems must adapt to reflect them in a fuller and more nuanced way, including by articulating the limits to transnational solidarity and its relationship to the national welfare state.

To conclude, Floris de Witte has written an extremely thoughtful, nuanced, and carefully argued work which will be of immense interest to all of those concerned with EU law and politics, and with the difficult and highly salient questions of solidarity and justice in and across Europe.

Gráinne de Búrca and Paul Craig

FOREWORD

Claims about injustices perpetrated by the European Union or to be rectified by it have become a central refrain about both the worth of the Union and what it should do in recent years. They lie at the heart of the agonizing surrounding its response to the sovereign debt crisis and the increasingly shrill arguments about the benefits and costs of migration of citizens within the Union. However, until recently, the relationship between EU law and justice was overlooked.[1]

This neglect is surprising. Some notion of justice must be present in EU law. It invites us to enter into relations with others. Any such relationship raises questions about what we owe both to each other and to those beyond the relationship. Historically, furthermore, redistributive questions can be traced back to the very beginning of the EU. The European Coal and Steel Community, after all, provided for price controls and wage floors to secure viable national coal and steel industries that treated their employees decently.

It is possible that this neglect emerged because, prior to the Lisbon Treaty, there was no explicit reference to justice in the Treaties. Even now, it is backgrounded. Article 2 TEU states that the Union is founded on a series of values of which justice is not one. These values are only present, however, in 'a society in which pluralism, non-discrimination, tolerance, justice, solidarity and equality between women and men prevail'. There is, thus, an ambiguous relationship. Justice is not one of the Union's founding values, but is central to the wider social environment that both gives rise to these values and allows them to be sustained.

How, then, is it possible to develop a theory of justice for EU law when EU law necessarily raises important questions of justice but does not address the question directly? Without acting too much as a spoiler for the work, I think Floris de Witte's monograph does this through a number of significant and original moves.

[1] Significant works, albeit with a very different take on this subject, are A. Williams, *The Ethos of Europe: Values, Law and Justice in the EU* (Cambridge: Cambridge University Press, 2010); J. Neyer, *The Justification of Europe: A Political Theory of Supranational Integration* (Oxford: Oxford University Press, 2012).

First, any theory must rely on a recognizable ethos of justice. Justice is a term of art that must be respected as such and cannot be reduced to an author's own sense of fairness. How is it possible to identify an ethos that both captures the claims asserted in EU law and serves as a suitable critique of these claims? The second move looks for the ethos that is most clearly immanent in EU law. European Union legal assumptions are made and reasoning developed that can be explained only through the prism of that ethos. The third move is to make sure that this ethos of justice is not too distorted by traditional assumptions born out of experience as to how justice operates within the nation state, as the latter might not be a good model for the EU. De Witte sees EU law's vision of justice as structured by its supranationality. Certain forms of justice can be replicated only through national structures, but these structures have limits that do not give sufficient expression to wider notions of justice. The supranational vision emerges from this paradox. Developing this, De Witte argues that if national systems are central to visioning justice as a collective good, EU law is concerned with locating the individual and the commitments owed to her within this settlement. The final move is to institutionalize this. Justice entails that commitments are owed to others when certain circumstances arise. These commitments are, furthermore, rarely owed to all others equally. A relationship must exist, based on solidarity, that gives rise to these commitments. De Witte identifies three forms of solidarity in EU law, based around ideas of the market place, community, and individual aspiration.

These moves provide the foundations for a work—and here I must declare my interest as one of the supervisors of the dissertation on which it is based—which reinterprets much EU law in subtle ways. I learned a lot about EU law reading it. It made me rethink many of my views on EU law. I found it, and continue to find it, unrelentingly provocative. Others, more dispassionate than I, will be better placed to assess its contribution. I hope you, the reader, enjoy it as much as I did.

Damian Chalmers
London
2015

ACKNOWLEDGEMENTS

With the support of good supervisors and good friends, writing a Ph.D. and then turning it into a book is not as difficult as it sounds. The former should be able to motivate; the latter distract and direct attention towards more important things than a stack of papers. I have had tremendous luck in having found both. The main fear that I had when starting this project—that I would spend years producing something that can be printed in ten minutes—was assuaged by all the other things that I did and learned in the meantime.

Many people have been important to me over the past years—for different reasons and at different times. I would first like to thank my Ph.D. supervisors. Damian Chalmers has done more than I could think possible in encouraging me to develop my ideas, in challenging me to push myself, and in teaching me to trust my instincts—both during the course of my dissertation and afterwards. His sense of perspective and unparalleled analytical skills have been a source of admiration and motivation, and my gratitude is immense. It is a pleasure and a privilege to be able to call him my colleague and friend these days. Many thanks also to Hugh Collins, whose challenge in our first supervision meeting, that he would not accept me trying to make sense out of nonsense, will probably guide me throughout my career. I am also very grateful to the staff at the LSE Law Department—both academic and administrative—for making it such a friendly and stimulating place to work. Finally, great thanks to Elinor Shields, Natasha Flemming, and the staff at OUP, whose professionalism and support helped me navigate the publishing process.

I wish to thank my friends for not caring about my book, for their affection, and for making my life richer and more interesting. I feel privileged to have such a fascinating group of friends. They have challenged and helped me in so many different ways to become who I am today. I simply hope that the next years of my life may be as happy as my previous years have been. So thank you Ali, Sam, Niko, Sarah, Luis, Marcel, Susanne, Pol, Bas, Will, Jules, Estelle, Hanno, Koen, Mike, Franck, Chris, Alex, Sacha, Jorrit, Moritz, Celinie, and JB. A final and massive thank you to my family: to Pauline, who has made writing this book, and everything else in my life, infinitely more fun and less important; to my *onnavolgbare* brother Marnix, who always makes me smile; and to my parents Veerle and Bruno, who gave me the world to play in.

F. de W.
London
December 2014

CONTENTS

TABLE OF CASES

Opinions of AG

LIST OF ABBREVIATIONS

AG	Advocate General
BverfG	*Bundesverfassungsgericht*
CFR	Charter of Fundamental Rights
CML Rev	Common Market Law Review
COM	Commission
CUP	Cambridge University Press
CYELS	Cambridge Yearbook of European Legal Studies
EC	European Community
ECB	European Central Bank
ECJ	European Court of Justice
ECR	European Court Reports
Ed/s.	Editor/s
EEC	European Economic Community
EJIL	European Journal of International Law
ELJ	European Law Journal
ELRev	European Law Review
EMU	Economic and Monetary Union
EP	European Parliament
ESM	European Stability Mechanism
EU	European Union
GLJ	German Law Journal
ICON	International Journal of Constitutional Law
ILJ	Industrial Law Journal
JCMS	Journal of Common Market Studies
JEPP	Journal of European Public Policy
LIEI	Legal Issues of Economic Integration
LEQS	LSE Europe in Question Paper Series
MJ	Maastricht Journal of European and Comparative Law
MLR	Modern Law Review
NLR	New Left Review
nyr	not yet reported
OJ	Official Journal of the European Union
OJLS	Oxford Journal of Legal Studies
OUP	Oxford University Press
PRD	Patients' Rights Directive
PWD	Posting of Workers Directive
TEU	Treaty on European Union
TFEU	Treaty on the Functioning of the European Union

Introduction

The question of justice is receiving more and more attention in the European Union. A ruling by the European Court of Justice in November 2014 in *Dano*, a case concerning access to minimum subsistence benefits for economically inactive EU migrants, made it to the front pages of *Le Monde*, *The Guardian*, *La Stampa*, and the *Frankfurter Allgemeine Zeitung* the following day.[1] In the discussion that ensued, the ruling was alternatively presented as 'saving the welfare state' by allowing Member States to exclude non-working EU migrants from accessing certain benefits, or as allowing for xenophobic and nationalistic narratives to be employed in limiting the emerging ideas of solidarity among the people of Europe.

European Union law generates these types of 'conflicts of justice' on a continuous basis throughout its territory. Properly understood, these conflicts suggest that the Member States and the EU have a very different idea of what justice is, means, and requires. This book has two objectives. First, it explains the differences between how Member States and the EU understand justice, in both institutional and normative terms. Second, it analyses to what extent these 'conflicts of justice' can be overcome by articulating forms of *transnational solidarity* that reflect the connections between citizens in the EU *across* borders.

Examples of the 'conflicts of justice' that EU law produces come in many different forms. A Hungarian doctor, for example, educated at the expense of the Hungarian taxpayer in order to ensure that the nation's citizens can access high-quality healthcare, moves to the UK to live with her Italian boyfriend, and finds employment there in the NHS. Does this create justice or injustice? Is it 'more' just that a Hungarian national is free to live and work

[1] Case C-333/13 *Dano* [nyr] ruling of 11 November 2014.

wherever she wants or 'less' just that Hungary cannot recoup the costs of training doctors, and UK doctors might be crowded out in access to a job? If the Hungarian national has a child with her Italian boyfriend, should she be eligible for childcare benefits in the UK, despite not being a national? And if so, is this on the basis of her residence or her employment? Should she still receive such benefits if she were to lose her job after two years? A Swedish pensioner, having worked his whole life in Sweden, decides to move to Spain to enjoy the sun and good food. After having lived in Spain for two years, he loses his eyesight. Should he be entitled to receive disability benefit from the Swedish state, where he paid taxes his whole life, or from Spain, where he now lives? And does Spain have to offer healthcare treatment to all resident pensioners—even if this imposes a disproportionate burden on their taxpayers and medical infrastructure? Does Greece have to refund its nationals if they go abroad to have open-heart surgery, on the basis that the domestic healthcare facilities are not adequate to guarantee high-quality treatment (courtesy of the troika)? Can an Estonian company build a school in Austria while paying its workers Estonian wages (thus protecting its competitive advantage) or should it pay Austrian minimum wages (thus protecting the Austrian *and* Estonian workers)? Can a French student who decides to study in Romania ask the Romanian state to offer student benefits, or should she direct that demand to the French state? Can a jobless German national who has lived in Poland for three years demand access to Polish minimum allowance provision, meant to allow citizens to live their life with a basic level of dignity, or should he be left to fend for himself?

It is very likely that the reader has an intuitive sense of how to answer these questions. It is also very likely that different readers come up with different answers. This is, simply put, the problem with justice: each person adheres to a different conception of what it is. In discussing the development of justice in the EU, moreover, we face an additional problem. While the Member States have come up with solid institutional mechanisms to mediate how different citizens think about justice, and are thereby able to articulate a *collective* idea of justice, the EU has not. The EU does not dispose a sufficiently sophisticated democratic structure that can settle the above 'conflicts of justice' in a legitimate manner and that can articulate an autonomous, supranational, and communal idea of justice. This book, instead, suggests an alternative way of settling the 'conflicts of justice' that emerge in the EU. It suggests that EU law implicitly articulates diverse types of *transnational solidarity*, which help us to make sense of these 'conflicts of justice' by telling us *why* we owe certain specific commitments of justice to individuals *beyond* our own political community. At the same time, these different forms of transnational solidarity tell us something about the 'idea' of justice that is emerging in the EU.

The Paradox of Justice

The development of the 'idea' of justice in modern societies is premised on a paradox. On the one hand, the claims made in the name of justice are necessarily universal. Something that is 'good' or 'bad', 'right' or 'wrong', 'appropriate' or 'inappropriate' is not logically confined to a particular spatial context. On the other hand, the institutions required to actually 'do' justice, in the form of democratic, administrative, or redistributive institutions, are tied to a particular territorial structure: the nation state. In other words, national institutions are indispensable in the attainment of justice, but can never fully realize the potential of justice. This paradox has led many commentators to argue that there is no space for a cosmopolitan or distinctly European 'idea' of justice as a result of the lack of sophisticated political communities and democratic institutions that transcend the nation state.[2] In fact, the question of justice is hardly ever explicitly discussed in the EU or in its law.[3] Of course, the integration project's original intentions of establishing lasting peace and generating economic prosperity on a shattered continent were not unrelated to ideas of justice and the 'good life', but the integration process was never meant to engage in what justice is, means, and requires. Those tasks were left to the Member States, where redistributive criteria are elaborated and legitimized through robust democratic institutions and public spheres.

At the same time, it has increasingly become clear in recent years that the EU, as a transnational institutional structure that situates itself between

[2] See e.g. T. Nagel, 'The Problem of Global Justice' (2005) 33 Philosophy and Public Affairs 113; A. Sangiovanni, 'Justice and the Priority of Politics to Morality' (2008) 16 Journal of Political Philosophy 137ff., and 'Global Justice, Reciprocity and the State' (2007) 35 Philosophy and Public Affairs 2–39. See, for the opposite view, J. Cohen and C. Sabel, 'Global Democracy?' (2005) 37 NYU Journal of International Law and Politics 763ff.

[3] Notable exceptions include A. Williams, *The Ethos of Europe* (Cambridge: CUP, 2010), whose understanding of justice does not go much beyond a commitment to liberal-democratic values, and A. Somek, *Engineering Equality* (Oxford: OUP, 2011), whose account is much more sophisticated but limited to the Union's non-discrimination agenda.

the nation state and the global level, almost inevitably engages in the redistribution of resources, and that its norms (and to a lesser extent its institutions) intuitively conform to some kind of ill-defined and *transnational* idea of justice. This expansion of ideas of justice beyond the structures of the nation state poses formidable problems, in both institutional and normative terms. While it opens our eyes to the associative ties between citizens across borders—be it in economic, social, or political terms—and suggests that these ties might be as valuable as the ties of nationality as a motive for sharing resources between individuals, it also clearly highlights that the institutions that can dependably produce justice have remained on the national level. The challenge, then, is to understand how national institutions can produce a type of justice that takes account of the relationships between citizens across borders.

This book argues that EU law can indeed serve as an instrument for the extension of the values of justice beyond the nation state. While the nation state 'does' justice, it does not, after all, fully exhaust what justice requires. The EU's tiered institutional settlement offers a novel and fascinating way of extending the values of social justice beyond the nation state. It does so by standing on the shoulders of the national welfare state construction, and adding a transnational dimension to its values. Such a tiered understanding of the idea of justice in Europe, however, raises three issues: (1) it challenges us to think beyond the contractarian reflex that equates justice with political self-determination of a *demos*; (2) it demands that we create a tiered institutional and normative model, involving both the nation state and the EU, that can make sense of the new ties between individual citizens that the process of European integration, and in particular its norms of free movement, continue to generate; and (3) it requires that we construct novel concepts of transnational solidarity that help us understand what those new ties—which may come in economic, social, or political forms—tell us about our transnational obligations of justice. This book attempts to address all three.

The Place of Justice

The first chapter focuses on how to think about social justice beyond the nation state. It suggests that justice requires us, primarily, to make sense of the very different conceptions of 'the good' that different participants in society adhere to. Some citizens might think that the 'good life' entails access to shelter and food; others that it entails being able to live a life without outside interference; others yet that it entails helping fellow citizens aspire to be whatever they want in life. The mediation between these different views, and the generation of collective ideas of 'the good' that can be enforced through the administrative machinery of the state, however, presupposes significant and long-term processes of social structuring. For justice to be 'produced', we need a sophisticated political system that is able to collect different voices, mediate between them, and legitimize a specific collective understanding of justice. This, in turn, requires closure of the boundaries of the polity, the creation of a strong centre, political loyalties, and cleavages in society that articulate distinct and competing conceptions of justice.

At the same time, the production of norms of justice entails the existence of a *motive* for individual citizens to share their resources with fellow citizens. Without such a redistributive commitment, usually referred to as 'solidarity', all ambitious conceptions of justice would collapse. Typically, solidarity is thought of as being inextricably linked to the nation state: the motive for sharing our resources with fellow citizens is that we are all Irish, or Spanish. The ethno-cultural similarities between citizens, built through history, language, and culture, and solidified by the creation of communities of fate and the nation state with its 'fiction of eternity', mean, in other words, that solidarity is primarily based on kinship. The motive for sharing our resources with one particular group of people is that they are 'like us'. Nationality or national citizenship, in turn, are shorthands for the definition of the citizens that fall within this category. It is unsurprising, then, that most academics, politicians, and citizens share the intuition that justice 'belongs' on the national level.

Some commentators have taken a more nuanced view of the interaction between the nation state and the development of justice, and have emphasized that it is the *state* (with its institutional connotations) rather than the *nation* (with its ethnic connotations) that is crucial in the development of justice. Simply put, this argument suggests that justice and solidarity follow not from certain ethno-cultural similarities, but from the specific associations or relationships between citizens. The *political* association between citizens to a polity, in other words, constitutes in itself a *motive* for sharing resources between the members of that group. As Thomas Nagel has put it:

> Sovereign states are not merely instruments for realising the pre-institutional value of justice among human beings. Instead, their existence is precisely what gives the value of justice its application, by putting the fellow citizens of a sovereign state

into a relation that they do not have with the rest of humanity, an institutional relation which must then be evaluated by the special standards of fairness and equality that fill out the content of justice.[4]

Properly understood, then, it is the associative connection between citizens that generates commitments of solidarity and sustains the production of norms of social justice. Perhaps the political association between citizens within the nation state is the most structured configuration in which justice and solidarity may occur. At the same time, understanding justice as a *relational commitment* between citizens that stand in a particular relationship with each other opens our eyes to new sites for the emergence of solidarity and the articulation of norms of justice.[5] More specifically, it suggests that the emergence of new types of association between citizens across borders—be it in economic, social, or political forms—come with claims of justice and solidarity of their own.

The emergence of these new associative connections between citizens across borders exposes a significant problem for the development of justice in the EU. The Union is unable to create a sufficiently sophisticated institutional framework that can legitimately 'translate' the new cross-border associative connections between citizens in Europe into specific norms of justice. At the same time, the only institutions that are sophisticated enough to undertake this exercise can be found on the national level, and are structurally insensitive to relational commitments (in economic, social, or political forms) across borders. The pursuit of justice in the EU thus has to contend with a fundamental asymmetry between the institutional mechanism that produces and stabilizes norms of justice (that has remained on the national level) and the nature of the relationships between citizens that give rise to claims of justice (which increasingly take place *across* borders).

Tiered Justice in the EU

The Union's incapacity to create an institutional structure that can translate the commitments between its citizens (in economic, social, or political

[4] Nagel, 'The Problem of Global Justice', 120.

[5] P. Rosanvallon, *The Society of Equals* (Cambridge, Mass.: Harvard University Press, 2013).

forms) into norms of justice does not, however, mean that the Union is agnostic when it comes to justice. The second chapter argues that the central norms of EU law—the free movement provisions—can be seen to articulate two very precise claims of justice. These claims attempt to overcome the normative problems created by the development of norms of justice through *national* institutions.

First, EU law suggests that national political communities are not very good at incorporating each citizen's idea of 'the good' in the collective structuring of society. To be precise, while every citizen has the periodic possibility of voting, in return that citizen is forced to adhere to a collective conception of 'the good' that may have little to do with his or her own needs, wishes, or desires. European Union law, and in particular the right to free movement, cut across this limitation to the individual's capacity to pursue his or her own conception of the 'good life'. The right to free movement allows all European citizens to move across borders and in doing so emancipates them from the constraints imposed by their own Member State—in both normative and practical terms. Citizens may choose to move to another Member State for reasons of love, for work, in order to understand a language, skill, culture, or cuisine; for reasons of tax legislation, the range of civic or social permissiveness, education, the weather, or simply the adventure. The first claim of justice that is implicit in EU law, then, is that the development of justice through national institutions is not sufficiently sensitive to the individual's preferences as to what constitutes a 'good life'.

The second justice claim that is implicit in EU law addresses equal citizenship. Free movement across borders in the EU upsets the internal dynamic within nation states: only nationals are allowed to vote in general elections, even if the outcome of such elections has consequences for the lives of non-national residents. The very criterion that creates 'justice' *within* the Member States—political deliberation between insiders—thus automatically excludes all non-nationals. The normative problem created by this mismatch can be explained in different ways. On the one hand, it violates the basic procedural condition of liberal democracy that equates objects and subjects of rule, in so far as it 'taxes' non-nationals without them being represented. On the other hand, it makes the domestic political system structurally insensitive to the life experiences of non-nationals, as well as to the associative connections *between* non-nationals and nationals. If justice is, after all, an associative obligation, physical co-presence of nationals and non-nationals in the territory of a Member State, or their economic interdependence in the market of that state, suggests that resident non-nationals should obtain certain rights in the host state. In other words, the associative connection between a resident non-national and fellow residents in his or her host state engenders specific obligations of justice that the national political process is unable to take into account. European Union law attempts to prevent this, and uses quite a blunt instrument to ensure that commitments internal to the nation state are extended to cover resident migrants: the prohibition of discrimination based on nationality. As soon as the mobile EU citizen finds him- or herself in the host state, he or she must be treated in the same manner as a national.

This brave attempt by EU law to ensure that the institutional system on the national level is sensitive to the associative connections between citizens *across* borders comes, of course, with problems of its own. To put it as simply as possible, while EU law is very sensitive to such associative connections, it is not sensitive to their *specific* nature and strength. The principle of non-discrimination presumes that a Spanish national who has worked in Hamburg for 20 years is in the same position as an unemployed Finnish citizen who has only just arrived in Ljubljana. Clearly, they do not stand in the same associative connection with nationals in their host state, and they cannot, in consequence, make similar claims on the basis of solidarity or justice. Simply extending, say, unemployment benefits to all EU citizens who reside in the territory of a host state means that EU law is insensitive to the *internal* commitments of justice between citizens on the national level. This possible blind spot of EU law—in so far as it is both disruptive of and parasitic upon the existence of domestic welfare entitlements—has led to claims that EU law destabilizes the workings of the welfare state. European Union law, in this argument, allows for welfare tourism, whereby migrants can extract resources from the communal pot without being forced to put anything in.[6] This argument is particularly resilient in British politics, where all mainstream parties are committed to limiting the right of mobile EU citizens to make use of UK welfare entitlements, even if empirical research suggests that the narrative of the 'welfare tourist' is a myth.[7]

[6] 'Editorial Comment: The Free Movement of Persons in the European Union: Salvaging the Dream while Explaining the Nightmare' (2014) 51 CML Rev. 729; and the pamphlet by D. Chalmers and S. Booth, 'A European Labour Market with National Welfare Systems: A Proposal for a New Citizenship and Integration Directive' (2014) Open Europe Policy Brief.

[7] At least in the institutional sense: EU migrants contribute more to the public purse than they take out. See C. Dustmann and T. Frattini, 'The Fiscal Effects of Immigration to the UK' (2014) 124 Economic Journal 563.

What these narratives suggest, at the same time, is that EU law needs to be sensitive to the stability of domestic welfare regimes. The Spanish national who has worked in Hamburg for 20 years needs to be treated differently from the jobless Finnish citizen who has only just arrived in Ljubljana. Each stands in a different associative connection to (the citizens of) his or her host state, and—given that justice is a relational or associative commitment—each should be incorporated in domestic welfare structures in a different manner. Differences such as length of residence in the host state, or economic activity in that state, may suggest that the Spanish national should more readily have access to social benefits in Hamburg (if necessary) than the Finnish national should in Ljubljana. In other words, in order not to destabilize domestic redistributive commitments, EU law must pay close attention to the specific commitments that link individuals to different polities—which might come in economic, social, or political forms.

The Court indeed increasingly incorporates such nuances in its case law when settling 'conflicts of justice'. In *Prinz and Seeberger*, for example, the Court had to decide when exactly a student can be considered as sufficiently integrated in a state to 'deserve' access to student benefits: 'That may be the case where the student is a national of the State concerned and was educated there for a significant period or on account of other factors such as, in particular, his family, employment, language skills or the existence of other social and economic factors.'[8]

The role of EU law, then, is to articulate not only which associative connections *across* borders have emerged since the start of the integration project (these come—as will be argued further—in economic, social, or political forms) but also which exact commitments of solidarity follow from such connections. The determination of the types of solidarity that are implicit in the EU, in other words, at once makes the Member States sensitive to the obligations of justice that have emerged by way of relationships between citizens across borders *and* rationalizes the limits of free movement and non-discrimination so as not to impose an unreasonable burden on the national welfare state. For EU law to be able to contribute to the pursuit of justice rather than obstruct it, then, we need carefully to articulate the different types of transnational solidarity that have emerged in the course of the process of integration as well as their limits.

[8] Joined Cases C-523/11 and C-585/11 *Prinz and Seeberger* EU:C:2013:524.

Three Worlds of Transnational Solidarity

The bulk of this book discusses the three different types of transnational solidarity that can be traced in the EU. It does not try to suggest that the EU institutions and the Court should decide to conform to them. Rather, it suggests that the EU institutions and the Court are *already* conforming to the norms of transnational solidarity (albeit in an implicit, incomplete, and incoherent manner). The objective of Chapters 3 to 5 is to rationalize and explain the emergence of transnational solidarity, and to problematize it by revealing its ambiguities and limits.

The process of European integration has generated three types of associative relationship between citizens across borders. The first involves the economic relationship between citizens on the internal market, the second the social relationship between residents in the same Member State (be it nationals or non-nationals), and the third the political relationship between all EU citizens by virtue of their (Member State's) participation in the integration project. Each of these new types of relationship constitutes a potential motive for citizens to share resources with each other; that is, each makes a distinct claim on the basis of solidarity. Each relationship, however, contains a distinct and specific claim of solidarity, with distinct and specific limits: the position of a Spanish national who has worked in Hamburg for 20 years is, after all, different from the position of a Finnish national who has only just arrived in Ljubljana.

The first transnational solidarity that will be traced throughout EU law reflects the relationships produced by interactions on the transnational internal market. This 'market solidarity' tells us something about the way in which transnational economic interactions—ranging from the right for workers to work in another Member State to the way in which the collectivities of 'labour' and 'capital' interact on the internal market—reshape our commitments of justice. It suggests that the economic relationship between actors alone (rather than their nationality, or the political and social links between them) constitutes a motive for sharing resources. It is reminiscent of Durkheim's concept of organic solidarity,[9] and argues that the mutually advantageous division of labour in a market engenders rights and obligations of solidarity. Market solidarity,

[9] E. Durkheim, *The Division of Labour in Society* (Basingstoke: Palgrave, 1984) 68–86.

then, serves to integrate the associative connections that emerge through economic interactions on the internal market within the domestic structures of the welfare state.

The second form of solidarity that can be traced throughout EU law can best be understood as 'communitarian solidarity'. It reflects the commitments of justice that have emerged by virtue of the social, quotidian, interaction between citizens across borders. On this view, residence alone—and the daily social interactions that are implicit in co-presence in a certain place—engenders a certain degree of solidarity that extends to all residents, whether national or non-national. The motive for sharing resources with resident migrants, in other words, is their social integration in the functioning of the host state society. The extent to which residence alone can justify access to welfare entitlements in the host state depends on both the depth and nature of the migrant's integration in the host state society, as well as the type of welfare benefit to which access is sought. In very simple terms: the Finnish national who lived in Ljubljana for four months without working may not have access to Slovenian student benefits, but he or she may be entitled to free emergency healthcare when hit by a car, simply by virtue of his or her residence. What communitarian solidarity demands, then, is not unconditional access for all residents to all welfare goods in the host state, but access that differs depending on the nature and function of a certain welfare good. Communitarian solidarity in the EU, in other words, is a normatively shallow but procedurally strong idea of membership, which serves to open up national systems of social sharing to *all* citizens (whether national or non-national) that demonstrate a social connection of a specific type to the host state's society.

Polities grant their citizens specific rights not only on the basis of their role as an economic or societal actor, but also in accordance with the polity's specific *political* aspirations. In the EU that specific aspiration has always been to check the coercive capacity of the state in limiting available realizations of the 'good life'. The third type of transnational solidarity follows from this political commitment and can best be understood as an instance of 'aspirational solidarity'. It suggests that Member States cannot in principle prevent their citizens from accessing the instruments that make up a 'good life'—such as the labour market, public goods, or welfare benefits. There is a dark side to aspirational solidarity, however, as it has the potential to pit individuals in society against each other. Aspirational solidarity therefore finds a limit when the aspirations of *individual* citizens risk undermining the capacity of *all* citizens to access welfare benefits. As will become clear by way of an in-depth analysis of the case law of the Court of Justice, aspirational solidarity can be traced in diverse areas of EU law—ranging from non-discrimination based on age to the right to export welfare benefits.

The precise elaboration of the nature and limits of each of these three different types of transnational solidarity serves both to reflect the new associations between citizens that have emerged in the course of the integration project, and to rationalize the extent to which national institutions, in their elaboration of norms of justice, need to take account of those new associations. Read together, the three types of transnational solidarity suggest that the EU *can* contribute in a meaningful sense to the pursuit of justice in Europe.

Conclusion

The EU has changed what justice is, means, and requires. European Union law, in turn, can be understood as a mechanism for the articulation of the ties that bind European citizens across borders, in economic, social, or political terms. As such, this book suggests that the European Union is an invaluable companion for the Member States in the pursuit of justice in three ways. First, EU law enhances the capacity of European citizens to move throughout the territory of the EU in search of their own version of the 'good life', whatever that may mean to the individual. As such, EU law resists the capacity of the nation state to oppress the individual by 'locking' him or her into very specific collective understandings of what such a 'good life' entails. Second, EU law offers an account of the associative commitments between citizens across borders in a way that the nation state cannot. If justice is indeed, as defended in this book, a *relational* commitment, engendered by the particular relationship between individual citizens, than we can no longer consider only the relationships that exist within the nation state relevant for the determination of what is 'just'. Indeed, the process of European integration has engendered different types of *transnational* relationships—in economic, social, and political terms—that need to be reflected in how we think about justice. Third, EU law offers an account of the way in which these emerging forms of transnational solidarity relate to national conceptions of justice. As such, it tells us something about the *limits* of transnational solidarity. Given that the development of justice in the EU is still to a large extent dependent on the institutions of the nation state, the articulation of the limits to transnational solidarity is vital to stabilize the welfare state and to legitimize the Union's involvement in its reorientation.

1

The Place of Justice

This chapter focuses on how to think about social justice beyond the nation state. At the highest level of abstraction, it seems that a commitment to social justice must take account both of the vastly different conceptions of the 'good life' that different citizens in society have, and their actual capacity to live such a life. In other words, both entitlements that help citizens to live autonomous and dignified lives, even in the face of adversity (such as healthcare resources or unemployment benefits), and the citizens' capacity to choose between different possible priorities in how to structure their lives are crucial components of the pursuit of justice. The production of the preconditions for the availability of both entitlements and choices, however, are dependent on significant and long-term processes of social structuring, which comprise both institutional elements—democracy, citizenship, mediation of differentiated interests—and symbolic or cultural elements, such as the creation of a 'community of fate' and the solidarity that allows for social integration, the crystallization of cleavages, and solidification of citizen loyalty to the normative project of the polity (section 1.1).

It is exactly this link between the pursuit of social justice and the processes of social and political structuring that has led many scholars to doubt the possibility of attaining social justice beyond the nation state. Properly understood, this critique does not necessarily challenge the universal nature of the claims of justice, but rather suggests that lifting the 'social question' outside the realm of the nation state, with its edified social structures, will destabilize any commitment to secure the entitlements and meaningful choices that are central in the *actual* pursuit of social justice. At the same time, it seems that the progressive dissolution of boundaries—in economic, cultural, and social terms—by way of processes of globalization and European integration, in particular in the aftermath of the euro-crisis, is in fact decreasing the nation state's capacity to answer the 'social question'. The economic processes to which the social question attaches, and the political–administrative processes that answer that question, are increasingly separated. While the social structures required to understand what citizens consider 'a good life', and the administrative structures required to implement any such conception have remained on the national level, the processes that influence the entitlements and life's choices of the individual have not. Scholars have long identified this gradual process of dissolution of the social question, and while some have warned of the instability and potential for rupture that such a system produces, others have heralded the dissolution of the social question as a way to prevent large-scale redistribution (which is seen as artificially skewing the market). It is uncontested, however, that globalization and European integration have changed the type of justice that institutions can deliver (section 1.2).

Other scholars see this development—while acknowledging the problems attributed to the dissolution of the social question—in a slightly more positive light. For them the gradual loosening of the nation state's grip on the life choices and entitlements that citizens can access is the first step towards a new, cosmopolitan type of society. The preoccupation here—which can be traced from the Stoics to contemporary scholars—is that state boundaries are morally arbitrary at best, and often produce significant processes of internal exclusion and external violence. In its most ambitious form, the cosmopolitan agenda is even seen as being able to reappropriate the social question by devising of political mechanisms that operate at the same spatial level as economic processes. The most sophisticated cosmopolitan thinkers, however, appreciate that the processes of social structuring that are required for the recreation of thick political structures on the European level (let alone the global level) are difficult to set in motion, and come with problems of their own. Instead, such scholars understand cosmopolitanism as a mechanism that operates in concert, rather than in competition, with the nation state. On this view, the promise of cosmopolitanism is about the reassessment, within the nation state, of categories of 'included' and 'excluded' citizens in the light of the new dynamics beyond the state, as well as the internal appropriation of cosmopolitan values. But how is it possible to realize—spatially, normatively, and institutionally—a structure whereby national institutions produce cosmopolitan norms of justice? This book focuses specifically on the conceptualization of a new mode of social integration that might serve to realize this 'new' type of justice. While the cosmopolitan tradition suggests that reliance on the simple concept of nationality is morally indefensible, as it does not take account of the relationships between citizens across borders, the importance of social structuring for the delivery of justice suggests that an individual's status as a human being alone does not suffice to give access to welfare benefits either—as it undermines the reproduction of the structures of social ordering upon which the welfare state depends. Rather, as will be discussed, solidarity, which constitutes a motive to share with others with whom one stands in a particular relationship, is based on relational dynamics. In other words, if we want to reintegrate cosmopolitan dynamics within the structures of the nation state in the pursuit of social justice, the concept of reciprocity, whether understood in economic, social, or political terms, might prove a good starting point, as it can conceptually accommodate relationships across borders while remaining sensitive to the preconditions for the reproduction of the welfare structures (section 1.3).

1.1 Justice on the National Level

That both welfare entitlements and the individuals' capacity of (private) choice are central to our understanding of justice is hardly a shocking statement. Indeed, both communitarians and liberals would subscribe to this view, even if their understanding of the relationship between entitlements and free choice, their relative importance, and the role of the state in their provision greatly differs. What Sen's view—espoused most explicitly in his book *The Idea of Justice*—adds to this discussion is the nuance that both elements are not mutually exclusive and indeed derive much of their moral appeal from a very similar conceptual starting point. Freedom, on this view, is both an object and a process that aids individuals—constituted both as independent actors and as acting in concert within society—in pursuing their understanding of the 'good life' (section 1.1.1). Every political project has to grapple with this problem, which is also central to the determination of justice: the irreducible plurality of conceptions of 'the good' that citizens adhere to. The traditional mechanism to mediate between different visions of 'the good', to placate tensions between them, legitimize one particular vision, and coerce conformity with that vision is the political system. On this view, the elaboration of what justice means requires not just elections and different political parties, but also significant and long-term processes of social and political structuring, which include boundary setting, centre formation, and sophisticated mechanisms for communication, cleavage management, and administration (section 1.1.2). The connection between the pursuit of justice and political structures means that the pursuit of justice has historically been tied to the spatial context of the nation state. It is unclear, however, to what extent the nation state itself plays an indispensable role in the elaboration of justice. For some scholars the contours of the nation state—with its 'community of fate' that reduces systemic complexity, its mode of social integration through shared values, and its ethno-historical connotations—are indispensable in providing the solidarity that is required to sustain the redistributive processes that are central to the welfare state. Other scholars, however, see the link between the nation state and justice as historically contingent, and highlight that the moral resources required for redistributive programmes can be secured by practices of democratic engagement. In other words, it is not the shared language, ethnicity, or nationality that sustains redistributive practices, but rather a shared political destiny and shared institutional system. The way in which we appreciate this difference will, of course, to a large extent inform the question if, and under what conditions, the pursuit of justice can be undertaken beyond the nation state (section 1.1.3).

1.1.1 *Justice and the Pursuit of the 'Good Life'*

The idea that the structure of society should contribute to 'justice' is premised on the basic preconception that society is an artefact made *by* its citizens, and thus also serves as an instrument *for* the realization of the citizen's values and ideals.[1] After all, by accepting that the citizen is the focal point of societal construction, '[t]he question of human suffering and human aspirations'[2] automatically becomes central to all such attempts.[3] In conceptualizing

[1] See M. Halberstam, *Totalitarianism and the Modern Conception of Politics* (New Haven, Conn.: Yale University Press, 1999) 16. Whether society is perceived as 'the all-encompassing social system that orders all possible communication between human beings' (N. Luhmann, *Political Theory in the Welfare State* (Berlin: de Gruyter, 1990) 30) or as 'the subjective expressions of requirements for social integration' (A. Honneth, 'Redistribution as Recognition: A Response to Nancy Fraser', in N. Fraser and A. Honneth, *Redistribution or Rec ognition: A Politico-Philosophical Exchange* (London: Verso, 2003) 174) the underlying theme is the same: society is mouldable around the ideals and values of its subjects, and does not serve a divine or 'natural' external objective.

[2] Halberstam, *Totalitarianism and the Modern Conception of Politics*, 17.

[3] Consider e.g. the radically different notions of *ubuntu* in African ethics and of 'autonomy' in liberal Western political thought, which nevertheless both emphasize that societal construction must centre on citizen well-being. See e.g. A. Shutte, 'Politics and the Ethics of *Ubuntu*', in M. F. Murove (ed.), *African Ethics: An Anthology of Comparative and Applied Ethics* (Scottsville: Kwazulu-Natal Press, 2009); T. H. Green, *The Political Theory of T. H. Green: Selected Writings*, ed. J. Rodman (New York: Appleton, 1964) 138–41.

justice in modern society, however, we run up against a basic and seemingly intractable problem, the interpretation of which has sparked different schools of thought in political theory and moral philosophy: every citizen has other needs, desires and aspirations. How to reduce this seemingly incredible plurality of ideas of 'the good' into clear norms of justice that guide, structure, inform and constrain society? The answers that theorists give to this question differ primarily in their starting point. Liberal theories start from the need to protect the individual's capacity to live life in a way that he or she prefers; while communitarian theories presume the capacity of the community to constrain individual choices with reference to the common good of the community to which the individual belongs. From this basic assumption follow insights into the appropriate role of the state, the suitable criterion for redistributive justice within a polity, and the definition of a core of rights that are insulated from encroachment by either market forces or public policy (depending on which theory is followed).[4] Despite these vast differences, however, it is evident that liberals and communitarians—as well as Marxists, republicans, and cosmopolitans—appreciate that both collective entitlements and the individual's freedom to prioritize life's choices are of importance in the pursuit of justice. What they disagree on, simply put, is the appropriate balance between these two approaches.

The work of Amartya Sen offers a sophisticated way of thinking beyond this seemingly intractable opposition between prioritizing the individual or the collectivity in the pursuit of justice.[5] Sen accepts that the pursuit of justice must accommodate the unimaginably and incommensurably different priorities and desires that citizens may have.[6] Each citizen has a different idea of the 'good life', and by placing this diversity at the centre of the way in which society ought to be structured, Sen automatically focuses attention on

[4] See, on the main theories, S. Mulhall and A. Swift, *Liberals and Communitarians* (Oxford: Blackwell, 2007) and F. Lovett and P. Pettit, 'Neorepublicanism, a Normative and Institutional Research Program' (2009) 12 Annual Review of Political Science 11. See, for other conceptualizations of these fault lines, I. Berlin, 'Two Concepts of Liberty', in H. Hardy (ed.), *Isaiah Berlin: Incorporating Four Essays on Liberty* (Oxford: OUP, 2002); R. Bellamy, 'The Liberty of the Post-Moderns: Market and Civic Freedom within the EU' (2009) LEQS No. 1.

[5] See also P. Rosanvallon, *The Society of Equals* (Cambridge, Mass.: Harvard University Press, 2013) 257.

[6] See, on irreducible plurality, T. Nagel, 'What is it Like to be a Bat?' (1974) 83 Philosophical Review 441–3, where he argues that we cannot possibly understand what other people value. See also A. Sen, 'Plural Utility' (1981) 81 Proceedings of the Aristotelian Society 193–215, where he shows that even the singular conception 'utility' is composed of many strands which are ordered in accordance with individual preferences.

the way in which society can help individual citizens to construe their own 'basket of happiness':

The various attainments in human functioning that we may value are very diverse, varying from being well nourished or avoiding premature mortality to taking part in the life of the community and developing the skill to pursue one's work-related plans and ambitions. The capability that we are concerned with is our ability to achieve various combinations of functionings that we can compare and judge against each other in terms of what we have reason to value.[7]

Crucially, Sen translates the individual notion of the 'good life' into a more structured and communal understanding of social justice. He uses the concept of freedom to make this connection. Freedom, on this view, is both an object and a process that aids individuals—constituted both as independent actors and as acting in concert within society—in pursuing their understanding of 'the good life'. In Sen's argument, a commitment to the 'good life' requires both the provision of the substantive entitlements for the individual (such as being well nourished) and the absence of outside interference in allowing citizens to lead their lives in accordance to their own perception of the 'good':

Freedom is valuable for at least two distinct reasons. First, more freedom gives us more opportunity to achieve those things that we value, and have reason to value. This aspect of freedom is concerned primarily with our ability to achieve, rather than with the process through which that achievement comes about. Second, the process through which things happen may also be of importance in assessing freedom. For example, it may be thought, reasonably enough, that the procedure of free decision by the person himself (no matter how successful the person is in getting what he would like to achieve) is an important requirement of freedom. There is, thus, an important distinction between the 'opportunity aspect' and the 'process aspect' of freedom.[8]

Both the emphasis on the insulation of the individual's capacity to choose how to live his or her life from the constraints imposed in the name of public policy (as central in liberal theories of justice) and the emphasis on redistributive criteria in order to achieve justice (as central in communitarian theories) are, in other words, conceptually linked. The moral intuitions that underlie both theories stem from different understandings of the same concept: freedom. Their mutual exclusivity, then, does not follow from a

[7] A. Sen, *The Idea of Justice* (Cambridge, Mass.: Harvard University Press, 2009) 233.

[8] A. Sen, *Rationality and Freedom* (Cambridge, Mass.: Harvard University Press, 2002) 585.

fundamentally contradictory account of what justice is, means, and requires, but simply from the fact that both cannot be implemented at the same time.

What Sen argues is, to put it as simply as possible, that welfare entitlements are indispensable in order to allow citizens to be free. Mere absence of obstruction—in the sense that I am *free* to jump from London to Amsterdam—is not a useful understanding of freedom. Freedom, rather, must be sensitive to our respective ability to achieve certain objectives. In this sense, a commitment to freedom can—perhaps counterintuitively—justify significant redistributive processes. To use the most obvious example, the availability of a valuable range of core entitlements, such as adequate housing, food, water, primary education, or emergency healthcare, can be seen as liberating individuals, *regardless* of personal normative values, from the chains of mere survival, and allow a more efficient pursuit of individual preferences as to how actually to live a 'good life', whatever this may entail:[9] 'some capabilities may be so basic to human welfare that they can be identified without any prior knowledge of the particular commitments that are held and expressed by an individual or group'.[10]

At the same time, Sen, in his thinking of the connection between freedom and justice, also makes us sensitive to the need to make available to citizens different possible realizations of the 'good life', and the need to respect the process through which individuals rank the available alternatives in terms of their relevance for their own personal understanding of the 'good life'. Sen reminds us that there is something inherently 'just' in generating the presuppositions for the individual to freely determine how (and where) to live his or her life.[11] Again, this tells us that the role of institutions is to facilitate the plurality of conceptions of 'the good' as well as their actual realization. In other words, justice is something that transcends and encapsulates institutions, rather than the other way around.[12] As we will see in the following sections, this insight is as much a theoretical nuance to the discussion of the term 'justice' as a claim for a different understanding of the role of the political process in its realization.

[9] See A. Sen, *The Idea of Justice* (Basingstoke: Penguin, 2010) esp. chs. 11–14 and 228–30; and Green, *The Political Theory of T. H. Green*, 138–41 and 111–16.

[10] S. Alkire, *Valuing Freedoms: Sen's Capability Approach and Poverty Reduction* (Oxford: OUP, 2002) 154.

[11] Sen, *The Idea of Justice*, 229.

[12] Rosanvallon, *The Society of Equals*, 273–4.

1.1.2 *Politics and the Pursuit of the 'Good Life'*

Both the availability of positive welfare entitlements, and the availability of a range of choices between alternative ways of living are thus crucial to our understanding of justice, in the sense that both accommodate the irreducible plurality of conceptions of 'the good' that a differentiated modern society produces. In one important way, however, this conceptualization is incomplete. How should we deal with the claims of justice that citizens make *against* other citizens or the state? How does a polity deal with the situation wherein a number of citizens thinks that the 'good life' consists of being able to fly to the moon, while another section of the population thinks that the 'good life' entails being able to fly to Mars? In principle, a guarantee that all citizens will be allowed, free of cost, to fly to the moon once in their lifetime may very well be undertaken by a polity. Such an entitlement, however, cannot but find its justification in the normative preferences of the people that compose a polity. A project entitling all citizens a journey to the moon is funded through the public treasury (that is, the citizens) and implies a limitation of other alternatives ('the state will *not* pay for my trip to Mars, or for me sitting in the pub, or living a year in Mozambique, instead'). Such financial participation and normative limitations are only legitimate if its outcome ('everyone to the moon!') incorporates and reflects the normative demands of individual citizens.

Any form of collective organization, then, requires an institutional mechanism that allows for discussion of, and mediation between, different conceptions of 'the good', that legitimizes the priority accorded to one idea of 'the good' over its alternatives, and that ties citizens together in pursuit of that larger 'common good'. Within the context of the modern nation state, the political system has traditionally played this role. In very general terms, the political system can be understood to play four key roles in structuring the attainment of justice.[13] Crucially, these reasons have also been used to argue that we cannot conceive of justice beyond the nation state, as will be discussed (section 2.1). In other words, these four reasons explain why the pursuit of social justice is to a large extent dependent on a specific institutional structure, and why the structures that we encounter beyond the state are not robust enough to sustain a commitment to transnational justice. First, the political process allows individuals to assume authorship and

[13] See also F. De Witte, 'Sex, Drugs and EU Law: The Recognition of Moral and Ethical Diversity in EU Law' (2013) 50 CML Rev. 1545.

ownership over the communal construction of society by offering a forum for contestation and communication that is inclusive and sensitive to the different understandings of the 'good life' of its subjects. The electoral system, based on the free and equal participation of citizens, offers each citizen a chance to voice his or her conception of 'the good' (albeit abstracted through the development of political parties).[14] Moreover, in the light of its 'categorical opening to normative viewpoints',[15] the political process ensures that society remains responsive to social discontent and newly generated social justice claims.[16] Second, the political process allows for the peaceful mediation between different conceptions of 'the good'. The structures of representative democracy and majoritarian politics ensure that citizens 'get what they want'. In this fashion, the political process legitimizes the eventual norm of justice decided on (everyone to the moon!) by internalizing dissent. This creates 'a sense of normative obligation that helps to ensure voluntary compliance with undesired rules or decisions of governing authority'.[17] Third, the political processes legitimize the coercive authority that follows from redistributive decisions. The collective will-formation that takes place through the political process is backed up by legal and administrative compliance mechanisms that enforce the redistributive choices. As Thomas Nagel has put it, the pursuit of justice 'depends on the coordinated conduct of large numbers of people, which cannot be achieved without law backed up by a monopoly of force'.[18] The coercive nature of such compliance mechanisms presupposes a degree of legitimacy that only comes from the outcome of a democratic debate on what is required in order to ensure access to the 'good life' and what is not. Fourth, the political process also plays an indispensable role in legitimizing the polity as the political space through which the citizen makes sense of life.[19] The capacity

[14] See, for critique, J. Buchanan, 'Social Choice, Democracy and Free Markets' (1954) 62 Journal of Political Economy 114–23, even if its institutionalization did allow for the more effective implementation of solidarity. See S. Stjernø, *Solidarity in Europe: The History of an Idea* (Cambridge: CUP, 2005).

[15] Honneth, 'Redistribution as Recognition', 134.

[16] As argued by G. Esping-Andersen (*The Three Worlds of Welfare Capitalism* (Cambridge: CUP, 1990) 15), 'democracy is an institution that cannot ignore majoritarian demands'.

[17] F. Scharpf, 'Legitimacy in the Multi-Level European Polity', in M. Loughlin and P. Dobner (eds.), *The Twilight of Constitutionalism* (Oxford: OUP, 2010) 89.

[18] T. Nagel, 'The Problem of Global Justice' (2005) 33 Philosophy & Public Affairs 115.

[19] The first welfare states were, in fact, largely devised in order to strengthen the nation state's territorial claims. Bismarck's *Soziaalstaat*, which can be seen as the first elaboration of the modern welfare state, was not an exercise in wealth redistribution or social recalibration,

of the state to structure the discussion about justice and the 'good life' facilitates a form of communication between citizens via the institutional structure, which not only strengthens associative ties between people, but also, structurally, 'institute[s] reciprocal obligations and entitlements and patterns of socialisation which allow a sense of equality, mutual respect and self-esteem to develop amongst the actors'.[20] In this sense, a political system allows for the continuous reconstruction of what a community 'means' to its members, and ensures that a polity is not simply seen as reflecting, but also as containing certain normative preferences. As a consequence, modern-day political institutions are almost exclusively concerned with the production and distribution of well-being,[21] not just to meet their subject's needs and desires, but also to consolidate their own role in the process.[22]

In other words, the attainment of social justice depends on social structuring. The political process, properly understood, is but the most evident result of such structuring. Institutionalizing the pursuit of justice also requires a support cast of organized cleavages, intricate structures for the mediation of conflict, an active civil society, public sphere and avenues for participation, and strong centrifugal loyalties that placate alternative sites for the management of the different conceptions of 'the good'.[23] As Ferrera and Bartolini have argued, social structuring presupposes two interrelated processes, which ensure the coincidence (that is, the perfect match) between 'cultural symbols, economic interactions, administrative regimes and physical coercion'[24] that—in very general terms—enable the political process to face the question of justice in the first place. First, social structuring requires the consolidation of territorial boundaries, which stabilize and generalize expectations of reciprocity between 'insiders'. This argument, in a nutshell, is that external closure is required for the formation of an internal system that is sufficiently sophisticated legitimately to settle the question of justice: 'the locking in of resources and actors in a bounded space oriented actor strategies towards the inside, focused them towards central elites, and promoted the formation of new

but a crafty state-building attempt. M. Ferrera, *The Boundaries of Welfare* (Oxford: OUP, 2005) 14 and 61–2.

[20] D. Chalmers, 'European Restatements of Sovereignty' (2013) LSE Law WP 14; A. Honneth, *The I in We: Studies in the Theory of Recognition* (Cambridge: Polity, 2012) 201–16.

[21] Esping-Andersen, *The Three Worlds of Welfare Capitalism*, 1.

[22] M. Ferrera, 'The JCMS Annual Lecture: National Welfare States and European Integration: In Search of a "Virtuous Nesting"' (2009) 47 JCMS 223.

[23] See generally S. Bartolini, *Restructuring Europe* (Oxford: OUP, 2007).

[24] Ibid. 109.

organisational vehicles for the exercise of voice and the strengthening of loyalty'.[25] After the external boundaries of a polity have been consolidated, processes of internal system sophistication are necessary. For Bartolini, this primarily consists of 'the formation of the centre and its internal hierarchy; the creation of loyalties and the formation of the system; the articulation of voice and the formation of specific political structures'.[26] These long-term processes ensure the trust, both horizontally between citizens of the polity and vertically between the citizens and the polity,[27] and the institutional homogeneity without which the functional differentiation of society and the creation of the cleavages that make competing claims of justice cannot emerge and cannot be sustained without endangering the stability of the polity as a whole.[28] In other (and simpler) words: without the significant and long-term processes of external closure and internal sophistication we cannot have a functioning political system; and without a functioning political system we cannot ensure the attainment of social justice.

1.1.3 *Moral Presuppositions of Justice*

The redistributive processes that are central to the welfare state and to the pursuit of justice need more than institutions alone. They also need symbolic or moral resources that are best captured under the term 'solidarity', in so far as they require a motive for individuals to share their resources with 'others' in the same community. It is uncontested that, historically speaking, this motive has developed a close tie with the spatial structure within which it has operated: the nation state. Every nation state has developed an idiosyncratic conception of justice, primarily as a result of the need to meet its own historically unique needs, circumstances, and institutional preferences, but also as the result of the particular strength and nature of the communal claims articulated by individual citizens. This explains the eight structural policy differences between the four welfare models that exist in Europe.[29] In

[25] Ferrera, *The Boundaries of Welfare*, 7.

[26] Bartolini, *Restructuring Europe*, 3.

[27] C. Tilly, *Democracy* (Cambridge: CUP, 2007).

[28] Bartolini, *Restructuring Europe*, 114.

[29] The four welfare models (three developed by Esping-Andersen, who distinguishes between the Scandinavian model, the Continental Model, and the Anglo-Saxon Model, to which the welfare model of former communist countries in central and eastern Europe may be added) differ in terms of eligibility and risk coverage, benefit structure and generosity, methods of financing, service intensity, family policy, employment regulation, logic of governance, and the regulation of industrial relations. See A. Hemerijck, 'The Self-Transformation of the European Social Model(s)', in G. Esping-Andersen (ed.), *Why We Need a Welfare State* (Oxford: OUP, 2002) 178.

other words, the nature and structure of the pursuit of social justice in the different nation states results from the associative connection between the individual citizens in a polity. As Nagel puts it:

> Sovereign states are not merely instruments for realising the pre-institutional value of justice among human beings. Instead, their existence is precisely what gives the value of justice its application, by putting the fellow citizens of a sovereign state into a relation that they do not have with the rest of humanity, an institutional relation which must then be evaluated by the special standards of fairness and equality that fill out the content of justice.[30]

These 'special standards of fairness and equality' suggest the existence of a modicum of solidarity between citizens. Social entitlements, after all, require the redistribution of resources, given that their financial burden is not usually shouldered by those who profit most from them. It presupposes that citizens care about the misery and happiness of their fellow citizens. Without such horizontal willingness to 'share' with 'others' within the same 'community', communal aspects of social justice cannot be sustained. If only 10 per cent of the electorate is willing to give up part of their finances for the establishment of certain welfare entitlements, such entitlements are unsustainable, both morally and financially. Even though whole libraries have been written on these notions, captured by the term 'solidarity', it remains a nebulous concept—stuck somewhere between rationality and emotion, between egoism and altruism.[31] Somek's conceptualization of solidarity as entailing both a sense of identification and one of societal transcendence captures these ambiguities nicely, and explains how the use of social solidarity as a moral vehicle for the development of social justice has increased the distinctly reciprocal and spatially bounded nature underlying participation in spaces of social sharing. *Solidarity as identification* implies that solidarity is essentially based on the recognition that fellow citizens 'endure what one abhors'.[32] This is the most classic form of solidarity, and underlies social policies in the sense that it rationalizes the pooling of resources in order to prevent general need throughout society. It is strongly self-referential in the sense

[30] Nagel, 'The Problem of Global Justice', 120.

[31] See, for a compelling chronological account of the development of the concept of solidarity, H. Brunkhorst, *Solidarity: From Civic Friendship to a Global Legal Community* (Cambridge, Mass.: MIT, 2005).

[32] A. Somek, 'Solidarity Decomposed: Being and Time in European Citizenship' (2007) 32 ELRev 807.

that it is centred on the individual's own desires and needs (if I were to get sick...), and thus assumes social protection set at the level beneath which the citizen would not him- or herself want to live.[33] Solidarity as identification is thus continuously vulnerable to 'negative des-identification', in the sense that greed, individualization, the privatization of welfare, ethno-cultural pluralism, and resentment can lead to decreased identification with those in need,[34] even if it seems that the common ethic aimed at alleviation of the worst of human suffering will always guarantee a basic level of solidarity.[35] The second aspect of solidarity is conceptualized by Somek as *solidarity as transcendence*.[36] In its theoretical core this entails identification with the life of the community as such, that is to say with capacities and opportunities that fellow citizens (do not) possess. This can be distinguished from solidarity as identification in the sense that it places the interests of society as a whole in the centre of the normative claims. The reasoning changes from an egocentric (if I were to get sick...) to one encompassing society as such (citizens in this community should be looked after when sick). Solidarity as transcendence requires a new frame of mind, identified by Stjernø as 'enlightened self-interest', in which not the individuals' own interest is placed to the fore, but the general interests and aspirations of the members of the organic community to which the individual belongs.[37]

Both senses of solidarity entail a 'moral commitment to "sharing with others", which is not easy to activate at the individual and primary group levels'.[38] The sustainability of the welfare state's strong redistributive character presupposes that inter-personal solidarity be 'thick' enough. Citizens must feel sufficiently connected to each other in order to have a motive to give up part of their finances for the 'communal good' of alleviating the suffering of, or creating opportunities for, fellow citizens. This

[33] It is, consequently, premised on a delicate balance: where the wants of those protected by social rights become higher than the egocentric abhorrence of the rest of society, solidarity as a concept fails, and the standard of social protection will be lowered in order to meet the new equilibrium between abhorrence and need.

[34] Somek, 'Solidarity Decomposed', 810. See also Stjernø, *Solidarity in Europe*, 2.

[35] J. Mayerfield, *Suffering and Moral Responsibility* (Oxford: OUP, 1999) 131. Somek ('Solidarity Decomposed') calls this the 'agapistic reflex' of solidarity.

[36] Somek, 'Solidarity Decomposed', 808.

[37] Stjernø, *Solidarity in Europe*, 201, and E. Durkheim, *The Division of Labour in Society* (Basingstoke: Palgrave, 1984) 150. See, for an interesting digression, P. Lafargue, *The Right to be Lazy, and Other Studies* (Chicago: Kerr, 1907).

[38] Ferrera, *The Boundaries of Welfare*, 46.

is where the connection between the pursuit of justice and the nation state becomes interesting. In simple terms, it raises the question whether the solidarity that is required to sustain vast redistributive processes is tied to the nation state because of the cultural homogeneity and ethnic identities that the nation state guarantees (which is often called 'ethnic solidarity') or because of the way in which the nation state ties together different individuals in the democratic determination of the common good (which is often called 'civic solidarity'). Or, to turn the question on its head, does solidarity (and by implication the pursuit of justice) require strong centrifugal identities and ethno-historical narratives to provide a *motive* for citizens to give up part of their resources to support 'others'; or does the mere co-presence of individuals in a democratic system provide for that motive—regardless of the heterogeneity of the population? If the former is true, the link between justice and *ethnos* would appear intractable. If the latter is true, on the other hand, the link between justice and *ethnos* is merely historically contingent, and the pursuit of justice beyond the state remains possible.

The process of nation building has certainly greatly contributed to the creation of 'thick' solidarities, by emphasizing the ethno-cultural similarities between national citizens and creating fictitious 'communities of fate'[39] that offer the 'fiction of eternity'.[40] Ethnicity, in this sense, is a 'historical deposit of collective experiences' that solidifies interpersonal relationships.[41] The binding property and identity-building capacity of concepts such as citizenship and nationality, as well as the closure provided by territorial boundaries, have allowed for social integration,[42] societal sophistication, and systemic simplification, both in terms of the creation of a 'cultural infrastructure',[43] and in terms of the cultivation of individual and collective identities and belongings.[44] This has generated strong horizontal solidarities based on a shared cultural, historical, and institutional heritage,[45] which

[39] D. Millar, *On Nationality* (Oxford: OUP, 1997) 22–7 and 184–5.

[40] C. Offe, 'Whose Good is the Common Good?' (2012) 38 Philosophy and Social Criticism 665.

[41] A. Smith, *The Ethnic Origin of States* (Oxford: Blackwell 1988).

[42] C. Calhoun, *Nations Matter: Culture, History and the Cosmopolitan Dream* (New York: Routledge, 2007) 154.

[43] Ferrera, *The Boundaries of Welfare*, 21; Smith, *The Ethnic Origin of States*, 133.

[44] Ferrera, *The Boundaries of Welfare*, 20.

[45] See T. Faist, 'Social Citizenship in the European Union: Nested Membership' (2001) 19 JCMS 37; M. Dougan and E. Spaventa, '"Wish you weren't here...": New Models of Social

have in turn led to the formation of very homogeneous social groups, strong centre–periphery relations, and institutional mechanisms, such as the political sphere and the welfare state, capable of reproducing these solidarities.[46] The ethnic tradition of the nation state, in this sense, locates the individuals' 'experience of belonging' in ways that other social or economic properties cannot, and is, as such, at the core of the solidarity that sustains redistributive processes.[47]

Other scholars have argued that the connection between the *ethnos* and solidarity is historically contingent. What matters, rather than a shared ethnicity, language, or cultural symbols, is the participation in a common political project. As Nagel has argued, a commitment to justice (and implicitly solidarity) emerges from the way in which political power is organized. Citizens that are subject to the same sovereign power, Nagel argues,

> have a duty of justice towards one another through legal, social, and economic institutions that sovereign power makes possible. This duty is *sui generis*, and is not owed to everyone in the world, nor is it an indirect consequence of any other duty of humanity. Justice is something we owe through our shared institutions only to those with whom we stand in a strong political relation. It is, in the standard terminology, an *associative* obligation.[48]

In essence this argument suggests that the *motive* for a citizen to give up part of his resources to alleviate the needs of fellow citizens, or to foster their aspirations, is the privileged position in which he finds himself vis-à-vis those specific citizens. In other words, only in respect of fellow citizens in a polity do citizens dispose of the institutional resources required to translate moral claims of justice into action. Since the alleviation of a fellow citizens' need or the facilitation of his aspirations

Solidarity in the European Union', in M. Dougan and E. Spaventa (eds.), *Social Welfare and EU Law* (Oxford: Hart, 2005) 185.

46 See D. Miller, *Citizenship and National Identity* (Cambridge: Polity, 2000) 31–2; C. Joppke, 'Transformation of Citizenship: Status, Rights, Identity' (2007) 11 Citizenship Studies 38.

47 Calhoun, *Nations Matter*, 149. See also D. Schnapper, *Community of Citizens: On the Modern Idea of Nationality* (New Brunswick: Transaction, 1995) 85. Balibar points out the paradoxes in this position. See E. Balibar, *We, The People of Europe* (Princeton, NJ: Princeton University Press, 2004) 55, 77.

48 Nagel, 'The Problem of Global Justice', 121, emphasis in original. See also A. Sangiovanni, 'Justice and the Priority of Politics to Morality' (2008) 16 Journal of Political Philosophy 137.

is, then, a political possibility, it becomes a potential claim for justice and the source for an associative obligation. The privileged position that binds citizens together in a common political destiny, on this view, is what creates and sustains the solidarity that is required for the vast redistributive processes that typify the welfare state. This can be best understood as civic solidarity, as opposed to the ethnic solidarity described above. Brunkhorst suggests that the increased complexity and functional differentiation of modern society destroys all forms of brotherly, ethnic solidarity. Redistribution can no longer be sustained by kinship or status—these strata are simply not powerful enough to reproduce themselves—and can only be sustained by the democratic engagement of people.[49] On this view, it is the constant normative reiteration of the associative connection between fellow citizens through a shared democratic engagement that sustains feelings of solidarity. Taking this civic view of solidarity has two important implications. First, it suggests that the pursuit of justice is not necessarily tied to the nation state. Given the appropriate institutional preconditions, solidarity can emerge at a level beyond the state. Second, it suggests that levels of solidarity do not necessarily (or automatically) decrease as the ethno-cultural composition of the state becomes more heterogonous as long as the newcomers participate in society. These two insights, as we will see in the next chapter, have important implications for the way in which we conceptualize justice in the EU.

This section has argued that both welfare entitlements and the individual's capacity of (private) choice are central to our understanding of justice. In fact, their moral appeal to a large extent derives from a different, but not mutually exclusive, interpretation of freedom. Giving more practical and actual content to the pursuit of social justice, however, requires long-term processes of social and political structuring, as well as the availability of significant moral resources that legitimize the vast redistributive agenda of the welfare state. These institutional and normative preconditions for social justice explain our deeply ingrained intuition that social justice belongs to the nation state—even if it seems that the civic structures of the *state* are more important than the ethnic elements of the *nation*.

[49] Brunkhorst, *Solidarity*, 105. See also J. Habermas, 'Democracy, Solidarity and the European Crisis', lecture delivered 26 April 2013 in Leuven.

1.2 Justice Beyond the State?

The above narrative of the pursuit of justice on the national level has not only been challenged by academics on moral grounds—typically arguing, as will be discussed below, that state borders are morally arbitrary and that commitments of justice are owed to *all* humans, and not just national citizens—but also by regulatory processes. Properly understood, this sees to the dislocation of the 'question' of social justice from the institutional structure of the nation state by processes of globalization, legal integration, and monetary integration. These three processes have decreased the capacity of states to 'lock in' agents and extract the resources required for redistributive programmes. In the simplest terms, this means that while the institutional structure that is sophisticated enough to answer the question of justice has remained on the national level, the administrative capacity to lock in resources and extract from them those required for the implementation of justice is situated at the level beyond the state (section 1.2.1). While this dislocation of the social question has been applauded on normative grounds (and indeed anticipated) by scholars such as Hayek, other scholars, such as Streeck and Polanyi, warn of the disruptive processes that emerge when economic processes are no longer mediated by the claims of justice produced within democratic states. Others yet—often thrown in the mixed bag of 'cosmopolitans'—stress the normative appeal of the nation state's loss of the monopoly in the pursuit of justice, often pointing at the deficiencies of popular sovereignty, such as parochialism, internal exclusion, and external violence. Finally, scholars such as Habermas argue that we should not attempt to reappropriate the social question by bringing back the capacity to 'lock in' resources on the national level, but, conversely, we should recreate the necessary political structures that can control economic processes on the level beyond the state (section 1.2.2).

1.2.1 *The Dislocation of the Social Question*

In the last section we saw that an effective pursuit of justice requires the coincidence of administrative control over resources and the political authority that legitimates a particular interpretation of what justice requires. While the latter mediates in answering the question of what a 'good life' consists of, the former ensures its implementation and enforcement through the coercive machinery of the state administration. This forced compliance to the answer of the 'social question' serves to make different processes—including the economy—sensitive to the electorate's needs and desires. Over the past decades, however, several structural processes have gradually divorced the political authority to answer the social question from the administrative control required to implement it.[50] Simply put, whereas the former has remained within the nation state, with its strong political and social structures; the latter has evaporated. On this view, the globalization of economic processes, integration through law in the European Union, and the creation of a common currency in Europe have robbed Member States of the instruments they require in order to implement their view of the 'good life'. Put more concretely, these processes have diminished the capacity of states to lock in resources. The increased porousness of boundaries makes it more difficult for states to enforce redistributive obligations—in particular in respect of mobile actors, who dispose of the legal right and economic capacity to 'exit' a certain polity. The social question, in consequence, is answered increasingly by the constraints imposed by global economic processes and transnationally mobile actors, not necessarily as a reflection of the needs, desires, and conceptions of the 'good' of the citizen. As Streeck puts it, 'the markets have begun to dictate in unprecedented ways what presumably sovereign and democratic states may still do for their citizens and what they must refuse them'.[51] This challenges not only the basic social and political assumption that the citizen is at the centre of the normative construction of society,[52] but also the nation state's institutional capacity to pursue social justice. More crucially, this process has demonstrated that emerging economic, social, or political connections *across* borders fit uneasily within the current institutional setting that 'does' justice.

The depoliticizing potential of globalization has been often discussed.[53] In the most simple terms, and at the risk of oversimplification, it postulates that the increased mobility of capital, that is, its capacity to skip (even virtually) between jurisdictions, which has been drastically increased both by the global programme of trade liberalization and technological progress, has a direct effect on the willingness of nation states to enact (and on their

[50] S. Bartolini, 'Old and New Peripheries in the Process of European Territorial Integration', in C. Ansell and G. Di Palma (eds.), *Restructuring Territoriality* (Cambridge: CUP, 2004) 23.

[51] W. Streeck, 'The Crises of Democratic Capitalism' (2011) 71 NLR 26.

[52] Halberstam, *Totalitarianism and the Modern Conception of Politics*, 17.

[53] See e.g. A. Glyn, *Capitalism Unleashed: Finance, Globalization and Welfare* (Oxford: OUP, 2007).

capacity to enforce) legislation or regulations that restrict or temper the power and potential of capital. To use a recent example, the threat by the UK government to impose a banking tax was met by the City of London with a simple counter threat: 'fine, we'll move to Zurich or Singapore'. It is, properly understood, not the actual mobility of actors that causes this effect, but its anticipated internalization by policy makers. This internalization has a cause, and it has an effect. The cause is, again in very general terms, that capital has become a 'fugitive power', which manages to elude the administrative and legal reach of the authority and enforcement capacity of nation states to bind them to a certain territory. This relates to both the intangible nature of many capital transactions (think of tax havens or mailbox cooperations), which, even though they may in reality take place within the territory of one particular state, manage to avoid the jurisdiction of that state, and to the global system of free trade, which to a large extent attributes effective control to the place of production over the place of consumption. The effect of this 'golden rule' of the global market, which disperses regulatory and administrative control out of reach of individual states, is that, given the inherent attraction that direct capital investment has on national governments, perennially worried about attaining an employment rate that is as high as possible, direct investment becomes top priority for many governments. In a mobile world, however, governments enter into competition with each other in attracting capital, a process that is often suggested to put pressure on wage and labour standards, which are considered to add to the costs of production. Both the incapacity to bind capital to its physical location and the interstate competition in the pursuit of direct investment has limited the capacity and willingness of nation states to answer the 'social question' in ways that impose significant redistributive obligations on capital, even if demanded by its citizens.[54] This asymmetrical effect is also discussed by Schäfer and Streeck, who argue that 'in the face of rampant tax competition, consolidation of public finances will have to be achieved overwhelmingly by spending cuts, apart from higher taxation of immobile assets—i.e. consumers and low-income earners'.[55] Globalization, then, systemically lifts the 'social question' out of the confines of political contestation and redistributive trade-offs, and instead decides which exact policies are acceptable

[54] J. Habermas, 'The Crisis of the European Union in the Light of a Constitutionalization of International Law' (2012) 23 EJIL 338; D. Held and A. McGrew, *The Global Transformation Reader* (Cambridge: Polity, 2000).

[55] A. Schäfer and W. Streeck, *Politics in the Age of Austerity* (Cambridge: Polity, 2013) 18

and which are not on the basis of their relative impact on mobile actors.[56] The economic and political structure of world trade, simply put, has become 'the generic alibi for surrender: every progressive alternative is derided on the ground that the constraints of globalisation make it impractical'.[57] Unger spells out what implications this process has: 'in European social democracy—with a well-developed social contract, [the citizens] have good reason to fear that the contract will be broken—not once, but over and over again in the name of economic necessity, described as competition and globalisation'.[58]

These two ways in which capital mobility has depoliticized the social question—in the sense that only a limited range of answers have remained available to the electorate—are even more blatant in the European Union, where the legally enforceable right to free movement of capital, establishment, and companies has institutionalized the practices described above. The notion of mutual recognition on the one hand, through which economic actors can 'export' home legislation into other Member States (which may have more stringent domestic standards), and regulatory competition on the other hand, which suggests that this legally condoned mobility further decreases the willingness of Member States to impose high social costs to the production process, have further limited the capacity of electorates to answer the social question in a way that involves, for example, high taxation on capital investments or on mobile industries, high social security obligations on (multinational) employers, and so on.[59] The increased ability of actors to 'exit' their own Member State through their rights to free movement, as Bartolini identified, not only affects 'the extent to which the state can extract resources for building/maintaining territorial structures, and the extent to which the political system can spread such resources to its weaker and peripheral strata, sectors and territories'[60] but it also 'leaves open the possibility that the dissatisfied mobiles—those who might exit—make the organisation particularly sensitive to their needs, and indeed, so much that the organisation tries to anticipate the course of action that will most likely prevent their exit'.[61] This has had particularly salient repercussions

[56] See D. Nicol, *The Constitutional Protection of Capitalism* (Oxford: Hart, 2010) esp. chs. 2 and 3.

[57] R. Unger, *The Left Alternative* (London: Verso, 2009) 133.

[58] Ibid. 39.

[59] M. P. Maduro, 'A New Governance for the European Union and the Euro: Democracy and Justice', RSCAS Policy Paper 2012/11, 14; D. Rodrik, *The Globalisation Paradox—Democracy and the Future of the World Economy* (New York: W. Norton, 2011).

[60] Bartolini, *Restructuring Europe*, 9. See also A. Somek, 'The Social Question in Transnational Context' (2011) LEQS 39, 21.

[61] Bartolini, *Restructuring Europe*, 11 and 337.

on the possible answers to the 'social question' as it affects the available policy choices regarding tax legislation, company legislation, and the transnational posting of workers, all of which play a fundamental role in the capacity of a Member State to enforce its answer to the 'social question' to all actors present on its territory.

Again, the challenge of legal integration to the pursuit of justice is that, of all the possible ways in which the social question can be answered, legal integration makes a number of them (to be precise, those that run against the interests of mobile actors—which is largely capital and not labour) unavailable. At the core, this boils down to the opportunity for 'exit' provided by free movement (which, oddly enough, does not even presuppose physical movement),[62] and can be traced back to the ordo-liberal origins of the integration project, which deliberately insulated the free movement provisions from political interference by their transnational codification and the subsequent interpretation of the free movement provisions by the Court.[63] This has led, as identified by Scharpf, to a double asymmetry on the European level.[64] On the one hand, negative integration (declaring illegal national regulations that restrict or make less attractive the mobility of capital) was more easily attained than positive integration (negotiating market correcting mechanisms on the political level) and, even more crucially, the absence of competences of the European Union in the more salient areas of social policy has led to a complete depoliticization. In the simplest terms, national answers to the social question that impose ambitious redistributive programmes are precluded by EU free movement law, and a European answer is precluded by lack of competences (and, of course, a sufficiently thick political sphere). Even within the sphere of the Union's competences, the ideological, institutional and economic preferences of the different Member States make imposing market-correcting mechanisms increasingly difficult.[65]

As if all of this was not enough, the recent euro-crisis has further confined the role of 'the political' to the national level in the answering of

[62] A. Saydé, 'One Law, Two Competitions: An Enquiry into the Contradictions of Free Movement Law' (2011) 13 CYELS 370.

[63] Ferrara, *The Boundaries of Welfare*, 118–24; D. Ashiagbor, 'Unravelling the Embedded Liberal Bargain: Labour and Social Welfare Law in the Context of EU Market Integration' (2013) 19 ELJ 303–24.

[64] F. Scharpf, 'The Asymmetry of European Integration, or Why the EU Cannot Be a "Social Market Economy"' (2010) 8 Socio-economic Review 217.

[65] F. Scharpf, *Governing in Europe: Effective and Democratic* (Oxford: OUP, 1999) ch. 2.

the social question.[66] Institutional, economic, and monetary constraints—constitutionalized through the six-pack, the two-pack, the ESM, Fiscal Compact, and the European Semester—make it all but impossible for Member States to answer the social question in ways that impose significant public *or* private redistributive obligations. Lowering fiscal obligations on market actors, we are told, is necessary to ensure economic growth; while public expenses need to be cut to diminish public debt rates.[67] Redistributive policies that cost too much, in simple terms, are unavailable not because they fail to convince the electorate, but because their implementation comes with the threat of political, administrative, and economic sanctions (whether in the form of Commission 'recommendations' or of 'spontaneous' changes in the financial markets of the state's yields, spreads, and bond prices).[68] What is left, then, is a commitment to austerity—not necessarily because citizens appreciate that this might be prudent, but because global market actors and supranational institutions think this might be prudent. As the crisis has progressed, moreover, the Union's focus has shifted from action geared towards remedying existing sovereign debt to action preventing *future* sovereign debt. Under the guise of long-term fiscal stability, preventing 'macro-economic imbalances' and issuing 'country-specific recommendations' in fields as diverse as healthcare, pensions, education, housing policy, and labour law, the Commission is structurally overseeing and substantively altering national answers to the social question.[69]

It lies beyond the scope of this book to analyse precisely how the three processes discussed—globalization, asymmetrical European integration, and the sovereign debt crisis—relate to each other, and to what extent they are more or less at the basis of the different positions in which the different Member States find themselves. The purpose of the above analysis is not to criticize the substantive direction in which these processes are pushing the pursuit of justice. Rather, it raises the concern that the processes of globalization and transnational cooperation, amplified by the economic crisis, have created a black hole that absorbs the social question, lifting it outside

[66] See, for an impressive account of the links between free movement, EMU, and the EU's political choices, A. Menendez, 'The Existential Crisis of the European Union' (2013) 14 GLJ 453. See also F. De Witte, 'EU Law, Politics and the Social Question' (2013) 14 GLJ 581.

[67] See Schäfer and Streeck, *Politics in the Age of Austerity* .

[68] Ibid. 19.

[69] See in depth M. Dawson and F. De Witte, 'Constitutional Balance in the EU after the Euro-crisis' (2013) 76 MLR 817.

the confines of political contestation that are essential to its very answer.[70] Answering the social question clearly requires both control over movement *and* political authority. Transnational processes have made these two drift apart—the former has shifted to the European or global level, while the former has remained on the national level—with obvious consequences for our commitment to the pursuit of justice.

1.2.2 *Justice Beyond the State: Four Normative Claims*

The dissolution of the social question away from the nation state and its political structures has sparked very diverse concerns and opinions. In very general terms, all opinions have one thing in common: they understand that we need to find a way to accommodate within our understanding of justice the transnational connections—of a social, economic, and political kind—that have emerged. For some, such as Hayek, the incapacity of the nation state to do so is to be applauded from a normative perspective, in so far as it prevents artificial redistributive processes. Others, such as Polanyi and Streeck, worry that this divorce could not only lead to the demise of capitalism (which needs to be socially embedded for its stable reproduction) but also to the demise of democracy and the pursuit of social justice (which need to be able to implement the desires of the electorate). Cosmopolitans, on the other hand, stress that the incapacity of the nation state to enforce its norms of justice might actually *help* the pursuit of justice by overcoming some of the nation state's in-built deficiencies, such as the moral arbitrariness of boundaries, the parochial biases of popular sovereignty, and the processes of internal exclusion and external violence. Finally, authors such as Habermas and Beck understand the inability of the nation state to engage with transnational dynamics as an opportunity to start building political structures beyond the nation state with the specific purpose of reappropriating the social question and ensuring that citizens remain central in the pursuit of social justice.

1.2.2.1 Hayek and Neo-liberalism

The dynamics of a globally and functionally integrated world have arguably permanently depoliticized the social question on the national level, subjecting matters of labour standards and redistributive justice to the logic of the

[70] Brunkhorst, *Solidarity*, 3.

transnational market and the relationships between market actors that it produces. In his work Hayek not only applauds this development, but in fact anticipates it with a foresight and precision that appears prophetic:

> [C]ertain kinds of coercion require the joint and co-ordinated use of different powers or the employment of several means, and, if these means are in separate hands, nobody can exercise those kinds of coercion. The most familiar illustration is provided by many kinds of economic control which can be effective only if the authority exercising them can also control the movement of men and goods across the frontiers of its territory. If it lacks that power, though it has the power to control internal events, it cannot pursue policies which require the joint use of both.[71]

From Hayek's perspective, lifting the social question out of the confines of the nation state thus ensures its dissolution.[72] Not only do states no longer possess the administrative means to enforce vast redistributive policies, but such policies are no longer attractive,[73] as the transnational regime would struggle to harness the popular support (or solidarity, if you will) *across* borders required to redistribute resources beyond the borders of the nation state—something that is becoming increasingly evident in the EU after the euro-crisis. For Hayek, the dissolution of the social question both protects individual freedom against state intervention and prevents redistributive mechanisms from distorting market interactions.[74] The neo-liberal project, in other words, has discovered (some would say created) a systemic flaw in our mode of governance, which structurally subordinates social policies to the economic power of market actors. The inability of the nation state to control transnational dynamics, on this view, *creates* justice by ensuring an undistorted market.

1.2.2.2 Polanyi, Steeck, and the End of Politics

Other scholars are much less optimistic about the inability of national processes to subject transnational (economic) processes to some form of justice. Polanyi and Streeck, for example, argue that when democracy and capitalism are not mutually embedded—that is, take account of the preconditions for each other's survival or reproduction—both struggle to survive, with obvious consequences for the pursuit of social justice. As

[71] F. von Hayek, *The Constitution of Liberty* (Chicago: University of Chicago, 1978) 184–5.

[72] Somek, 'The Social Question in Transnational Context', 4.

[73] See also M. Höpner and A. Schäfer, 'Embeddedness and Regional Integration: Waiting for Polanyi in a Hayekian Setting' (2012) 66 International Organisations 429.

[74] J. Buchanan, 'Federalism and Individual Sovereignty' (1996) 15 Cato Journal 266.

Delanty argues, 'a key aspect of the shape of European modernity was the prevalence of strong politics of solidarity emanating from class struggle and a relation between state and capitalism that set limits to the capacity of either to dominate entirely the social order'.[75] Traditionally, this balancing between politics and capitalism—which gives content to the notion of social justice—took place through what Polanyi has called a 'double movement' and Streeck 'democratic capitalism', whereby politics ensures that economic processes are constrained by commitments to social justice, so as to prevent mass social discontent and systemic instability. In this fashion, politics ensures the 're-embedding [of] the market economy to make it compatible with a liveable life'.[76] At the same time, this process of re-embedding is also necessary in order to make capitalism 'work'. As Streeck summarily puts it, 'society is not a *product* of competitive contracting but its *precondition*'.[77] Without the reservoirs of equity, solidarity, equality, and redistribution, the emergence and existence of which depend on the political sphere, capitalism quickly consumes the structures of inclusion, access, stability, trust, and exchange upon which it crucially depends.

The gradual separation between the social question and the transnational economy, then, as described in the previous section, might endanger the survival of capitalism, but also of politics. Properly understood, our incapacity to 'fit' transnational economic processes within national answers to the social question not only challenges the social and political criteria of self-determination, in the sense that it removes political agency, authorship, and ownership over the conditions of life from the citizens, but also destabilizes the legitimacy of the political system that imposes those norms. Without meaningful choice, politics becomes vacuous, and the relationships between citizens become exposed to arbitrary market forces.[78] Equally, the incapacity of institutions to accommodate transnational economic, but also social and political, commitments within its answer to the social question entails that transnational processes might increasingly be perceived as creating, or mandating, 'injustice'. This feeds the process of political instability, through which social conflict—typically in support of different

[75] G. Delanty, *Formations of European Modernity* (London: Palgrave Macmillan, 2013) 21.

[76] W. Streeck, 'Taking Capitalism Seriously: Towards an Institutionalist Approach to Contemporary Political Economy' (2011) 9 Socioeconomic Review 158.

[77] Ibid. 154. Emphases original.

[78] J. Schumpeter, *Capitalism, Socialism and Democracy* (London: Routledge, 2010) ch. 22.

understandings of social justice—moves from the institutional sphere onto the streets, and through which political institutions and the norms that they propagate quickly lose legitimacy. The first signs of systemic political instability are visible in the mass protests throughout the Continent, the decreasing trust in political institutions, increased anti-European rhetoric in debtor and creditor states alike (a sure sign of the incapacity of the European political settlement to mediate in transnational social conflicts), and also in decreased voter turnouts,[79] higher voter volatility,[80] and the rise of what have been called 'anti-political political parties'. In the absence of an institutional forum (whether on the national or European level) that can articulate and settle social conflicts, history tells us, anomie, political instability, and/or a repressive state might follow. Radical as this may sound, any response quickly becomes so once an institutional system can no longer accommodate the citizen's voices and articulate avenues for the mediation of structural conflicts of justice.[81] For Streeck and Polanyi, then, the dissolution of the social question beyond the nation state is problematic because it has led to a situation whereby the conflicts that a differentiated and complex market society produce can no longer be accommodated institutionally.

1.2.2.3 Cosmopolitanism and the Moral Limits of the Nation State

Other scholars *celebrate* the fact that the nation state is no longer capable of enforcing its norms—and that actors can easily exit the polity and form transnational economic and social relationships. Scholars who adhere to the cosmopolitan tradition are deeply suspicious of the modern nation state, and in particular its practices of exclusion and aggression. On this view, the nation state comes with severe normative drawbacks—and removing its capacity to enforce moral claims vis-à-vis citizens goes some way towards remedying these drawbacks. While the earliest cosmopolitans in particular highlighted the moral arbitrariness of state boundaries, arguing that obligations of justice extend to all human beings and not only to national citizens,

[79] See, on all these issues, D. Chalmers, 'The European Redistributive State and a European Law of Struggle' (2012) 18 ELJ 667.

[80] See W. Streeck, 'How Will Capitalism End?' (2014) 87 NLR 40.

[81] Streeck ends his article entitled 'How Will Capitalism End?' by arguing that increased societal fragmentation will occur, 'not necessarily but quite possibly on the scale of the global breakdown of the 1930s' (ibid. 64). See also M. Wilkinson, 'The Specter of Authoritarian Liberalism: Reflections on the Constitutional Crisis of the European Union' (2013) 14 GLJ 527.

modern cosmopolitans have highlighted the practices of parochialism, internal exclusion, and external aggression that seem inextricably connected to the mechanics of popular sovereignty.

The claim that state boundaries perpetuate a sort of moral arbitrariness can be traced back to the Stoic tradition. Seneca famously argued that 'there are two communities—the one, which is great and truly common, embracing gods and humans, in which we look neither to this corner nor to that, but measure the boundaries of our citizenship by the sun; the other, the one which we have been assigned by the accident of our birth'.[82] Attributing too much importance to the latter, the argument runs, underestimates what human beings have in common, and arbitrarily limits the application of universal moral claims that underlie the construction of society only to citizens of a particular polity.[83] Sen—in a more modern interpretation of this arbitrary exclusion—demonstrates why this is so problematic:

> A person belongs to many different groups (related to gender, class, language group, profession, nationality, community, race, religion and so on), and to see them merely as a member of just one particular group would be a major denial of each person to decide how exactly to see himself or herself. The increasing tendency towards seeing people in terms of one dominant 'identity' (…) is not only an imposition of an external and arbitrary priority, but also the denial of an important liberty of a person who can decide on their respective loyalties to different groups.[84]

Modern cosmopolitans have focused more on the element of coercion that Sen has also picked up. For them, the power of the nation state to enforce parochial measures, employ exclusionary practices, or inflict violence on insiders and outsiders alike needs to be limited. Divorcing the political apparatus of the state from its capacity to enforce its norms, on this view, goes a long way towards limiting the potentially negative effects of the construction of society through the institutional structure of the nation state. Indeed, Parker traces this process back to the mid-eighteenth century, where a decisive turn in political economy was made in favour of market freedom. Market freedom was seen as an instrument that would allow the power of money and private interests to displace the capacity of the state (originally in the form of absolute monarchs and later of popular democracy) to subject its citizens to invasive constraints or wage war on its neighbours. Market

[82] Reproduced in J. Sellars, *Stoicism* (Chesham: Acumen, 2006) 131–2.

[83] See Sen, *The Idea of Justice*, 116.

[84] Ibid. 246–7.

freedom was thus presented as an *ethical good*—not simply as a purpose per se, in allowing for personal autonomy and private interest, as neo-liberals cast it these days—but rather as a mechanism to ensure the efficient management of the population, and to allow for the flourishing of both individuals and collectivities. Its objective was not freedom as such, but what such freedom prevented: sovereign violence—both violence of the sovereign in restricting the capacity of the individual to partake in the development of society[85] and violence in the name of the sovereign, directed towards internal minorities or external 'others'.[86] The awareness of the need for internal security and external stability, of course, became ever more pronounced in the aftermath of the Second World War, which crushingly demonstrated the incapacity of the existing institutional structures to prevent both external violence and internal (ethnic) segregation.[87] Indeed, as Jan-Werner Müller has suggested, the structure of the integration process was explicitly meant to tame the power of popular sovereignty and *constrain* its capacity for violence.[88] This is not far from the cosmopolitan position. Its purpose was to allow the population to flourish by structurally incorporating 'the other' within societal structures and creating a space of freedom for all subjects. The idea here is that until we manage sufficiently to incorporate appreciation for the differences between people, and for 'the other' within ourselves, we can neither prevent the ethnic biases and sovereign violence that scar democratic self-government nor can we create sufficient space for individual self-determination and stable internal cooperation.[89] As Kristeva has put it, 'in the long run, only a thorough investigation of our remarkable relationship with both the other and strangeness within ourselves can lead people to give up hunting for the scapegoat outside their group'.[90] This, of course, strongly resonates within the European context, where 'the other' is geographically close and 'borders' have shifted throughout history. In the

[85] To which we may associate negative, or both negative and positive, rights. See Sen, *The Idea of Justice*, for a persuasive argument towards the latter.

[86] O. Parker, *Cosmopolitan Government in Europe* (Abingdon: Routledge, 2013) 28. See, generally, F. De Witte, 'Union Citizenship and Constrained Democracy', in M. De Visser and A. P. van der Mei (eds.), *The Treaty of European Union: Reflections from Maastricht* (Antwerp: Intersentia, 2013) 357.

[87] Balibar, *We, The People of Europe*, 183–5.

[88] J. W. Müller, 'Beyond Militant Democracy' (2012) 73 NLR 44, and *Contesting Democracy* (New Haven, Conn.: Yale University Press, 2011).

[89] Parker, *Cosmopolitan Government in Europe*, 177.

[90] J. Kristeva, *Nations without Nationalism* (New York: Columbia University Press, 1993) 51.

cosmopolitan position, then, the divorce between political authority and the coercive machinery of the state is not necessarily problematic. For the cosmopolitan, the inability of the nation state to 'lock in' resources—and the concomitant capacity of actors to move in and out of different polities and form relationships across borders—goes some way towards preventing the negative consequences of the moral arbitrariness of political boundaries.

1.2.2.4 Habermas and the Reappropriation of the Social Question

For some cosmopolitans—who find any difference in treatment between citizens on the basis of their presence in a particular territory problematic—the creation of a supranational government on the European level is also problematic, as it recreates the same structures of exclusion at the level beyond the state. On this view, the undemocratic nature of the EU itself is understood as a deliberate strategy to prevent the reproduction of the risk of sovereign violence and practices of exclusion on the level beyond the state.[91] For others, such as Somek, the absence of democratic structures in the EU is, in itself, an answer to the social question—a renunciation on the part of the EU governments and their citizens to a redistributive agenda that is more ambitious than preventing the most egregious of suffering.[92] Others yet have forcefully argued for the construction of a democratic space beyond the state in order to bring the 'social question' back under political control. Only by political action on the transnational level, after all, can 'the social forces of nature that have been unleashed at the transnational level—i.e. the systemic constraints that operate without hindrance across national borders, today especially those of the global banking sector—also be tamed'.[93] For Habermas, for example, the attraction in elaborating democratic structures in the EU is based on simultaneously transcending the nation state paradigm without renouncing the social question, that is, without allowing the economy to colonize the citizens' life-worlds. Beck is more explicit about the ultimate objective of the reconstruction of a political community at the level beyond the state: 'the goal is rather to make the situation of others—their fears, hopes, disappointments, feelings of humiliation, and anger—comprehensible through social relations between individuals, encounters, joint action, conversations and

[91] Parker, *Cosmopolitan Government in Europe*, ch. 4.

[92] Somek, 'The Social Question in Transnational Context', 13.

[93] J. Habermas, *The Crisis of the European Union* (Malden, Mass.: Polity, 2012) 10.

observations, and shared involvement'.[94] As discussed above, such a thick political community requires a significant amount of social structuring. Some scholars argue that in the EU the basic structures that would allow for full transnational engagement already exist. Risse, for example, highlights that the diffuse identity and transnational public sphere that are necessary for the generation of democratic solidarity are already present,[95] while Delanty argues that modern societies are very good at 'articulating new relations to the world' that 'make possible solidarity and egalitarianism at least as an aspiration'.[96] As will be discussed in Chapter 2, however, it is doubtful whether the structures that Risse identifies, and the aspiration that Delanty describes, are sufficient to overcome the primacy of the national political process in capturing the individual's political loyalty. In other words, while the gradual divorce of the political authority to answer the social question from the administrative means to enforce such an answer has opened up the possibility for its reconfiguration on the European level so as to ensure that the citizen—and his or her needs and aspirations and new relationships across borders—remains central to the way in which society functions, it would appear that in empirical terms, the level of social structuring required on the European level, as well as the strong hold of such national structures on the political imagery, resist such a development.

1.3 Institutionalizing Justice Beyond the State

Any modern conception of justice needs to take seriously the structural and normative claims that have emerged through the gradual dissolution of the social question away from the nation state. A project aimed at 'bringing justice back in' cannot, it seems, be solved by exclusively relying on processes *within* the nation state (such a solution is normatively unappealing on account of the nation state's exclusionary practices and also would fail to acknowledge the emerging economic and social ties between citizens beyond the state); nor

[94] U. Beck, 'The European Crisis in the Context of Cosmopolitanism' (2012) 43 New Literary History 659.

[95] Even if what is missing is mass politics. See T. Risse, *A Community of Europeans? Transnational Identities and Public Spheres* (Ithaca, NY: Cornell University Press, 2010) 8.

[96] Delanty, *Formations of European Modernity*, 18.

can it be solved by exclusively relying on processes beyond the nation state (where the institutional and normative preconditions for a commitment to justice are lacking). Indeed, it seems that the question that many scholars have grappled with is how to square reliance on the national institutional framework for the production of norms of justice with the need to ensure that the content of such norms takes account of claims of justice beyond the state. Only by doing so, after all, can the pursuit of justice—centred as it is around both entitlements and free choices—internalize the increased mobility of actors entering and exiting the nation state's territory without renouncing the internal political processes that legitimize redistributive practices and ensure that citizens (and their needs, desires, and aspirations) remain central in the pursuit of justice.

A tiered understanding of justice—wherein the institutional and normative structure of both the nation state and the level beyond the state are represented—requires us to rethink the relationship between the individual citizen and public authority. How can we, after all, at once strengthen the nation state's capacity for redistribution (which seems to be based on a clear demarcation between 'insiders' and 'outsiders' to the reproduction of the political system) while at the same time promoting the capacity of actors to move between states, and thereby overcome the moral arbitrariness of boundaries (and all the problems that are attached to it) which is based on the *absence* of a clear demarcation between 'insiders' and 'outsiders'? In other words, how can we reintegrate the mobile actor within domestic processes of rule-setting, will-formation, and—central to this book—redistributive practices without undermining the state's capacity to pursue social justice?

From the outset it appears clear that neither the individual's status as a national to a particular polity nor that individual's status as a human being are useful instruments to reintegrate the mobile actor in domestic redistributive practices. The former is not only morally arbitrary but also fails to take account of the emerging links between citizens and other polities than the one of which they are nationals—links that can be described in economic, social, political, or cultural terms. The latter faces a problem of legitimation and fails to take account of what Nagel calls the associative obligations between citizens, that the specific links between individuals—again to be described not necessarily in political terms,[97] but also possibly in social, cultural, or economic

[97] Nagel, 'The Problem of Global Justice', 119.

terms—engender heightened obligations of justice. Both the national and the cosmopolitan position, in other words, are too 'flat' to take the emergent transnational political, economic, and social links into account while remaining sensitive to the institutional preconditions for the pursuit of justice.

More sophisticated cosmopolitan thinkers have suggested that this paradox of the necessity to use national institutional structures to produce a type of justice that transcends the national framework is a false one. Kostakopoulou summarizes: 'the belief that a liberal democratic state must give priority to the claims of nationals and direct its cultural and material resources in order to protect the common societal culture is not necessarily antithetical to the idea of global equal concern'.[98] Instead, as Kymlicka puts it, the purpose of cosmopolitanism is not to transcend the nation state but to *tame* it.[99] This is further articulated in the work of scholars such as Benhabib, Habermas, and Delanty, who have all offered theories on how to structure the obligations of cosmopolitan justice within the nation state. Their focus seems to be on the need to reproduce the narrative of the nation state in inclusive and civic terms rather than in ethnic terms. As such, their focus lies on disentangling the *demos* from the *ethnos*. Benhabib offers an excellent starting point: 'from a universalist and cosmopolitan point of view (...) state boundaries and frontiers, require moral justification', which entails that the articulation of cosmopolitan claims 'increases the threshold of justification to which formerly exclusionary practices are now submitted'.[100] Cosmopolitan legal norms, in Benhabib's view, will foster a dynamic and reflexive process through which national legal norms internalize the demands of cosmopolitanism. More specifically, this will take place both by processes of democratic iteration and jurisgenerative politics—that is, political contestation and strategic litigation.[101] Delanty and Habermas, on the other hand, have focused less on the mechanisms for the reintegration of cosmopolitan norms within the nation state, and more on new modes of social integration within nation states that are categorically open

[98] D. Kostakopoulou, 'European Union Citizenship: Writing the Future' (2007) 13 ELJ 630. See also K. C. Tan, *Justice without Borders* (Cambridge: CUP, 2004); A. Gutman, 'Democratic Citizenship', in J. Cohen (ed.), *For Love of Country: Debating the Limits of Patriotism* (Boston, Mass.: Beacon, 1996) 66; G. Delanty, *Citizenship in a Global Age: Society, Culture, Politics* (Milton Keynes: Open University Press, 2000) 64–6.

[99] W. Klymica, 'Liberal Nationalism and Cosmopolitan Justice', in: S. Benhabib, *Another Cosmopolitanism* (Oxford: OUP, 2005) 128; and Delanty, *Formations of European Modernity*, 255.

[100] S. Benhabib, *Another Cosmopolitanism* (Oxford: OUP, 2006) 71.

[101] Ibid. 49.

to 'outsiders' without renouncing the structural closure required for the reproduction of the social and political structures that sustain redistributive processes. As such, Delanty's concept of 'civic cosmopolitanism'[102] and Habermas's 'constitutional patriotism'[103] attempt to rethink the relationship between individual citizens in ways that rely less on concepts such as nationality, ethnicity, and cultural identity and more on commitments to democratic values, human rights, and residence. The upshot of this reconceptualization would be that cosmopolitan values could be reproduced through the existing *national* political frameworks.

This book suggests a different approach. It focuses on *relational* criteria, that is, on the way in which global (and in particular European legal) processes have recast the economic, social, and political relationships between citizens—whether 'insider' or 'outsider' in the traditional sense of the word. In the simplest terms, this means that citizens have specific obligations of justice vis-à-vis those citizens with whom they stand in a certain sufficiently meaningful relation—whether in economic, social, or political terms. This allows us simultaneously to incorporate and transcend the commitments between national citizens. Properly understood, this connects the cosmopolitan claim that commitments of justice in principle extend to all human beings with the recognition that the realization of justice prioritizes those citizens with whom one stands in a particular relationship—be it social, economic, or political. In fact, this position can be traced in the Stoic tradition and even in Kant's cosmopolitan principle of hospitality: both understood that universal claims of justice must reflect nuances in relational or associative status:

> as we develop as rational beings we do not narrowly associate our self-preservation with our own physical survival. One obvious example is a parent's desire to protect their children, which the Stoics conceive as a natural widening of our circle of concern. A further widening would be concern for one's extended family and friends, and then concern for one's whole community or society.[104]

This need to be sensitive to the associative or relational interaction between citizens nudges us towards theories of reciprocity. Reciprocity is a particularly useful conceptual tool, as it allows, to use Rosanvallon's words,

[102] Delanty, *Formations of European Modernity*, 112.

[103] J. Habermas, *The Inclusion of the Other* (Cambridge, Mass.: MIT, 1998) 105ff.

[104] Sellars, *Stoicism*, 131, with reference to Cicero, *De Finibus*, J.26. Kant's principle of hospitality, equally, makes a clear distinction between those citizens who are allowed to 'visit' and those who are allowed to 'stay'.

the articulation of a 'type of society whose mode of composition is neither abstract universalism nor identity-based communitarianism but rather the dynamic construction and recognition of particularity'.[105] In other words, it allows us to take account of national particularity, transnational commonality, *and* interpersonal relationships in our assessment of the rights and obligations of justice. Reciprocity, in Rosanvallon's work, takes two forms.[106] On the one hand we can find reciprocity based on exchange (the transaction of material or symbolic goods with the obligation to return the favour). On the other hand we find reciprocity based on equality of involvement: '[r]eciprocity of involvement refers to another type of parity. Its object is the social relation itself, which is simultaneously produced and consumed. It may take various forms, including coproduction of relational goods and parity of social engagement.' Rosanvallon's remarkable insight is that the concept of reciprocity, as such, is sensitive to different settings in which it is produced, and as such allows for the reconfiguration of how 'ideas of commonality, similarity and equality relate to each other'.[107] The concept of reciprocity, moreover, not only suggests that rights to justice are relational, but that obligations of justice are relational, too. Simply put, reciprocity requires involvement so as to ensure its commitment to equality and its own reproduction.[108] Reciprocity thereby allows for the reconfiguration of justice on the national level so as to take account of the transnational relational commitments that have emerged in economic, social, or political forms.

This book is devoted to the thorough exploration of these new relational dynamics, which will be explained as instances of transnational solidarity, and which, as Kostakopoulou was the first to pick up, are deeply engrained in EU free movement and non-discrimination law.[109] The way in which relational dynamics are rearticulated through EU law has different facets—including the way it sets up economic interactions (which will be explained as instances of transnational *market* solidarity); social interactions (which lies at the basis of emerging norms of transnational *communitarian* solidarity); and political interactions (which will be described as *aspirational* solidarity). Through these

[105] Rosanvallon, *The Society of Equals*, 261.

[106] Ibid. 271. [107] Ibid. 291. [108] Ibid. 273–4.

[109] Kostakopoulou, 'European Union Citizenship', 628. Note that my understanding of reciprocity sees to the way in which European integration and EU law reshapes the relationship between citizens, not between states. Sangiovanni has articulated a concept of justice and solidarity in Europe that is also based on reciprocity, but focuses on obligations between states. A. Sangiovanni, 'Solidarity in the European Union' (2013) 33 OJLS 220.

three emerging forms of transnational solidarity, it will be argued, the EU can contribute to the pursuit of justice by simultaneously insulating the national dynamics that sustain redistributive processes while at the same time offering citizens more opportunities to pursue their idea of the 'good life'.

1.4 Conclusion

This chapter has set the scene for the thorough investigation of the emergence of norms of transnational solidarity in EU law. It has answered the first of our central paradoxes in the pursuit of justice: how to think about justice beyond the nation state. As such, this chapter has made three claims. First, it highlighted that a commitment to justice entails a commitment both to welfare benefits and to the creation of meaningful choices for individuals as to how to live their lives. Both, it was argued, are central in the pursuit of justice in so far as they allow citizens to live a 'good life'—whatever that may mean or entail for a particular citizen. Second, this chapter demonstrated that the pursuit of justice presupposes significant and long-term processes of social and institutional structuring, as well as a reservoir of moral resources often called 'solidarity', which explains the deeply intuitive connection between the pursuit of justice and the institutional context within which it usually is expressed: the nation state. The third claim made in this chapter indicated the limits to this 'national' understanding of justice. Such an understanding is not only normatively unattractive, in so far as it arbitrarily limits universal claims of justice and potentially generates processes of parochial justice, internal exclusion, and external violence, but also fails to accommodate the increasingly transboundary nature of migration flows, economic interactions, and legal integration. In order to overcome this, it was argued that we need to rethink how the national processes that are indispensable to the production of justice can serve to articulate norms of justice that transcend the nation state. It seems that interpersonal claims of solidarity based on relational dynamics might be a useful method of conceptually reintegrating cosmopolitan dynamics within the structures of the nation state. This would allow for the pursuit of social justice without falling into the traps of nationalism or universalism. The norms of transnational solidarity that structure this type of reintegration are deeply ingrained in EU law—and in particular in its norms of free movement and non-discrimination based on nationality—as will be discussed in the following chapters.

2

The Tiered Concept of Justice in Europe

This chapter analyses the interaction between national conceptions of justice, which are primarily expressed through the institutions of the welfare state, and the process of European integration. It will be argued that the integration process articulates several distinct claims of justice, which are conceptually very different but not necessarily in conflict with those articulated on the national level. While both the welfare state and the integration process share the ambition to produce a stable and prosperous society, they traditionally have been governed separately. This separation reflects their respective institutional capacities. The European Union, for example, lacks the most elementary democratic and institutional preconditions for the legitimate production of norms of justice. This limits the type of justice that the EU can legitimately articulate, which has become particularly evident since the start of the euro-crisis. Only a vast institutional and normative rethinking of the integration project can help overcome this limitation (section 2.1). Notwithstanding the inherently limited capacity of the European Union to engage in the development of justice, this chapter will highlight that more and more transnational elements of justice have emerged. European Union law, on this view, serves not to challenge the nation state as the site for the production of norms of justice, but instead serves to mitigate the normative deficiencies of the development of justice norms within national communities. As such, EU law can be understood to express three claims of justice. First, EU law serves to extend the capacity of citizens to live 'good lives' *beyond* their own Member State through its rights to free movement. Second, EU law protects the principle of equal citizenship by extending a right to non-discrimination on the basis of nationality to all mobile EU citizens. Third, EU law needs to be (and is) sensitive to the ways in which its demands of justice affect domestic redistributive processes. As will be discussed, the EU's claims of justice are parasitical on the existence of such processes, and their stability thereby becomes a concern for EU law (section 2.2). Over the past decades, then, the narratives of justice developed on the national level and that of the integration project have become intertwined. The functional and political separation between the projects has become tenuous, and the question of coherence between the normative claims they produce is increasingly significant. In order to ensure that the tiered concept of justice in Europe—whereby the nation state redistributes, and the EU offers more choices and possibilities to its citizens—enhances rather than decreases the capacity of citizens to live 'a good life', a conceptual framework that allows for the reintegration of the different norms of justice is required. Such a framework must be sensitive to national particularities and emerging transnational relational dynamics and be committed to creating the presuppositions for citizens to be able to live a 'good life'. The final section of this chapter will explain how the economic, social, and political ties that bind citizens in the EU have generated commitments of *transnational solidarity*. Such commitments serve to integrate the Union's claims of freedom and equality beyond the state with the relational structures of justice on the national level (section 2.3). In the simplest terms, transnational solidarity serves to ensure that the type of justice that is produced by national institutions takes account of the transnational economic relationships on the internal market, the social connections between mobile citizens and their host state, and the collective political commitments undertaken by Member States. The following chapters will distinguish between these three types of transnational solidarity, and describe them as instances of market solidarity, communitarian solidarity, and aspirational solidarity respectively.

2.1 The EU's Inability to 'Do' Redistributive Justice

As a consequence of the distinctly national character of the pursuit of justice, as discussed in the previous chapter, it should not come as a surprise that welfare competences have remained on the national level notwithstanding half a century of European integration. In fact, much of the success of the project of European cooperation and its objective of creating 'peace and prosperity' depended on their retention on the national level. In the run-up towards the negotiations on the Treaty of Rome, it was thought that *both* the creation of a common market, which would stimulate economic growth and increase living standards while intertwining the different polities in order to create political stability,[1] *and* the national welfare state with its solidarity mechanisms, which would continue to look after the well-being and specific social needs of its citizens, were necessary in order to create a stable, efficient, and 'just' Europe.[2] In other words, the structure of the integration process was meant to create a common market while at the same time supporting the Member States' autonomy in welfare policy.[3] This 'separate track' solution would, especially 'when account is taken of the strength of the trade union movement in European countries and of the sympathy of European governments for social aspirations',[4] serve as a guarantee against unacceptable social consequences of economic integration and thereby 'socially embed' the European integration project on the national level in accordance with the justice claims of the national electorates.[5] Even though the Union's legislative competences in the social area have gradually increased over time in order to meet new functional challenges in the establishment of the internal market, they still do not extend beyond a merely complementary role in labour law,[6] and an even more restricted mandate in fields covering redistributive welfare.[7] That the primary task of welfare redistribution remains on the national level is also reflected by the lack of taxation powers for the Union, and by the fact that the Treaty obliges the Union to respect the Member States' autonomy in core welfare areas, explicitly prohibiting harmonizing measures.[8] Several aspects of the Member States' welfare

[1] Official summary of the 'Ohlin Report' (1956) 74 International Labour Review 101.

[2] D. Damjanovic and B. De Witte, 'Welfare Integration through EU Law: The Overall Picture in the Light of the Lisbon Treaty', in U. Neergaard, R. Nielsen, and L. Roseberry (eds.), *Integrating Welfare Functions into EU Law* (Copenhagen: DJOF, 2009) 59. See also M. Ferrera, *The Boundaries of Welfare* (Oxford: OUP, 2005) 94.

[3] In fact, it is felt that the main concern of the Ohlin Group, which discussed the need for social harmonization as a precondition for effective economic integration, was that of 'guaranteeing the maintenance (and progressive expansion) of highly developed and autonomous systems of social protection within individual Member States'. See S. Giubboni, *Social Rights and Market Freedom in the European Constitution: A Labour Law Perspective* (Cambridge: CUP, 2006) 42 and more generally 157–8.

[4] Report by a Group of ILO Experts, 'Social Aspects of European Economic Co-operation' (Geneva: ILO, 1956) para 210.

[5] Official summary of the 'Ohlin Report' 108 and 112, claiming that social policies as such have an impact on international trade, but their content would not reduce the benefits that any Member State derives from free trade.

[6] Article 153 TFEU. [7] Article 156 TFEU.

[8] Articles 149 TFEU and 153 (2)(b) TFEU. See also Declaration 31 attached to the Treaty of Lisbon.

models, such as the fundamental principles underlying the social security systems, or the right to strike, have even been intentionally ring-fenced from Union interference.[9] The refusal of Member States to transfer welfare competences to the Union is informed both by the preoccupation that such transfer would reduce the legitimacy of the national political process, which strongly depends on its central role in the generation and distribution of policies related to citizen well-being,[10] and by the more normative preoccupation that the Union is institutionally incapable of sustaining redistributive welfare tasks. Such claims highlight the absence on the European level of the two essential institutional preconditions for effective and 'just' social structuring discussed in the previous chapter: a functioning system of representative democracy, and (consequently) the capacity to generate and sustain interpersonal solidarities and communal redistributive arrangements.[11]

The first limitation lies in the fact that the European institutional structure is not democratic enough to determine the normative content of social policies correctly. The requirement of a strong democratic process is essential given that the legitimacy of, and participation in, redistributive welfare as an expression of social justice is premised on the dynamic—institutionalized through the electoral process—that the citizens' normative preferences must eventually be translated into social policy.[12] This holds true especially in relation to questions of great normative salience and political contestation such as social justice and redistributive welfare. Simply put, as citizens must be able to get what they want, whichever polity decides on matters of welfare must ensure that its institutions are capable of actually determining (and implementing) its citizens' needs and desires. The *Bundesverfassungsgericht* (*BverfG* or German Constitutional Court) has conceptualized this in terms of the individual's right to (political) self-determination.[13] It argues that in order to ensure such self-determination, 'the right, and the practical possibilities of action, to take conceptual decisions regarding systems of social security and other social policy and labour market policy decisions',[14] must remain on the national level, given that the Union's system of representative

[9] Article 153 (4) and (5) TFEU.

[10] See e.g. S. Bartolini, 'Old and New Peripheries in the Processes of European Territorial Integration?' in C. Ansell and G. Di Palma (eds.), *Restructuring Territoriality* (Cambridge: CUP, 2004) 25.

[11] See section 1.2.

[12] A. Heritier, 'Elements of Democratic Legitimation in Europe: An Alternative Perspective' (1999) 6 JEPP 278, and *Lisbon* ruling of BVerfG 2 BvE 2/08 of 30 June 2009 paras 208 and 256.

[13] Article 38 of the German *Grundgesetz*.

[14] *Lisbon* ruling of BverfG para 399.

democracy cannot guarantee that the social policy decisions potentially made accurately reflect the normative wishes of the electorate.

The *BverfG* essentially lays down the democratic benchmark for the legitimate exercise of welfare competences. Most of the elements identified as lacking in the EU had already been discussed at length in academia. The democratic benchmark includes the requirement that the main legislative body be directly elected[15] on the basis of free and equal elections,[16] through an organized competition between political forces,[17] which are open to the participation of all citizens,[18] and are conducted in a space of public and free opinion-forming.[19] Any government established through such election must moreover be sure to represent the will of the majority of the electorate,[20] and be challenged by an unhindered opposition that may come to power upon a shift of the electorate's opinion.[21] It is evident that the European Union does not meet these requirements. The limited powers of the European Parliament (EP), as the body representing the European electorate,[22] the insulation of the European executive and the agenda-setting from the vote,[23] the entrenchment of national interests in the decision-making process,[24] the digressively proportionate composition of the EP,[25] and consequently its incapacity to guarantee simple majority decision making,[26] the absence of genuine European political parties,[27] the limited political participation in

[15] Ibid. para 210.

[16] Ibid. paras 212 and 270; C. Lord and J. Pollak, 'Unequal but Democratic? Equality According to Karlsruhe' (2013) 20 JEPP 190ff.

[17] Ibid. paras 213 and 270; A. Follesdal and S. Hix, 'Why there is a Democratic Deficit in the EU: A Reply to Moravcsik' (2006) 44 JCMS 533.

[18] Ibid. para 250. See on the need for mass mobilization T. Risse, *A Community of Europeans? Transnational Identities and Public Spheres* (Ithaca, NY: Cornell University Press 2010) ch. 10.

[19] Ibid. paras 213, 250, 268, and 270.

[20] Ibid. paras 209, 210, 250, and 270; C. Lord, 'The Democratic Legitimacy of Codecision' (2013) 20 JEPP 1056.

[21] Ibid. paras 213, 268, and 270.

[22] Ibid. paras 284 and 286.

[23] P. Dann, 'European Parliament and Executive Federalism: Approaching a Parliament in a Semi-Parliamentary Democracy' (2003) 9 ELJ 558–60, see also *Lisbon* ruling of BverfG 2 BvE 2/08 of 30 June 2009 paras 270 and 280.

[24] R. Bellamy and D. Castiglione, 'Three Models of Democracy, Political Community and Representation in the EU' (2013) 20 JEPP 217.

[25] *Lisbon* ruling of BverfG paras 277 and 280; Lord, 'Democratic Legitimacy' 1070.

[26] Ibid. paras 280 and 284; G. Majone, *Rethinking the Union of Europe Post-Crisis* (Cambridge: CUP, 2014) 236–9.

[27] Ibid. para 280, S. Bartolini, *Restructuring Europe* (Oxford: OUP, 2005) 41.

European elections,[28] lack of accountability in the legislative process,[29] and the absence of a European public sphere[30] all severely restrict the legitimacy of Europe's potential assumption of welfare competences.

The second institutional problem faced by the Union follows from its lack of a robust political space. As Brunkhorst has convincingly argued, democratic structures are indispensable in producing (or, less cynically, capturing) the feelings of solidarity that exist in a polity.[31] And while it may be true that we are 'linked with each other through trade, commerce, literature, language, music, arts, entertainment, religion, medicine, healthcare, politics, news reports, media communication',[32] the kind of general, long-term, undisputed, thick solidarity that sustains actual, *positive* welfare entitlements cannot be found or administrated in such transnational settings. While some scholars have argued that the thickness of solidarity required for stable redistribution of resources can only be found on the national level, and that in fact the ethnic concept of nationality is a vital factor in the creation of a 'community of fate', and in the reproduction of commitments of solidarity towards others within that community,[33] other scholars have (more convincingly) argued that the development of solidarity is primarily dependent, not on ethno-cultural links, but on democratic structures that connect individuals within the same polity.[34] Habermas and Brunkhorst, for example, argue that solidarity emerges as a by-product of the interpersonal links created, strengthened, and reproduced by way of a democratic process. Their argument against the development of European norms of justice, then, would not be that the Union lacks a *demos*, a homogenous ethno-cultural identity or 'community of fate',[35] but rather that the EU lacks a political system that

[28] The most recent EP election (in 2014) had a voter turnout of 43% on average, taking into account that in two Member States voting is compulsory.

[29] See J. Neyer, *The Justification of Europe: A Political Theory of Supranational Integration* (Oxford: OUP, 2012); Lord, 'Democratic Legitimacy' 1085.

[30] H. Brunkhorst, *Solidarity: From Civic Friendship to a Global Legal Community* (Cambridge, Mass.: MIT, 2005) 119ff., and D. Grimm, 'Does Europe Need a Constitution?' (1995) 1 ELJ 293–4.

[31] Brunkhorst, *Solidarity*.

[32] A. Sen, *The Idea of Justice* (New York: Penguin, 2010) 172–3.

[33] See D. Miller, *On Nationality* (Oxford: OUP, 1995) 48; D. Miller, *Citizenship and National Identity* (Cambridge: Polity, 2000) 31–2. This position finds little empirical support. See e.g. M. Wright and T. Reeskens, 'Of What Cloth are the Ties that Bind? National Identity and Support for the Welfare state across 29 European countries' (2013) 20 JEPP 1443.

[34] See Brunkhorst, *Solidarity*, esp. ch. 3.

[35] Grimm, 'Does Europe Need a Constitution?' 282.

is sophisticated enough to produce the patterns of socialization and engagement that produce the political solidarity that is required to sustain redistributive practices.[36] The *BverfG* collapses these two sources of solidarity in its assessment of the democratic deficit in the EU, arguing that the development of a 'just' social condition presupposes a degree of vertical identification. As long as the patterns of vertical and horizontal identification and interaction that underlie the determination of welfare policy remain inextricably tied up with national characteristics such as a shared language, culture, and history, social policies cannot be transferred to the European level:

> Even if due to the great successes of European integration, a joint European public that engages in an issue-related cooperation in the rooms of resonance of their respective states is evidently growing, [...] it cannot be overlooked [...] that the public perception of factual issues and of political leaders remains connected to a considerable extent to patterns of identification which are related to the nation-state, language, history and culture. The principle of democracy [...] therefore require[s] to factually restrict the transfer and exercise of sovereign powers to the European Union in a predictable manner particularly in central political areas of the space of personal development and the shaping of the circumstances of life by social policy.[37]

This claim, which suggests that the legitimacy of redistributive policies is directly correlated with the strength of the identification between polity and *demos*, makes sense. Whether this requires a shared language, history, and culture is, of course, another story. Without doubt, however, the absence of democratic structures in the EU is directly related to the absence of a type of solidarity that is thick enough to sustain redistributive policies.[38]

That redistributive practices were practically impossible to legitimize on the supranational level had in fact been clear from the beginning of the integration process. Yet, since the outbreak of the euro-crisis, the EU has engaged in exactly that: unprecedented and explicit redistributive practices dictated on the supranational level.[39] By way of the excessive deficit procedure, the macro-economic imbalance procedure, and the European Semester and its country-specific recommendations, the Commission has

[36] J. Habermas, 'Democracy, Solidarity and the European Crisis', Lecture delivered 26 April 2013 in Leuven.

[37] See *Lisbon* ruling of *BVerfG* para 251.

[38] Bartolini, *Restructuring Europe*, 104.

[39] M. Dawson and F. De Witte, 'Constitutional Balance in the EU after the Euro-crisis' (2013) 76 MLR 817, and 'Self-Determination in the Constitutional Future of the EU' (2015) 20 ELJ (forthcoming).

gained significant influence in domestic budgetary structures and national welfare policies, typically suggesting a scaling back of expenditure and welfare benefits. These mechanisms exist for all Member States, regardless of their economic situation. For the Member States that have had to ask for a bail-out, the imposition of transnational redistributive preferences is even more glaringly obvious. The Memoranda of Understanding that such Member States are asked to sign with the troika, composed of the Commission, ECB, and IMF, typically demands vast welfare changes: from the liberalization of public services to pension cuts, and from the demand that all collective agreements be rescinded to severe decreases in standards of healthcare.[40] Since such vast redistributive realignments cannot be justified and legitimized through democratic structures in the EU (they do not exist), the EU has increasingly looked at the Commission and the European Council for another type of legitimacy, this time based on executive power and authoritarian liberal practices.[41] In fact, most scholars suggest that the EU should increase this transfer of power from representative institutions to executive institutions in order to legitimize the redistributive convergence programmes that the euro-zone Member States are required to undergo in order to stabilize the monetary union.[42]

What this shift since the euro-crisis demonstrates, more than anything, is the inadequacy of the Union's institutional system in dealing with highly divisive and salient policy questions: its institutional set-up is simply not sophisticated enough to be able to legitimize redistributive practices or sustain commitments of solidarity. The changes required in order to enable the EU to engage in such practices in a democratic and legitimate manner are significant, and go to the very nature of the integration process. Beyond remedying the institutional problems already identified,[43] what seems to be required is the vast re-enfranchisement of the European citizens by

[40] Dawson and De Witte, 'Constitutional Balance in the EU' (2013) 76 MLR 825, and F. Scharpf, 'Monetary Union, Fiscal Crisis and the Preemption of Democracy' (2011) 36 LEQS 22.

[41] M. Wilkinson, 'The Specter of Authoritarian Liberalism: Reflections on the Constitutional Crisis of the European Union' (2013) 14 GLJ 527.

[42] Dawson and F. De Witte, 'Self-Determination', with reference to J. C. Piris, *The Future of Europe: Towards a 2-Speed EU?* (Cambridge: CUP, 2012) 106–20; G. Majone, *Rethinking the Union of Europe Post-Crisis* (Cambridge: CUP, 2014) 118–24; M. Poiares Maduro, 'A New Governance for the European Union and the Euro: Democracy and Justice' (2012) 11 RSCAS Policy Papers.

[43] See earlier in this section.

strengthening the role of the representative institutions in the EU, and by recreating, on the transnational level, the cleavages in society that generate distinct and competing claims towards the appropriate level of redistribution that is required in the pursuit of justice.[44] This would require a radical overhaul of the Union's normative, institutional, and legal framework,[45] and would entail a great shift in democratic authority from the national level to the supranational level—which appears neither a feasible nor a particularly attractive option for most governments.[46]

2.2 Enter Europe: Justice Norms Beyond the Nation State

Notwithstanding these fundamental limitations to the EU's capacity to contribute to the attainment of the normative objectives of 'social justice' and 'citizen well-being' pursued by the nation state, the EU clearly possesses certain social policy competences,[47] and, as the *BverfG* highlighted, it *must* even be social.[48] This apparent contradiction between the Member States' clear prerogative in welfare construction and the simultaneous development of Europe's social dimension can be best explained in terms of their respective spatial predisposition. Simply put, while it is true that the EU cannot reproduce the institutional and normative preconditions for the development of the type of justice that is produced on the national level; the development of justice within nation states also, as we saw in the previous chapter, produces some significant normative deficiencies. The EU, simply put, is much better positioned to tackle such deficiencies, and the claims of justice that it

[44] M. Dawson and F. De Witte, 'From Balance to Conflict: A New Constitution for Europe' (2015) 20 ELJ (forthcoming).

[45] Ibid. Bartolini, *Restructuring Europe*, 248.

[46] D. Chalmers, 'Democratic Self-Government in Europe: Domestic Solutions to the EU Legitimacy Crisis' (Policy Network Paper 2013); F. Scharpf, 'Political Legitimacy in a Non-optimal Currency Area', in O. Cramme and S. Hobolt (eds.), *Democratic Politics in a European Union under Stress* (Oxford: OUP, 2014).

[47] *Lisbon* ruling of BverfG, para 393.

[48] *Lisbon* ruling of BverfG, para 258: 'Germany's participation in the process of integration depends, inter alia, on the European Union's commitment to social principles. Accordingly the Basic Law not only safeguards social tasks for the German state union against supranational demands in a defensive manner but wants to commit the European public authority to social responsibility in the spectrum of tasks accorded to it.'

produces specifically serve to do so. The first concern about the development of norms of justice within Member States is that its dependence on normative closure and its articulation of *one* type of justice (mediated through the political system) means that it is not very good at respecting the individual's vision of the 'good life'. The individual can voice such a vision in the political process, but is—in return—bound to the outcome of that process, even if it does not conform to his view of the 'good life'. European Union law, and in particular its free movement provisions, can be understood as remedying this problem: it allows individuals to chase whichever type of life they consider 'good', regardless of the normative and spatial limitations imposed by their own Member State (section 2.2.1). The second deficiency implicit in the development of justice on the national level follows from its political closure. Simply put, only *insiders* receive political rights that allow them to engage in the communal elaboration of what is 'just'. This potentially creates a structural parochial bias that discriminates against mobile citizens by not incorporating their needs, concerns, and experiences in the elaboration of norms of justice, and by not reflecting the different ways in which they contribute to society in the host state. European Union law, and in particular its obligations of non-discrimination on the basis of nationality, can be understood as correcting this, and as committing the development of justice on the national level to the principle of equal citizenship *beyond* the nation state (section 2.2.2). In correcting the generation of norms of justice on the national level, however, the EU needs to remain sensitive to the way in which it destabilizes domestic structures of justice. As was discussed in the previous chapter, commitments of justice emerge primarily from the associative connection between individual participants in the same political project. The Union's claims of justice are *parasitic* on that connection (the EU cannot sustain redistributive practices on its own) but at the same time reformulate that connection by insisting on free movement between political projects and the incorporation of 'outsiders' in its functioning. A third claim of justice that is emerging on the European level, then, sees to the stabilization of domestic redistributive commitments by way of EU law. In simple terms, this means that the demands of free movement and non-discrimination on the basis of nationality must be made sensitive to the commitments of justice undertaken by national citizens (section 2.2.3). As will be discussed in the next chapters, the way in which this takes place is by integrating the associative ties that bind citizens beyond the Member State within national claims of justice. This process, as will become clear, can best be conceptualized as the emergence of different forms of transnational solidarity.

2.2.1 *Free Movement as a Commitment to Individual Freedom*

The first way in which EU law serves the demands of justice is by extending the capacity of individual citizens to pursue their conception of 'the good life'. The right to free movement, on this view, not only allows citizens to choose to move to another Member State for professional, personal, social, or cultural reasons; it also categorically prevents Member States from 'locking in' their own citizens and subjecting them to a type of life that is not conducive to the 'good life' (of a particular citizen). In other words, EU free movement law extends individual choices beyond the confines of political boundaries. The justice claim inherent in free movement is that it—much like the whole integration project—unshackles individual behaviour, and the pursuit of the individual's aspirations, from the limitations imposed through the national decision-making process. The liberating effect of this lies in the fact that—since individual preferences are incomplete, must allow for future changes of mind, and are abstracted through the political process[49]—*one* national political process can never fully reflect and respect the normative demands placed on it by individuals. As Amartya Sen's work on the concept of justice suggests, living a 'good life' is not only about social entitlements, and political participation, it is also about the possibility of making valued choices in life:

> In assessing our lives, we have reason to be interested not only in the kind of lives we manage to lead, but also in the freedom that we actually have to choose between different styles and ways of living.[50]
>
> Our motives [for living any particular life] are for us to choose—not, of course, without reason, but unregimented by the authoritarianism of some context-independent axioms or by the need to conform to some canonical specification of 'proper' objectives and values. The latter would have had the effect of arbitrarily narrowing permissible 'reasons for choice', and this certainly can be the source of a substantial 'unfreedom' in the form of an inability to use one's reason to decide about one's values and choices.[51]

The extension of opportunities and choices for Europe's citizens beyond those offered within the national context by way of free movement, in other words, can be seen to be 'just' because it expands the capacity of citizens to

[49] See A. Sen, *Rationality and Freedom* (Cambridge, Mass.: Harvard University Press, 2002) 77.

[50] Sen, *The Idea of Justice*, 227. See also J. Griffin, *On Human Rights* (Oxford: OUP, 2008) 167.

[51] Sen, *Rationality and Freedom*, 5–6.

attain their *own* conception of 'the good life'. This insight from social choice theory, which focuses on ranking available realizations in terms of their relevance for the individual's ('good') life, shows how limited the nationally bounded conception of justice is. The political structure through which it is articulated is not very good at accommodating the irreducible plurality of conceptions of 'the good' that exists in society. Even though all citizens can express their diverse views in the electoral process,[52] in return they are expected to abide by the (majoritarian) outcome—even if it does not conform to their personal preference.

The rights to free movement serve to overcome this limitation. As such, EU law liberates the individual from 'his' or 'her' political community and encourages him or her to *choose* to pursue his or her own interpretation of a 'good life', wherever that may lie and whatever that may prioritize.[53] On this view, as highlighted by Benhabib, 'crossing borders and seeking entry into different polities [becomes] (…) an expression of human freedom and the search for human betterment in a world which we have to share with our fellow human beings'.[54] The reason for exercising individual movement is irrelevant—exactly *because* it is meant to reflect the irreducible plurality of conceptions of 'the good'.[55] The individual exercise of the free movement rights is thus seen as expressing what a citizen thinks constitutes a 'good life'. The Stoics already appreciated this connection between individual preferences and the capacity to act on them: 'the best indication of a person's

[52] Such variations are important given that we can never predict how different citizens will value the same outcome, even if they have voted for it. See on this problem of subjectivity T. Nagel, 'What is it Like to be a Bat?' (1974) 83 Philosophical Review 441–3.

[53] See IP/06/389: 'Europeans move for love and a better quality of life.' See Favell for a whole book full of reasons why citizens move to another Member State: A. Favell, *Eurostars and Eurocities* (Oxford: Blackwell, 2008). See also A. Favell and E. Recchi, 'Social Mobility and Spatial Mobility' in A. Favell and V. Guirandon (eds.), *Sociology of the European Union* (Basingstoke: Palgrave 2011).

[54] S. Benhabib, *Rights of Others* (Cambridge: CUP, 2004) 177. Within the EU, however, the reason for mobility seems to be no longer economic necessity but choice. See Favell, *Eurostars and Eurocities*, 84.

[55] Voltaire already captured this centuries ago. Candide and Cacambo, after having suffered from blatant injustice in any country they had visited, arrived in El Dorado—a place better, fairer, more beautiful and more just than any they had visited or could possibly imagine. The realization that they would never have it better, however, did not prevent their desire to move on. Irrational as it may ultimately be, a change of scenery felt necessary: 'the desire for freedom of movement, to cut a figure amongst their own people, and to tell their travellers' tales, induced these fortunate beings to forsake their good fortunes'. Voltaire, *Candide, ou L'Optimisme* (New York: Penguin, 2006) 52.

philosophy is not what they say but how they behave'.[56] Free movement, in this sense, suggests that the capacity to decide on what constitutes a 'good life' should be conceptually distinct from the individual's participation in the political process.[57] The former encapsulates and transcends the latter. European Union law, in other words, extends the potential scope for the individual's realization of the 'good life' beyond a Member State's spatial and normative boundaries, and as such can be understood to help overcome the limitations of the development of justice through national political structures.

From the start of the integration process, the most dynamic and pervasive provisions of EU law have been the free movement provisions, which allow factors of production (and in a later stage, citizens) to move around freely throughout the territories of the Member States. This logic of free movement originally served as an instrument to take the sting out of nationalism,[58] and it has always been understood as a tool to increase economic efficiency.[59] Increasingly, however, it is conceived as an instrument to generate citizen well-being and pursue ideas of justice. Rights to free movement provide a 'trampoline' for individuals to vault over the limitations imposed by the national decision-making process,[60] and encourage the individual to choose to pursue his or her own interpretation of a 'good life', wherever that may lie. The free movement provisions thus translate the importance of individual choice in the European context and institutionally entrench it. As Weiler and Lockhart have put it: '[p]art of the Community ethos (...) lies in the important civilizing effect [which] (...) is achieved through the intended inability of Member States, practical and legal, to screen off different social choices, legally sanctioned, in other Member States'.[61] This

[56] See J. Sellars, *Stoicism* (Chesham: Acumen, 2006) 32.

[57] Rawls collapses the two: J. Rawls, *A Theory of Justice* (Oxford: OUP, 1971) 415–16. See also M. Sandel, *Liberalism and the Limits of Justice* (Cambridge: CUP, 1998) 163–7.

[58] See M. P. Maduro, 'Reforming the Market or the State? Article 30 and the European Constitution' (1997) 3 ELJ 62, where he highlights the 'inevitable connection between the aims of individual freedom and the avoidance of nationalism'.

[59] M. P. Maduro, 'European Constitutionalism and Three Models of Social Europe', in M. Hesselink (ed.), *The Politics of a European Civil Code* (Alphen aan den Rijn: Kluwer, 2006) 128–9.

[60] T. Kingreen, 'Fundamental Freedoms', in A. Von Bogdandy and J. Bast (eds.), *Principles of European Constitutional Law* (Oxford: Hart, 2008) 561; D. Halberstam, 'The Bride of Messina: Constitutionalism and Democracy in Europe' (2005) 30 ELRev 777; P. Pescatore, 'The Doctrine of Direct Effect: An Infant Disease of Community Law', (1983) 8 ELRev 158.

[61] J. Weiler and N. Lockhart, "Taking Rights Seriously" Seriously: The European Court of Justice and its Fundamental Rights Jurisprudence' (1995) 32 CML Rev 604.

logic of opportunity and choice underlies, of course, the construction of the European economic constitution. It is also reflected in the Court's understanding of free movement of students.[62] Fundamentally, however, EU law is agnostic as to the reasons for the exercise of free movement. Whether for love, better weather, work, the adventure or a certain language, skill, or cuisine—EU law devolves such choices to the individual. A good life, after all, means and requires different things for each citizen.[63]

This more aspirational interpretation of the rights to free movement is also strongly reflected in the Court's attitude towards the right of all EU citizens to move throughout the Union. Article 21 TFEU reflects this right: '[e]very citizen of the Union shall have the right to move and reside freely within the territory of the Member States, subject to the limitations and conditions laid down in the Treaties and by the measures adopted to give them effect.' The limitations and conditions to which Article 21 TFEU refers can be found in the string of directives enacted in the early 1990s, which essentially conditioned free movement upon the citizen not making use of the welfare system of the host Member State.[64] This way, it was thought, the extension of free movement beyond the 'market citizen' would not produce unreasonable burdens on the national welfare systems. In essence, it extended the aspirational promise of free movement to cover 'rich' Europeans, excluding those who did not have enough resources to sustain themselves while resident in other Member States. Over the course of 15 years, however, the Court consistently lowered this threshold by widening the personal and material scope of Article 21 TFEU, and by insisting on the prohibition of discrimination on the basis of nationality in its application.[65] The requirements of sufficient resources and sickness insurance, central in the attempt of the directives to protect the national welfare state, are relegated, through the application of the principle of proportionality, to simple formal requirements

[62] Cf. the language of the Court used in *Bressol*, where it held that the '*opportunity* for students coming from other Member States to gain access to higher education' constitutes the 'very essence of the principle of free movement of students' which is protected by the Treaty. See Case C-73/08 *Bressol* [2010] ECR I-2735 para 79. My emphasis.

[63] See, on the last point, F. De Witte, 'Sex, Drugs and EU Law' (2013) 50 CML Rev 1545.

[64] Articles 1 to Directive 90/364, Directive 90/365, and Directive 93/96; now recast as Article 8 (4) of Directive 2004/38.

[65] See e.g. Case C-413/99 *Baumbast* [2002] ECR I-7091; or Case C-408/03 *Commission* v *Belgium* [2006] ECR I-2647. See, more generally, M. Dougan, 'The Constitutional Dimension of the Case Law on Union Citizenship' (2006) 31 ELRev 613.

that citizens can easily meet.[66] More stringent requirements imposed by Member States have been consistently invalidated by reference to the unconditional character of Article 21 TFEU,[67] as have attempts to mitigate this lack of welfare protection by expelling foreign citizens making claims on the national welfare state.[68] The recent *Dano* case, however, might herald a more restrictive interpretation of those requirements.[69] The Court has generally interpreted Union citizenship as a new individual freedom to be protected by the European constitutional order. This emphasis on choice and opportunity, allowing Union citizens to move to the state in which they think their 'good life' can be found, is the first justice claim that is implicit in Europe's make-up. In essence, it is premised on the recognition that national processes of collective will-formation are not very good at respecting the individual's preferences.

2.2.2 *Non-discrimination as a Demand of Equal Citizenship*

The opening up of spatial boundaries for all Union citizens through free movement has highlighted a more systemic problem of justice in the EU. Simply put, the development of justice within segregated political units is strongly contingent on the procedural demand of equal political citizenship for 'insiders'.[70] This mechanism ensures that each national citizen's needs and desires (and conception of 'the good life') are equally incorporated within the development of the norms that govern society and that such norms are free from bias in favour of certain groups in society. At the same time, this demand for internal political equality *excludes* non-members (such as mobile EU citizens) from the political process altogether. While migrant EU citizens obtain electoral rights for municipal and European elections,[71] they do not obtain the right to vote in nation-wide, general elections. The latter, however, are indisputably the most crucial when assessed from the

[66] R. Bellamy, 'The Liberty of the Post-Moderns? Market and Civic Freedom within the EU' (2009) 1 LEQS Paper Series 17–18.

[67] See Dougan, 'Constitutional Dimension of the Case Law', 613, and A. Somek, 'Solidarity Decomposed: Being and Time in European Citizenship' (2007) 32 ELRev 795.

[68] See Somek, 'Solidarity Decomposed', 796–7, and Case C-184/99 *Grzelczyk* [2001] ECR I-6193 paras 42–3; Case C-456/02 *Trojani* [2004] ECR I-7573 para 45.

[69] Case C-333/13 *Dano* [nyr]. See also section 4.3.3.

[70] C. Joppke, 'Transformation of Citizenship: Status, Rights, Identity' (2007) 11 Citizenship Studies 38.

[71] Article 20 (2)(b) TFEU.

perspective of the incorporation of the individuals' needs and desires within the way society is structured, even in federal states. In other words, only Dutch nationals get to vote on what is 'just' within the Dutch territory, even though it has an effect on the lives, needs, and desires of non-national residents.

This disconnect between the subjects and objects of rule is problematic in so far as it possibly allows for the exact bias that the political process was meant to prevent, where the normative preferences, social experiences, and associative commitments of a particular group in society are excluded from consideration.[72] To use familiar vocabulary, migrant Union citizens are taxed without being represented in the political process in their host state. This is particularly problematic in the elaboration of welfare standards. Given that such policies typically express nationally bounded solidarities (be it in ethic or civic terms),[73] the procedural exclusion of non-nationals risks creating a substantive normative bias that discriminates against non-nationals in access to social entitlements, and that fails to reflect their economic or social engagement in the host state polity. The very requirement for effective redistribution on the national level—political deliberation by insiders—thus creates injustice when perceived from the transnational perspective.[74]

The second way in which EU law serves the demands of justice is by safeguarding the principle of equal citizenship in these situations. It does so by attaching a right to non-discrimination on the basis of nationality to the individual exercise of free movement. This is meant to prevent parochial biases in national decision-making and to ensure the inclusion of the experiences, needs, desires, commitments, and interest of mobile EU citizens in the national political process. As Joppke has correctly identified, it is the liberal-democratic principle—which requires congruence between the

[72] M. Kumm, 'The Idea of Socratic Contestation and the Right to Justification: The Point of Rights-based Proportionality Review' (2010) 4 Law & Ethics of Human Rights 157.

[73] See section 1.3.

[74] The defence of equal citizenship here differs fundamentally from the more traditional recourse in EU law to the 'argument from transnational effect', which understands EU law as correcting the effect of democracies vis-à-vis other democracies, that is, *outside* its territorial borders. In this section, equal citizenship is not under threat because of a democracy's external effect, but because of *internal* biases. See, for the 'traditional' understanding of the argument from transnational effect, J. Neyer, *The Justification of Europe: A Political Theory of Supranational Integration* (Oxford: OUP, 2012), and for a thorough critique, A. Somek, 'The Darling Dogma of Bourgeois Europeanists' (2014) 19 ELJ 688.

subjects and objects of rule—that plays a central role here.[75] The justification for the development of this second claim of justice implicit in EU law, then, is to re-establish the essential procedural notion that the development of justice norms be guided by objective criteria free from parochial bias.[76] Kumm helps to explain:

> On a high level of abstraction it is possible to state a relatively uncontentious criterion: The structure, composition, and practices of political institutions must reflect a commitment to free and equal citizenship. It is clear that a process which entrenches structures that tend to privilege a particular class of actors in each jurisdiction does not fulfil this requirement. [...] The structural bias provides a reason—a weak *prima facie* case, not a conclusive reason—for the federal legislator to consider intervention. [77]

The most evident solution to the problem of 'exclusionary neglect' would be to extend full electoral rights to 'outsiders' that reside in a host Member State. That way, impartiality would be restored within each Member State, allowing citizens to move, vote, and participate in the outcomes wherever they wish. Yet, the full equalization of migrants with nationals in terms of political rights remains very problematic, for both normative and legal reasons. Tying electoral rights to residence somewhat dissolves the bond between membership and the nation state, which asks fundamental questions about the role of collectivities in the expression of state sovereignty, and about the role of the integration process, that the EU is not willing to ask (or answer). In addition, much resistance is to be expected by national institutional actors, as it fundamentally changes the perception of what the 'state' is for.[78] Rather than the institutional

[75] Joppke, 'Transformation of Citizenship', 40. See also C. Offe, 'Whose Good is the Common Good?' (2012) 38 Philosophy and Social Criticism 680.

[76] At the conceptual basis of each theory of justice lies a demand of impartiality on its elaboration. Rawls's 'veil of ignorance', Sen's focus on public deliberation and rational scrutiny, or Smith's 'impartial spectator' are all attempts to ensure that decisions be free from biases and prejudices, equally incorporate everyone's views, and be based on objective reasoning. See specifically Sen, *The Idea of Justice*, 138–52 and 54 where he argues that the foundational idea of fairness and justice 'must be a demand to avoid bias in our evaluations, taking note of the interests and concerns of others as well, and in particular the need to avoid being influenced by our respective vested interests, or by our personal priorities or eccentricities or prejudices. It can broadly be seen as a demand for impartiality.'

[77] See M. Kumm, 'Constitutionalising Subsidiarity in Integrated Markets: The Case of Tobacco Regulation in the European Union' (2006) 12 ELJ 513–4, even though his argument dealt with the scope of (what is now) Article 114 TFEU.

[78] One need only think of the *BverfG*'s insistence on the inalienable right to political self-determination of *German* citizens.

and normative manifestation of a *demos* (if not necessarily an *ethnos*), and the container of certain intangible values associated with membership of a political community, the nation state would become an instrument for the effective realization of functional demands. Consider the example of Luxembourg, in which migrant Union citizens make up 33.5 per cent of the (potential) electorate.[79] Extending voting rights to such citizens may or may not have a (large) impact on decisions concerning taxation, migration, or nuclear energy. What is more problematic, however, from a constitutional perspective, is how it would affect answers to the question if the *Grand-Duc* should remain the head of state, or whether Luxembourg should form a new republic with Wallonia and parts of Germany. Opening political participation to all residents destabilizes the basic assumption that collective self-determination is a tool not just for the functional construction of society but also for the elaboration and constant normative reiteration of what the nation state 'means' to its citizens, and that such a privilege is reserved for those citizens that can demonstrate a particular commitment to the normative project of the polity.[80] In other words, polities not only facilitate but also contain normative claims. At the same time, *not* extending electoral rights to migrant residents may also seem unjust. Surely someone who has lived in Luxembourg for six years should both be able to decide how his or her taxes are spent and, in particular, have access to the social structures he or she helps to finance? If not taken seriously, the 'exclusionary neglect' of the national political process could severely hamper the individual migrant's capacity to make use of his or her right to free movement and *at the same time* still enjoy positive welfare entitlements to—say—education, healthcare, or disability benefits.

European Union law has found a remarkably easy solution to this conundrum. Instead of extending political rights to migrant EU citizens, EU law offers them a right to non-discrimination on the basis of nationality during their stay in the host state. Whenever a Union citizen finds himself in another Member State, he or she must be treated the same as nationals of the host state. In other words, his or her needs and desires are not incorporated

[79] Assuming an equal proportion of minors among Luxembourgers and nationals of other EU Member States. See for numbers: <http://www.migrationinformation.org/Feature/display.cfm?id=587>, accessed February 2015.

[80] See, for a good discussion, R. Baubock, 'Why European Citizenship?' (2007) 8 Theoretical Inquiries into Law 471–80.

in the construction of society by *ex-ante* participation in the political process, but by *ex-post* access to whatever the nationals consider 'just' and 'fair'. These rights to non-discrimination on the basis of nationality are laid down in Regulation 492/2011, Directive 2004/38, Article 18 TFEU, and have been read into the five free movement provisions. The choice to move to another Member State is thus accompanied by a guarantee that the migrant can access the social entitlements that the citizens of the host state consider necessary for themselves to live a 'good life', and that serve to alleviate their needs and accommodate their desires.

On this view, the principle of non-discrimination on the basis of nationality becomes an instrument to correct distributive outcomes on the national level to account for the associative obligations towards those excluded from participation in the national decision-making process. Azoulai calls this the review function of EU free movement law, which 'helps the Member States to "recontextualise" the decision-making process at national level to force them to take account of interests coming from or situations in other Member States, which are not only interests of firms but also of citizens, workers or students'.[81] Equal access to the outcome of the political process, thus, goes some way towards the incorporation of the needs and desires of outsiders[82] and towards teasing out parochial biases, as it forces Member States to take account of the individuals beyond their closed circle of 'membership', and of the associative ties that such individuals have built up in the host Member State.[83] Properly understood, then, the principle of non-discrimination is a political right to representation that serves to internalize the voices of resident migrants.[84] The principle of non-discrimination on the basis of nationality thus seems to mitigate the exclusionary potential of the concept of political membership, which plays a central role in processes of redistribution on the national level. As such, EU law serves to re-establish the basic notion that all residents are equal.

[81] L. Azoulai, 'The Court of Justice and the Social Market Economy: The Emergence of an Ideal and the Conditions for its Realisation' (2008) 45 CML Rev 1342–3.

[82] Cf. Somek who argues that 'so long as outsiders are not discriminated against they can be said to be virtually represented in the political process'. See A. Somek, 'The Argument from Transnational Effects I' (2010) 16 ELJ 323.

[83] Azoulai, 'The Court of Justice', 1342–3.

[84] See C. Joerges, 'European Law as Conflict of Laws', in C. Joerges and J. Neyer (eds.), *Deliberative Supranationalism Revisited* (2006) 20 EUI Working Paper 22–3. See, in the context of the free movement of goods, M. P. Maduro, *We, the Court* (Oxford: Hart, 1998).

2.2.3 *EU Law and the Stability of the Welfare State*

So far we have looked at how EU law attempts to remedy the normative deficiencies of the pursuit of justice on the national level. On this view, EU law enhances the capacity of individuals to pursue their conception of 'the good life' and ensures the principle of equal citizenship. The way in which EU law does this, by attaching strong normative consequences to the individual exercise of free movement, however, potentially creates a very *divisive* and *parasitic* notion of justice.

Tying access to social benefits in a host Member State to the act of an individual is divisive for a very simple reason: it is not couched in communal decision-making processes that can legitimize its effects. The recent political challenges to the way in which EU law skews national distributive arrangements, with reference to the potential threat of 'welfare tourism', is but a symptom of this process.[85] European Union law recalibrates the locus for the elaboration of what justice means and requires away from the political process, which is exactly the process that serves to legitimize redistributive arrangements. Attaching normative importance to the individual's decision to move to another Member State generates a bias because it does not represent the plural conceptions of the 'good', but rather singles out one particular conception. It does not force Member States to incorporate the views of 'all Europeans' in any particular divisive social question, but only the views, and by proxy the needs and desires, of those that actually make use of the rights to free movement (even if they do not necessarily physically move!).[86] Several studies have shown that the *actual* exercise of free movement rights contains significant distortions and asymmetries, which are both the result of the *use* of EU law by repeat players and private litigants,[87] and the *way* in which rights to movement operate.[88] Given that national policies

[85] 'Editorial Comment: The Free Movement of Persons in the European Union: Salvaging the Dream while Explaining the Nightmare' (2014) 51 CML Rev 729, for examples of political challenges to welfare tourism. See also 'The Free Movement of Citizens', 29th Report of the House of Commons European Scrutiny Committee, 2014.

[86] A. Saydé, *Abuse of EU Law and Regulation of the Internal Market* (Oxford: Hart, 2014).

[87] M. P. Maduro, 'European Constitutionalism and Three Models of Social Europe', in M. Hesselink (ed.), *The Politics of a European Civil Code* (The Hague: Kluwer, 2006) 130. Fligstein shows that those exercising their rights under free movement are mostly professional, white-collar, middle-class citizens. See N. Fligstein, *Euro-Clash: The EU, European Identity and the Future of Europe* (Oxford: OUP, 2010) 170–86.

[88] F. Scharpf, 'The Asymmetry of European Integration, or: Why the EU cannot be a "Social Market Economy"' (2010) 8 Socioeconomic Review 218–20.

automatically incorporate such asymmetries (as a result of the obligations of non-discrimination), they structurally favour (in the most general terms) the much more mobile capital and the richer citizens over immobile labour and poorer citizens by making policy choices that go against the interests of such mobile actors unavailable. This process has been described in company law,[89] labour law,[90] and regulation of the marketing of goods[91]—where policy outcomes are structurally biased towards the interests of global (and mobile) capital. It is also visible, however, in access to social entitlements such as education, where 'the reality is that (poor and usually non-mobile) taxpayers from the host countries are supporting the education of (middle class) students from other Member States with whom they share little by way of community of interests'.[92] In certain fields of social policy, then, domestic collective choices are restricted by the need to respect the individual agency of those who actually move across borders. Such partial de-politicization is problematic *as such*, given that collective agency was exactly meant to tame such (often the very same) particularistic interests, but more fundamentally because it shows that the obligation of non-discrimination is *not* normatively neutral. The paradox is thus that allegedly non-represented external interests become over-represented in the internal elaboration of the just distribution of scarce resources. More fundamentally, it means that a polity might no longer be sensitive to the precise strength and nature of the associative commitments between citizens within the polity. In other words, the individual rights that companies and citizens derive from EU law have the potential to subvert—on the national level—the political structures that are meant to represent collective ideas of what is 'good'.[93]

Moreover, EU law, in its attempt to overcome the normative deficiencies of the national elaboration of what justice requires, has created a parasitic type of justice. In simple terms, the capacity of free movement and non-discrimination to enhance the pursuit of 'the good life' is dependent on the stability and continued existence of national welfare entitlements. If that latter crumble, the former are meaningless. An equal entitlement

[89] S. Deakin, 'Reflexive Harmonisation and European Company Law' (2009) 15 ELJ 224ff.

[90] S. Deakin, 'Regulatory Competition after *Laval*' (2008) 10 CYELS 581.

[91] Maduro, 'European Constitutionalism', 141–3.

[92] C. Barnard, 'EU Citizenship and the Principle of Solidarity', in M. Dougan and E. Spaventa (eds.), *Social Welfare and EU Law* (Oxford: Hart, 2005) 178.

[93] F. Scharpf, 'Legitimacy in the Multilevel European Polity' (2009) 1 European Political Science Review 173ff.; Deakin, 'Regulatory Competition after *Laval*', 581–609; A. Somek, 'The Social Question in a Transnational Context' (2011) 37 LEQS.

to nothing, after all, entitles you to nothing: EU law can entitle an Italian migrant to equal access to German universities, but if the German electorate does not wish financially or morally to sustain such structures, the claim of justice on the basis of EU law is utterly meaningless. This parasitic nature of the Union's justice claims on the *actual* availability of welfare structures has important consequences, as it suggests that EU law must be sensitive to the associative or reciprocal commitments between 'insiders' to the national system that sustain the welfare state. Simply extending, say, a right to unemployment benefit to all unemployed Union citizens who reside in Sweden without regard to the structures of reciprocity that sustain and legitimize such benefits, may lead to the Swedish electorate deciding no longer to support unemployment benefits financially, if such an extension is perceived to extend solidarity to those who do not 'deserve' it, that is, *if the relative associative relationship between different citizens is not taken into account.*[94] As Bellamy explains:

> whether justified or not, citizens have demanded governments pursue politics that guard against putative welfare 'scroungers' and have been sensitive to 'economic' immigration if that is felt to detract from the employment opportunities available to existing citizens or to place additional burdens on social services such as housing, hospitals, schools without any compensating gain in tax revenue towards their maintenance and improvement. [95]

If citizens evaluate a certain claim as extending solidarity and reciprocity to those who do not 'deserve' it, they may simply be inclined to reduce their own (no longer reciprocated) commitments to communal sharing.[96] The real problem, then, is that demands of EU law in its pursuit of justice risk limiting the willingness of national citizens to sustain the positive welfare entitlements that are instrumental to any conception of 'the good life'. As AG Sharpston has recently put it:

> the financial burden of making a social advantage widely available may compromise its existence and overall level. In such circumstances, concerns about budgetary

[94] See e.g. Ferrera, *The Boundaries of Welfare*, 229; S. Giubboni, 'Free Movement of Persons and European Solidarity' (2007) 13 ELRev 361; A. Sangiovanni, 'Solidarity in the European Union' (2013) 33 OJLS 227; P. Rosanvallon, *The Society of Equals* (Cambridge, Mass.: Harvard University Press, 2013) 274.

[95] Bellamy, 'The Liberty of the Post-Moderns?', 14 with reference to C. Pattie, P. Seyd, and P. Whitely, *Citizenship in Britain: Values, Participation and Democracy* (Cambridge: CUP, 2004).

[96] See A. Falk and U. Fischbacher, 'A Theory of Reciprocity' (2001) CESifo WP No. 457 3–4 for a theoretical explanation, and 5–19 for economic analysis.

implications are intrinsically linked with the existence and objective of the social advantage itself and cannot therefore be wholly disregarded. Member States might otherwise forgo altogether providing particular forms of social advantage, to the detriment of the public interest.[97]

If this occurs (and little empirical evidence exists to support that claim),[98] it is not only the migrant Union citizens that lose out on social benefits, but also immobile national citizens—that is, nationals who do not move from their own state. The parasitic nature of the EU's claims of justice, in other words, has the potential to limit the capacity of national institutions to pursue social justice. Sen explains why limiting the capacity of institutions to offer welfare entitlements is problematic: '[w]hy should we regard hunger, starvation and medical neglect to be invariably less important than the violation of any kind of personal liberty?'[99] Indeed, if we take the capacity of individuals to live a 'good life' as central to our conceptions of justice, it seems we must be primarily concerned with what we are actually able to do, rather than what we can potentially do. Even though we are all free to jump from London to New York, in the sense that no one is preventing us from doing so, we are evidently not able to do so.[100] Any conception of freedom or justice, it would appear, requires us to incorporate our respective ability to enjoy those things in life which we value. Those values can be realized only 'if [individuals] also have access to and enjoy a bundle of rights and entitlements which are necessary for them to lead lives of human dignity and autonomy'.[101] In other words, positive welfare entitlements are important because they enable us to live a type of life that freedom alone would not allow for.[102]

Both these reasons—the divisive potential and parasitic nature of EU law's claims of justice—entail that EU law can significantly decrease the

[97] Opinion of A. G. Sharpston in Case C-542/09 *Commission* v *Netherlands* EU:C:2012:346 para 88.

[98] See e.g. C. Dustmann and T. Frattini, 'The Fiscal Effect of Immigration to the UK' (2014) 124 The Economic Journal 563; Centre for Research and Analysis, 'Assessing the Fiscal Costs and Benefits of A8 Migration to the UK', Discussion Paper Series CDP 18/09; European Commission, 'Impact of mobile EU citizens on national social security systems' available at <http://ec.europa.eu/social/BlobServlet?docId=10972&langId=en>, accessed February 2015; European Commission, 'Free Movement of EU Citizens and their Families: Five Actions to Make a Difference' (COM (2013) 837 final).

[99] Sen, *The Idea of Justice*, 65, 296.

[100] Example stolen from Raymond Plant's plenary address at the IGLRC, King's College London, 7 April 2011.

[101] Benhabib, *Rights of Others*, 111.

[102] T. Judt, *Ill Fares the Land* (New York: Penguin, 2010) 12.

capacity of the nation state to pursue social justice. Unless we consider transnational cooperation as an antidote against redistributive arrangements on the national level, as Hayekian scholars tend to do, it is argued that EU law must be sensitive to the way in which justice is elaborated on the national level, and must allow for the effective elaboration of such arrangements by stabilizing national welfare entitlements. The next section sets out how this is possible, focusing on the integration of the EU's claims of justice within the associative connections of reciprocity that structure and stabilize the national welfare state.

2.3 Reintegrating Tiered Justice: Transnational Solidarity

The tiered concept of justice in Europe—whereby national political structures legitimize internal redistributive criteria, while EU legal norms ensure equal citizenship and individual freedom beyond the state, is, as was discussed above, inherently unstable. The latter is parasitic upon, and potentially disruptive of, the former. What is required, then, is a method to integrate these diverse claims of justice so that the EU enhances rather than decreases the possibility for its citizens to live 'good lives'. As discussed in the previous chapter, such a method must be *relational*, that is, sensitive to the relationship between individuals, in economic, social, or political terms. Only such relational concepts—typically referred to as reciprocity—can rearticulate what national belonging, European integration, and social justice mean and require in a tiered system: they allow us to confront and transcend the link between the pursuit of justice and the institutions of the nation state. For that purpose, this book formulates a theory of transnational solidarity, which serves to integrate the Union's claims of freedom and equality beyond the state with institutional and normative framework of the nation state that is indispensable in the production of norms of justice. Solidarity, after all, serves to institutionalize justice: it is a normative reason for action, a motive for sharing resources—and as such it becomes a mechanism that allows for the translation of obligations of justice into actual rights and entitlements. The function of transnational solidarity, then, is not to structure a framework for distributive justice beyond the nation state, but to reflect and articulate the new forms of association that have emerged horizontally between individual Union citizens and vertically between such citizens and the different

Member States with which they share economic, social, or political affinities. This book argues, essentially, that the process of European integration has generated new associative connections that need to be reflected in the way we think about justice in the EU. Three such associative connections will be discussed. Together, they offer a prism through which to describe and understand, and a conceptual framework through which to implement, the idea of justice that exists in the EU.

The first transnational solidarity that can be traced reflects the relationships produced and generated by interactions on the transnational internal market. This *market solidarity* tells us something about the way in which transnational economic interactions—ranging from the right for workers to work in another Member State, to the way in which the collectivities of 'labour' and 'capital' interact on the internal market—reshape our commitments of justice. It suggests that the economic relationship between actors alone (rather than their nationality, or the political and social links between them) constitutes a motive for sharing resources. This concept of market solidarity is in many ways a transnational variant of the solidarity upon which many of the first national welfare rights were based. It is reminiscent of Durkheim's concept of organic solidarity,[103] and argues that the mutually advantageous division of labour in a market engenders rights and obligations of solidarity. In the European context, this has—as will be highlighted in the next chapter—significant implications. Economic interactions, after all, are no longer bound by national boundaries. This entails that the way in which we need to reshape our commitments to justice domestically needs to take account of the economic relationships that take place on the transnational level. Or, to put it in simpler terms, market solidarity serves to integrate the associative connections that emerge through economic interactions on the internal market within the domestic structures of the welfare state.

Europe is more than a market, however. It also offers economically inactive citizens—students, pensioners, and unemployed citizens—the possibility to reside in another Member State. *Communitarian solidarity* is the solidarity that follows from this novel idea(l) of community, and describes the rights that citizens derive by virtue of their social, quotidian, interaction with citizens in the host state. Communitarian solidarity, in other words, strips Member States of the capacity to differentiate in welfare access on the

[103] E. Durkheim, *The Division of Labour in Society* (Basingstoke: Palgrave, 1984) 68–86.

basis of criteria of nationality or residence alone. Instead, it requires that eligibility criteria are drafted in a way that reflects the social associative links between resident citizens. Such an obligation serves to contextualize the demands of migrant citizens within the structures that sustain welfare entitlements on the national level. What communitarian solidarity demands, then, is not unconditional access for all migrants to domestic welfare goods, but a system that differs depending on the nature and function of a certain welfare good. To put it in simple terms—the connection between a migrant citizen and his or her host state polity that is required before publicly funded emergency healthcare can be accessed is different from the type, nature, and depth of the connection that is required before the migrant can access student grants. This entails that—at least as far as access to social benefits goes—the shape and size of political communities are context-specific: they expand according to the social function of the different welfare goods. Communitarian solidarity in the EU, then, is a normatively shallow but procedurally strong idea of membership, which serves to open up national systems of social sharing to all citizens that demonstrate social connection of a specific type to the host state polity.[104]

Polities grant their citizens specific rights not only on the basis of their role as an economic or societal actor, but also in accordance with the polity's specific political aspirations. In the EU, that specific aspiration has always been to check the coercive capacity of the state in limiting available realizations of the 'good life'. This objective at once lies at the core of the Union's legitimacy and explains the peculiar role of law and centrality of individual rights in the integration process.[105] European Union law, as such, can be seen as rationalizing the limits of public power. *Aspirational solidarity* tells us about the rights and obligations that follow from this shared political commitment. It suggests that Member States cannot prevent their own nationals or migrant EU citizens from accessing the instruments that make up 'a good life'—such as the labour market, public goods, or welfare benefits. Aspirational solidarity is easily the most divisive type of transnational solidarity, as it has the potential to pit individuals in society against each other: there are simply not enough jobs, hospital beds, and resources for

[104] See also F. De Witte, 'The Ends of EU Citizenship and the Means of Non-Discrimination' (2011) 18 MJ 86–107. For a recent restatement of the case law, see Case C-503/09 *Stewart* [2011] ECR I-6497 paras 78–90.

[105] J. Weiler, 'Van Gend en Loos: The Individual as Subject and Object and the Dilemma of European Legitimacy' (2014) 12 ICON 94.

unemployment benefits in the Member States to employ, cure, and sustain all the Union's citizens. As discussed above, then, EU law needs to be sensitive to its limits—to the point where it inhibits the elaboration of associative commitments between citizens. Aspirational solidarity, then, is conditional. Its conditionality is entirely consequentialist and depends on the factual circumstances: when the aspirations of individual citizens risk undermining the associative commitments *between* citizens, the demands of aspirational solidarity find their limit. As such, aspirational solidarity commits the state both to the rationalization of public power and to the reorientation of the precise categories of citizens that undertake associative commitments.

2.4 Conclusion

This chapter has attempted to break down the complexity of Europe's social dimension in order to distil how to best develop justice beyond the nation state without renouncing the redistributive commitment that underlies the national welfare state. The picture that emerges is that of a model of justice that is tiered, both institutionally and normatively. On the one hand, Member States remain the most legitimate *locus* for the generation and distribution of well-being and material resources. On the other hand, the EU has, without challenging the primary mandate of the national welfare state in the elaboration of welfare policy, developed its own transnational claims of justice, which centre on increasing the individual's autonomy, incorporating external interests within national political processes, and stabilizing national distributive balances. This chapter has argued that the welfare state and the Union in fact cooperate to provide the preconditions for the individual expression of a 'good life', and that such a perspective offers a much richer framework to understand what justice is and how it can be achieved. It offers a 'moral narrative' that not only articulates how the Union can help to overcome the institutional limitations of the pursuit of justice on the national level, but also creates avenues for the incorporation of new types of interaction engendered by the project of integration—in economic, social, or political terms.

The conception of justice espoused here accepts that institutional structures, on the national level, serve an important justice function (the generation of the willingness to redistribute scarce goods that enable citizens to live good lives) that cannot easily be provided outside national boundaries.

At the same time it posits that the process of European integration has created transnational commitments in the economic, social, and political sphere. Such commitments—and the associative obligations of justice that they imply—cannot easily be expressed within domestic political systems. As such, then, the EU and its Member States cooperate to lay down a normative framework that serves to attain the objectives of justice beyond the nation state. In doing so, it was argued, the transnational solidarities, which extrapolate what citizens owe each other beyond the confines of the nation state *as a result of new relational connections between them*, are helpful in structuring the normative dimension of a European project that actually increases all citizens' chances of living what they perceive to be a 'good life', and not exclusively the chances of those who make use of their rights to free movement. The following chapters detail the theoretical background and conceptualization, as well as the legal implementation, of each of the three transnational solidarities.

3

Market Solidarity

The first transnational solidarity that can be traced in the evolution of the integration process can best be termed 'market solidarity'. It articulates transnational economic interactions—ranging from the right for workers to work in another Member State to the way in which the collectivities of 'labour' and 'capital' interact on the internal market to reshape our commitments to justice. Market solidarity is at the same time engendered by, and a stabilizing factor for, interactions on the market. Fundamentally, it affects the way in which obligations of justice embed, or alter, the functioning of the market. Traditionally, such norms are articulated and enforced through the national political process (section 3.1). Within the European context, market solidarity operates differently. Economic interactions, after all, are no longer limited by national or political boundaries, which entails that the way in which we reshape our commitments to justice domestically must take account of the economic relationships that take place on the transnational level. Or, to put it in simpler terms, market solidarity serves to integrate the associative connections and relational commitments that emerge through economic interactions on the internal market within the domestic structures of the welfare state.

Market solidarity can be traced in three areas of integration. First, EU law has been concerned with extending domestic norms of market solidarity to include non-national EU citizens that work in a host state. Market solidarity, after all, suggests that the economic relationship between actors alone (rather than their nationality, or the political and social links between them) constitutes a motive for sharing resources. As such, EU citizens that are economically active in another Member State can access the same welfare rights as national workers—regardless of their nationality, the limited period of residence, or even the absence of residence (section 3.2). Second, EU law has attempted to infuse certain norms of market solidarity directly within the functioning of the transnational market, and in particular has tried to construe the rights and obligations that the collectivities 'labour' and 'capital' owe each other when acting transnationally. This is a role for which the EU is not particularly well equipped, given the absence of a political system that is sophisticated enough to articulate the appropriate balance between 'labour' and 'capital'. In consequence (and problematically), the task of articulating an autonomous, transnational understanding of market solidarity has fallen on the Court. Worryingly, it appears that the Court fundamentally misreads the concept and function of market solidarity, which has led to the remarkable assertion that justice requires that capital be protected from the power of labour, rather than the other way around (section 3.3). The third way in which the logic of market solidarity manifests itself in EU law is more surprising. In the area of healthcare, it seems that the internal market has been used as a mechanism to *enforce* domestic obligations of market solidarity. Free movement law, here, has been used by the Court to allow patients to enforce the conditions of the healthcare contract that they have entered into with their Member State (section 3.4).

All in all, it seems that market solidarity is well developed and uncontentious in most areas of EU law. It reflects the rights and obligations that are implicit in the economic interaction between citizens on the European market, primarily by extending *domestic* norms of solidarity to include migrant workers or cross-border transactions. European Union law struggles much more when it needs to create autonomous norms of transnational market solidarity, that is, to directly prescribe how interactions on the market alter our commitments of justice.

3.1 The Normative Premise and Legal Structure of Market Solidarity

The primary policy objective of European integration was the creation of a single market. It was thought that by intertwining the economies of the different Member States political conflict could be minimized and economic productivity increased. As in any market, however, the interaction of actors on the new European market had to be normatively embedded, so that the outcome of market transactions would be socially acceptable. This insight links the concepts of market and solidarity: for the functional division of labour on a market to work properly, a degree of solidarity is indispensable. Durkheim has conceptualized this as 'spontaneous' or 'organic' solidarity, which results from the interdependencies between actors and the mutually advantageous nature of their transactions.[1] Bluntly put, it entails that the butcher and the brewer, by exchanging the goods that they produce, enter into a fictitious relationship that is governed not only by the financial transaction between them but also by a tacit acknowledgement of their respective obligations and rights that ensure that their engagement is stable and remains mutually advantageous.[2]

The political origins of this market solidarity can be traced back to the late nineteenth century, when the rapid industrialization of European processes of production, and the simultaneous demise of agrarian societies and their corporatist regulatory mechanisms mainly based on kinship and voluntary obligations, drastically changed societal structures, creating a functionally differentiated society in which the efficient exploitation of resources, including labour, became increasingly important. The ensuing power asymmetry between capital and labour led to the imposition of harsh working conditions and to the exclusion of certain less efficient societal groups—the young, the old, and the sick—from the manual labour process, and thereby condemned them to subsistence. This 'social insensitivity' of the market led to the mobilization of large numbers of dissatisfied citizens. It was felt that the externalities of this new, asymmetrical 'division of labour' endangered the basic level of material resources required to protect the individual's autonomy and his or her potential to live a 'good life', and not be trapped in poverty or social status undercurrents.[3] As Hyman argued:

> this [asymmetry] derives from the very fact that the productive system is, in the main, the private property of a tiny minority of the population. Confronting this concentrated economic power, the great majority who depend on their own labour

[1] E. Durkheim, *The Division of Labour in Society* (Basingstoke: Palgrave, 1984) 68–86.

[2] See also Adam Smith, *An Inquiry into the Nature and Causes of the Wealth of Nations* [1776] (Oxford: Clarendon, 1976) 26–7; A. Somek, 'Solidarity Decomposed: Being and Time in European Citizenship' (2007) 32 ELRev 812.

[3] See K. Polanyi, *The Great Transformation* (Boston, Mass.: Beacon, 2002) 136–40; J. Habermas, 'Struggles for Recognition in the Democratic Constitutional State', in A. Gutmann (ed.), *Multiculturalism: Examining the Politics of Recognition* (Princeton, NJ: Princeton University Press, 1994) 45–58 and 108–9.

for a living are at an inevitable disadvantage. Put simply, the employer can normally survive without labour longer than the worker can survive without employment.[4]

In the most functional terms, then, the objective of market solidarity is to stabilize—in spontaneous ways or through political mediation—the relationship between actors in the market by embedding the meritocratic logic of the market so that it leads to socially acceptable outcomes.[5] In doing so, market solidarity generally gives expression to three core claims:[6] it (1) seeks to prevent the exploitation of the individual worker by capital, (2) tries to ensure equality of bargaining power between labour and capital,[7] and (3) seeks to create a space of negative freedom from the market where the individual's hopes, needs, and aspirations can be articulated and fulfilled. These objectives are typically met by the imposition of limits to competitive contracting; the extraction of resources for redistribution from the production process and the protection of the workers' health; and collective labour rights. Market solidarity thus compensates market actors, typically in the form of social entitlements, for their submission to the meritocratic logic of the market, and guarantees them a *juste retour* on the depletion of their wage-earning potential through their continuous engagement with the market. In consequence, *all* actors who engage in the division of labour on the market automatically accrue certain rights and obligations under market solidarity. Market solidarity, then, describes the normative aspect of interactions on the market.

It is hardly surprising that a transnational market requires a degree of transnational market solidarity in order to function properly, in both normative and economic terms. Given that the spatial enlargement of national markets through economic integration has changed the dynamic and structure of, and opportunities generated by, market interactions, the sense of

[4] R. Hyman, *Industrial Relations: A Marxist Introduction* (Basingstoke: Macmillan, 1975) 22–3. See also S. Webb and B. Webb, *Industrial Democracy* (Basingstoke: Macmillan, 2003) 654–60.

[5] S. Bacharach and E. Lawler, *Bargaining: Power, Tactics and Outcomes* (San Francisco: Jossey-Bass, 1981) 4–7.

[6] See also Lukes, who convincingly argues that regulatory intervention is generally warranted in three different situations: where an unregulated market would lead to commodification of the workforce, where it would create inequality of power and rights between labour and capital, or where it restricts general citizenship rights. S. Lukes, 'Invasions of the Market', in M. Miller (ed.), *Worlds of Capitalism* (London: Routledge, 2005) 302ff.

[7] O. Kahn-Freud, 'Labour Law', in M. Ginsberg (ed.), *Law and Opinion in England in the 20th Century* (London: Stevens, 1959) 224.

justice and solidarity that governs such interactions has changed accordingly. The drafters of the Treaty of Rome, in fact, while acknowledging that almost all social policy competences were to remain in the hands of the Member States, already realized that an *inter-national* market that is not regulated centrally could be inefficient *and* unjust.[8] What is 'just' in interactions on the national market (and therefore institutionalized by national political processes) is simply not necessarily 'just' on a transnational market (and vice versa). What a European market would require, really, is a political system that could internalize what would be considered fair on a market without internal boundaries.

Yet, a sufficiently robust transnational political system does not exist (see section 2.2). Instead, the regulation of the market is tiered, partially devised in national capitals and partially in Brussels. This absence of centralized political authority has led to the manifestation of many different instruments that serve to implement transnational market solidarity. On the most abstract level, market solidarity is reflected in the objectives of the Union, which refer to a 'social market economy', and in the horizontal clause that calls for the incorporation of social and labour protection in all European policies.[9] This sense of market solidarity can also be traced on the highest political level, where schemes compensate market actors and indeed entire (groups of) Member States for the justice externalities of the internal market through the establishment of the CAP,[10] Social Funds,[11] or cohesion funds[12] and accession agreements.[13] Equally, the bailouts and establishment of structural fiscal supervision arrangements are explicitly justified

[8] Article 119 of the Treaty of Rome, demanding that Member States introduce the principle that men and women receive equal pay for equal work, for example, was premised on the logic that differences in pay-structures within a single Member State would upset the dynamics of interstate integration. See Ohlin Report paras 104-10 and 156.

[9] See Article 9 TFEU.

[10] The Common Agricultural Policy redistributed common resources on the basis of the need to 'ensure a fair standard of living for the agricultural community, in particular by increasing the individual earnings of persons engaged in agriculture'. Article 39 (b) EEC: 'to ensure a fair standard of living for the agricultural community, in particular by increasing the individual earnings of persons engaged in agriculture'.

[11] See Article 123 EEC, and its function of 'rendering the employment of workers easier and of increasing their geographical and occupational mobility within the community'.

[12] See Article 174 TFEU: 'the Union shall aim at reducing disparities between the levels of development of the various regions and the backwardness of the least favoured regions'.

[13] Through which the Union in essence negotiates access to new markets by the exchanges of vast funds.

by reference to the interdependence between the Member States' fiscal and economic policies.[14] The Union legislator also automatically incorporates market solidarity in its function as market (re-)regulator. Given that market regulation cannot take place in a normative vacuum and is always 'about something else as well',[15] the regulation of, say, roaming charges or environmental regulation entails making a normative assessment of the contractual positions and demands of operators and consumers in different Member States, and its regulation on the European level therefore automatically entails the incorporation of transnational market solidarities.

The peculiar nature of governance of the European market—whereby market rules are decided on the transnational level, and the social rules that embed the market on the domestic level—has led to an equally peculiar form of market solidarity.[16] European Union law incorporates the demands of transnational market solidarity, that is, how economic mobility reshapes the rights and obligations of actors, in three ways. First, it extends national understandings of market solidarity to include intra-EU mobile workers. Article 51 of the Treaty of Rome already highlighted that it might be necessary to coordinate the social entitlements of migrant workers in order to ensure that the transnational mobility of labour conforms to ideas of market solidarity.[17] It seems quite natural, for example, that an Italian worker who is employed in Germany should be entitled to the same social benefits as his fellow German workers. Both are engaged in the effective division of labour in Germany, and both should derive the same social entitlements from that economic engagement. There is no reason to assume that the Italian is less deserving of the entitlements that reward such engagement or serve to protect the dignity and autonomy of the worker inside and outside the workplace—whether in the form of minimum wages, healthcare benefits, or childcare allowances. In this transnational context, then, market solidarity

[14] The preamble to the Fiscal Compact highlights that the 'need for governments to maintain sound and sustainable public finances (…) is of an essential importance to safeguard the stability of the euro area as a whole'. See Article 3 of that same compact for more examples.

[15] B. De Witte, 'Non-Market Values in Internal Market Legislation', in N. Nic Shuibhne (ed.), *Regulating the Internal Market* (Cheltenham: Edward Elgar, 2006) 75.

[16] See D. Damjanovic, 'The EU Market Rules as Social Market Rules: Why the EU Can Be a Social Market Economy' (2013) 50 CML Rev 1685.

[17] See Article 51 EEC, which reads: 'The Council, acting by means of a unanimous vote on a proposal of the Commission, shall, in the field of social security, adopt the measures necessary to effect the free movement of workers, in particular, by introducing a system which permits an assurance to be given to migrant workers and their beneficiaries'.

entails that transnational labour mobility must in principle be accompanied by access to social entitlements in the host state (section 3.2).

The second way in which EU law incorporates demands of market solidarity lies in the management of the structural tension between labour and capital on the internal market. Originally, EU law sought to do this by insulating domestic understandings of market solidarity from the pressures and (capital-friendly) dynamics of regulatory mobility. Increasingly, however, the Court is developing autonomous, EU-wide norms that decide on the appropriate balance between labour and capital on the internal market, and that challenge domestic understandings of the normative limits to the interaction between economic actors.[18] As will be discussed further, the absence of a political system that can legitimize such a balance has exposed the development of market solidarity in the EU to the asymmetrical power advantage of capital over labour, rather than insulating it (section 3.3).

The third and most innovative way in which the creation of a transnational market has altered rights and obligations of justice is by understanding the rights of free movement as allowing citizens to enforce their rights to welfare. This comes through most clearly in the area of healthcare, where the Court allows patients to access cross-border treatment with retention of their right to reimbursement whenever their own Member States cannot guarantee them the healthcare for which they are insured (section 3.4). Market solidarity, as this chapter will indicate, is deeply embedded in the way we think about free movement. The new economic relationships between citizens in the internal market produce new rights and obligations of justice—which are incorporated on both the national and the European level. The absence of a sophisticated political system of the latter, however, severely limits the capacity of the EU to find the appropriate balance of rights and obligations.

3.2 Rights for Migrant Workers on the Basis of Market Solidarity

The first way in which EU law incorporates market solidarity sees to the extension of domestic welfare benefits to include mobile workers. In other

[18] See, structurally, J. Snell, 'The Internal Market and the Philosophies of Market Integration', in C. Barnard and S. Peers (eds.), *European Union Law* (Oxford: OUP, 2014) 300ff.

words, it is not about creating a catalogue of rights that all workers in the EU should receive, nor is it about altering the range of rights that Member States offer their citizens and workers. Member States remain free to define the range and nature of social rights offered on their territory. Market solidarity simply extends the personal scope of such rights to include non-national workers. Such workers, after all, stand in the same economic relation with the host state polity as national workers. This understanding of market solidarity has long been accepted, even if conceptual tensions are emerging at its edges—for example concerning the definition of a 'worker', the rights for family members of the worker, frontier workers, and involuntarily unemployed workers.

This logic of market solidarity—if an migrant engages with the host state's economy, he is entitled to welfare benefits on equal terms as nationals of that state—has been elaborated by the Union legislator and the Court since the 1960s. Market solidarity, as such, 'imposes responsibility in the social sphere on each Member State with regard to every worker who is a national of another Member State and established in its territory'.[19] The absolute obligation on the part of the state for equal treatment in employment is implemented differently for different policy areas. At times, EU legislation prescribes detailed assimilation rules that depend on the worker's past insurance records,[20] or the occurrence of specific events,[21] while in the absence of detailed legislation the Court falls back on the more general equal treatment provisions, to be found in Article 4 of Regulation 883/2004, Article 24 of Directive 2004/38, and Article 7 (2) of Regulation 492/2011, which have been interpreted to extend the right to equal treatment for economically active EU citizens to cover all welfare benefits.

[19] Case 235/87 *Matteucci* [1988] ECR 5589 para 16.

[20] Article 6 of Regulation 883/2004 is a good example of this approach. It forces host states whose legislation requires the completion of a period of insurance, employment, or residence before access is given to social security benefits to take account of the insurance record which the migrant worker has built up in other Member States. The state of employment thus pretends that the past insurance records of the workers were accrued in the state of employment, thereby ensuring complete equal treatment of migrant workers with nationals.

[21] For benefits that are less directly connected to the insurance record of the worker, such as disability or maternity benefits, Article 5 of Regulation 883/2004 provides another assimilation rule: 'where, under the legislation of the competent Member State, legal effects are attributed to the occurrence of certain facts or events, that Member State shall take account of like facts or events occurring in any Member State as though they had taken place in its own territory'.

From the moment at which the economic activity starts, then, and for as long as it lasts, the worker has a right to access the same social security and social assistance schemes as nationals, and the host state is precluded from demanding additional criteria, such as periods of residence, or minimum financial resources, to be met. The relational economic connection between the mobile worker and the state alone, on this view, justifies access to welfare benefits. The *Levin* case emphasizes the absolute and unconditional character of market solidarity, and also shows that the reason for this demand of equal treatment is not so much the specific financial contribution of the migrant to the host state's finances, but rather his or her general engagement with, and participation in, the economic life of the host state. The *Levin* case dealt with a British national who resided and worked in the Netherlands—but earned less than the level that the Netherlands considered as the minimum required for subsistence. The Netherlands argued that, in consequence, Mrs Levin could not be classified as a worker and would therefore not qualify for social assistance on equal terms with Dutch nationals. In other words, what the Netherlands argued was that the right to equal treatment for workers (market solidarity) depended on their individual contribution to the host society, rather than their general engagement with the market and their status as economic agents.[22] The Court held, however, that the only relevant requirement was one of engagement with the host state's economy, thus including all workers whose activities could be classified as 'effective and genuine', and excluding workers who performed 'marginal and ancillary' activities.[23] The individual contribution of a migrant worker to the state's public purse was immaterial. Accordingly, the concept of 'worker', including privileges of equal treatment, extends to cover even those workers whose income is less than the minimum required for subsistence—which possibly entails an obligation upon the host state to grant social assistance.[24] This was confirmed in *Trojani*, which dealt with a French national who had obtained a job as part of a reintegration programme with the Salvation Army in Brussels. The Court held that the pivotal test was not whether the job undertaken was part of the labour market, but rather that it was '*capable* of being regarded as forming part of the normal labour market'.[25] In other words, it is not the functional

[22] Case 53/81 *Levin* [1982] ECR 1035.

[23] *Levin* para 17. See also Case C-138/02 *Collins* [2004] ECR I-2703 para 26; Case C-507/12 *Saint Prix* EU:C:2014:2007 para 35; Case C-46/12 *L.N.* EU:C:2013:97 para 40.

[24] *Levin* para 15; Joined Cases C-22/08 and C-23/08 *Vatsouras* [2009] ECR 4585 para 28; Case C-345/09 *Van Delft* [2010] ECR I-9879 para 89.

[25] Case C-456/02 *Trojani* [2004] ECR I-7573 para 24. My emphasis.

contribution of the migrant worker, but his or her personal engagement with the labour market in the host state that counts. As the Court put it:

> neither the *sui generis* nature of the employment relationship under national law, nor the level of productivity of the person concerned, the origin of the funds from which the remuneration is paid or the limited amount of the remuneration can have any consequence in regard to whether or not the person is a worker for the purposes of [Union] law.[26]

This conforms to the theoretical discussion on the scope of market solidarity above, where it was argued that it is the interdependence between the worker and the host state in the division of labour that engenders a normative obligation on the latter to extend all social entitlements to cover the worker—not the nature, degree, or function of that engagement, nor the reason for which a migrant moved to the host Member State.[27] In other words, as long as a migrant worker engages in the division of labour in the host state, 'the worker is guaranteed the possibility of improving his living and working conditions and promoting his social advancement' by access to welfare entitlements. [28]

It is the scope of market solidarity, rather than its existence, that has been vigorously contested by Member States, in particular with reference to access to benefits for family members of the worker, non-resident workers, and (in)voluntary unemployed migrants.[29] In all such situations, the link between the applicant for welfare benefits and the employment market of the host state is tenuous. The Court, however, has traditionally been receptive for expansive interpretations of the scope of market solidarity—including within its scope dependent family members, non-resident workers, and (in) voluntary unemployed migrants. The emergence of communitarian solidarity, however, which grants different but autonomous rights to residence and equal treatment to economically *in*active citizens on the basis of their social (rather than economic) connection to the host state, has led to a reassessment

[26] Ibid. para 16.

[27] *L.N.* para 46: 'factors relating to the conduct of the person concerned before or after the period of employment are not relevant in establishing the status of worker'.

[28] Recital 3 of the preamble to Regulation 1612/68. See e.g. Case 207/78 *Even* [1979] ECR 2019; Case C-237/94 *O'Flynn* [1996] ECR I-2617; or Case 137/84 *Mutsch* [1985] ECR 2681 para 17. See, for an overview, A. P. Van der Mei, *Free Movement of Persons within the European Community* (Oxford: Hart, 2003) 31–4.

[29] See also examples mentioned in 'Editorial Comments: The Free Movement of Persons in the European Union: Salvaging the Dream while Explaining the Nightmare' (2014) 51 CML Rev 729. See also section 2.3.

of the scope of derivative rights under market solidarity.[30] This has led to a degree of conceptual confusion in the case law of the Court.

The first question that tests the limits of market solidarity is whether a migrant worker's engagement with the host state's society constitutes a reason for extending equal treatment to welfare benefits to his family members. Does the unemployed child of a migrant worker have a right to jobseeker allowance in the host state? Regulation 883/2004 only explicitly extends the right to equal treatment to include family members in respect of sickness benefits[31] and family benefits,[32] while Article 10 of Regulation 492/2011 explicitly guarantees equal access to all levels of education for the children of economically active migrants.[33] In the absence of more specific provisions that guide the scope of application of market solidarity, the catch-all provision in Regulation 492/2011, which entitles the worker to the same 'social and tax advantages as national workers',[34] has been used to argue that the right to equal treatment for family members of the economically active migrant should be extended to cover all social benefits.[35] This line of reasoning is contingent on establishing a connection between the worker and the social benefit. In other words, it must be argued that, say, a jobseeker allowance for an unemployed child is a social advantage for the worker,[36] or, more precisely, that the engagement of the worker with the host state's economy warrants access to entitlements for family members who are economically dependent on him or her.

Indeed, in *Lebon* the Court excluded benefits for financially *independent* family members from the scope of the obligation of equal treatment in Regulation 1612/68,[37] as such benefits have no effect on the worker's

[30] See, for a (convincing) argument of how this has confused the Court's case law, S. O'Leary, 'Developing an Ever Closer Union Between the Peoples of Europe?' Edinburgh Mitchell Working Papers 6/2008.

[31] Article 17 of Regulation 883/2004.

[32] Article 67 of Regulation 883/2004.

[33] See, previously, Article 12 of Regulation 1612/68.

[34] Article 7 (2) of Regulation 492/2011, and previously Article 7 (2) of Regulation 1612/68.

[35] In the early *Michel S*, *Cristini*, and *Even* cases the Court moved from one end of the spectrum to the other, first finding that only the benefits which 'are to benefit the worker themselves' were covered by Regulation 1612/68 (Case 76/72 *Michel S.* [1973] ECR 457 para 9) and later that they 'include all social and tax advantages, whether or not attached to the contract of employment' (Case 32/75 *Cristini* [1975] ECR 1085 para 13) before finding a middle ground in its interpretation, including social advantages which 'are generally granted to national workers primarily because of their objective status as workers or by virtue of the mere fact of residence on the national territory' (in Case 207/78 *Even* [1979] ECR 2019 para 22).

[36] Case C-212/05 *Hartmann* [2007] ECR I-6303 para 25.

[37] Case 316/85 *Lebon* [1987] ECR 2811 para 13.

economic position. Conversely, it appears that social benefits meant to alleviate the economic burden of taking care of dependent family members *do* fall within the scope of market solidarity. This view seems congruent with the logic underlying market solidarity. Its purpose is to both reward and protect the worker's engagement with the host state by financially compensating for social risks and responsibilities. Market solidarity, as such, stretches to include all social advantages that have a direct effect on the worker's financial situation. This line of reasoning seems to have been accepted by the Court in *Hartmann*, which dealt with the question whether a childcare allowance, typically given to the child's mother, constituted a 'social benefit' for the working (male) spouse. The Court emphasized that such an allowance:

> enables one of the parents to devote himself or herself to the raising of a young child, by meeting family expenses, [and] benefits the family as a whole, whichever parent it is who claims the allowance. The grant of such an allowance to a worker's spouse is capable of reducing that worker's obligation to contribute to family expenses, and therefore constitutes for him or her a 'social advantage'.[38]

The real test, then, seems to be a factual assessment of whether or not the benefit affects the economic position of the worker, either by meeting the expenses that would be covered by the worker, or substituting his or her support of other family members.[39] The right to equal treatment under market solidarity, in other words, can only be extended to cover the worker against the social risks that have struck dependent family members.[40] This criterion of economic dependence is particularly problematic when it comes to student benefits. In fact, it is based on an untenable legal fiction, whereby students can derive a right to student benefits from the state of employment of their parents only when their parents would have supported them financially in the first place.[41] Students whose parents are unable or unwilling to offer financial support are, after all, not 'dependent' on the worker, and would have no claim to equal treatment under market solidarity. As will be argued in the following chapter, this tension in the area of student benefits mirrors the tension between different welfarist traditions in the EU, and should be solved by approaching students as EU citizens whose autonomous claims to

[38] *Hartmann* para 26. [39] See also, very explicitly, *Lebon* paras 22 and 24.

[40] See also Article 1 (i) (2) and (3) of Regulation 883/2004, which highlights the dependence criterion.

[41] See F. De Witte, 'Who Funds the Mobile Student? Shedding Some Light on the Normative Assumptions Underlying EU Free Movement Law: *Commission v Netherlands*' (2013) 50 CML Rev 203; and Case C-542/09 *Commission* v *Netherlands* EU:C:2012:346.

equal treatment depend on their social links to a particular polity, not their parents' engagement with a certain employment market.[42]

The second category of workers whose rights under market solidarity have been contested are frontier workers. Logically, given that rights accrued under market solidarity are exclusively attached to the engagement of the migrant worker with the labour market of the host state, they cannot be made conditional upon residence in that state.[43] Yet, the extension of market solidarity to cover frontier workers has been criticized on two accounts. First, it has been argued that it overplays the economic link between the worker and the state of employment. Since income tax is paid in the state of residence rather than in the state of employment,[44] the argument runs, the migrant worker does not contribute to the public purse in the state of employment, and should not be able to obtain benefits paid from that purse.[45] Second, the Court has long rhetorically justified the rights under market solidarity in terms of 'facilitating the mobility of such workers within the Community',[46] and promoting their 'integration in the society of the host country'.[47] Frontier workers, however, would evidently not require access to social benefits from their state of employment for these purposes if they reside in another state.

The Court and Union legislator have generally not been impressed with such criticisms, and as a rule extend all benefits to frontier workers. Regulation 883/2004 indeed ensures that, regardless of place of residence, workers obtain, from their state of employment, healthcare insurance,[48] sickness benefits,[49] benefits in respect of accidents at work and occupational diseases,[50] invalidity benefits,[51] and family benefits.[52] In its case law

[42] See section 4.4. [43] Case C-160/96 *Molenaar* [1998] ECR I-849 para 43.

[44] See OECD Double Taxation Treaty; available at: <http://www.oecd.org/tax/treaties>, accessed March 2015.

[45] The Court got this wrong in *Commission* v *Netherlands*, where it argued that non-resident workers could derive benefits from their state of employment because they paid taxes there. See *Commission* v *Netherlands* para 66.

[46] Case 207/78 *Even* [1979] ECR 2019 para 22.

[47] Joined Cases 389/87 and 390/87 *Echternach and Moritz* [1989] ECR 723 para 35. See, for a similar argument, Opinion of AG Geelhoed in *Hartmann* paras 41 and 47–9.

[48] The bill being sent to the state of employment even if the worker decides to undergo treatment in the state of residence. See Article 19 (1) of Regulation 883/2004.

[49] Articles 21 and 35 of Regulation 883/2004. See *Molenaar* para 43, and (explicitly) Case 41/84 *Pinna* [1996] ECR 1.

[50] Articles 36 and 41 of Regulation 883/2004.

[51] Article 44 of Regulation 883/2004.

[52] See, very explicitly, Article 67 of Regulation 883/2004: 'A person shall be entitled to family benefits in accordance with the legislation of the competent Member State, including for

on Regulation 1612/68 (now codified in Regulation 492/2011), moreover, the Court has always followed, and recently confirmed, this prima facie presumption of exportability.[53] Economic engagement thus seems to function as a master-key to unlock the closed nature of sharing arrangements within the host Member State, regardless of the place of residence. This master-key is delivered to migrant workers from the moment that the migrant worker starts to work in the host state. It is not premised on financial parity, as discussed above, nor on the payment of taxes in the state of employment (as the Court seems to think),[54] but on the basis of the migrant's engagement in economic interactions in the host state. It is his or her relational economic status in the host state, and not his or her residence or social relationship, that warrants a range of rights under market solidarity. Indeed, as recently highlighted by the Court in a series of cases concerning student benefits, economic activity alone in principle justifies claims of equal access to welfare resources.[55] Lack of residence, as in the case of frontier workers, cannot detract from such a claim.

It is even stranger, then, that the Court has at times indicated that frontier workers cannot export certain welfare benefits. The Court took its cue (if not its conceptual rigour) from AG Geelhoed, who has repeatedly argued for a dissociation of 'the migrant citizen as a person from what he represents in economic terms'.[56] What Geelhoed means, essentially, is that the frontier worker is—for lack of residence—nothing but an economic agent in his or her state of employment, and should only be allowed to access social benefits meant to cover risks related to his or her status as a worker. This is really an argument for the reassessment of the allocation of social responsibility: while the state of employment is responsible for employment-related benefits, for which the worker has insured him- or herself by participation in sharing schemes, the state of residence should cater for the social benefits that are unrelated to employment, such as childcare benefits.[57] Such benefits,

his family members residing in another Member State, as if they were residing in the former Member State'. See also Case C-312/94 *Hoever & Zachow* [1996] ECR I-4895.

[53] Case C-206/10 *Commission* v *Germany* [2011] ECR I-3573 paras 34ff. See also *Hartmann*; Case C-57/96 *Meints* [1997] ECR I-6689 paras 49–50.

[54] See *Commission* v *Netherlands* para 66. Perhaps this confusion was caused by the fact that the members of the Court do not pay full rates of taxation in their state of employment or in their state of residence.

[55] *Commission* v *Netherlands* 63; and Opinion of AG Sharpston in *Commission* v *Netherlands* paras 72ff.

[56] Opinion of AG Geelhoed in *Hartmann* para 41.

[57] Opinion of AG Geelhoed in *Hartmann* para 51.

and the reciprocity that they express, so the argument runs, are inextricably tied to territorial policy objectives (such as demographic concerns), not economic objectives, and should therefore not be exportable from the state of employment.[58]

In *Hendrix* and *Geven*, the Court indeed followed AG Geelhoed's approach and limited the scope of market solidarity. The latter case is particularly instructive. It concerned a Dutch national who resided in the Netherlands and worked in Germany for between 3 and 14 hours a week. While, the Court argued, this classified her as a 'worker' under Regulation 1612/68,[59] it did *not* necessarily entitle her to have a right to equal access to all social advantages. The Court allowed Germany to impose an additional requirement of 'more than minor' employment, before the child-raising allowance could be exported.[60] In other words, if Ms Geven had lived in Germany her 'minor employment' would not have barred her from accessing the childcare benefit.[61] And, indeed, as is argued below, it is uncontested that childcare benefits cannot be exported by economically *in*active citizens.[62] What is at stake here, however, is the nature and scope of market solidarity. Is it, as the bulk of the Court's case law and the theory of market solidarity would have it, an unconditional requirement, whereby the only relevant question is whether a migrant stands in an economic relationship with the host polity, or does market solidarity impose a quantitative or qualitative requirement as well? It is argued that the Court's interpretation in *Geven* is unfortunate, not only for the leeway it gives Member States in defining such quantitative requirements, but also in that it fails to engage with the more profound question whether the emergence of different forms of transnational solidarity besides market solidarity warrant, not a reassessment of the absolute nature of market solidarity, but rather a coherent mechanism for the allocation of welfare responsibilities *between* states when individual citizens have different claims vis-à-vis different Member States.[63] In other

[58] See, explicitly, Opinion of AG Geelhoed in *Hartmann* paras 66 and 69.

[59] Case C-213/05 *Geven* [2007] ECR I-6347 para 17.

[60] Ibid. paras 23–8.

[61] *Geven* para 29; thereby overturning the ruling in *Levin* para 11; and Case 139/85 *Kempf* [1986] ECR 1741 para 15. See also Opinion of AG Geelhoed in *Geven* para 36.

[62] See section 5.3.

[63] See Rennuy on how the principle of proportionality is used to reallocate welfare responsibility. N. Rennuy, 'The Emergence of a Parallel System of Social Security Coordination' (2013) 50 CML Rev 1234.

words, a more appropriate interpretation of the limits of market solidarity might be that while Ms Geven is entitled to childcare allowance on the basis of her (limited) economic activity in Germany, her status as a resident and national in the Netherlands constitutes a much stronger (social) ground for claiming access to childcare allowances, in particular given the nature and purpose of the social benefit.[64] Indeed, in *Hendrix*—the sole case so far where a worker received minimum subsistence benefits from his state of employment which he would *not* receive from his state of residence—the Court was visibly ill at ease in limiting the absolute nature of market solidarity and instead expressly required the national court to come to a 'fair' outcome, regardless of the express prohibition of exportability of minimum subsistence benefits for frontier workers in Regulation 883/2004.[65] Properly understood, then, it seems that this very limited exception to the absolute nature of market solidarity in case of frontier workers is not a denial of the existence of a right under market solidarity as such, but simply a mechanism for coordination—giving priority to the social relationship that the migrant has with the state of residence over the economic relationship that he or she has with the state of employment.

The third category of citizens whose rights under market solidarity have long been contested are (in)voluntarily unemployed citizens. Given that the right to equal treatment is functionally tied to the migrant's status as an economic agent in the host state, one would expect that the loss of such status would automatically have consequences for the social benefits enjoyed. In principle, in the case of unemployment the social responsibility to provide social benefits falls on the state of residence of the citizen on the basis of a social rather than economic connection.[66] At the same time, the Union legislator and Court have repeatedly emphasized that market solidarity can, in certain specific instances, have effects beyond the period of employment.[67] The first is when a migrant worker loses his job. Can the migrant worker claim social benefit on the basis of prior engagement with the market? The second sees to prospective engagement with the market. Can migrant workers who interrupt

[64] See Chapter 4.

[65] Case C-287/05 *Hendrix* [2007] ECR I-6909 para 57. See also section 4.3 and Rennuy, 'The Emergence of a Parallel System', 1238.

[66] See Case 275/96 *Kuusijarvi* [1998] ECR I-3419 para 73.

[67] See Article 7 (3) of Directive 2004/38; *Meints* para 40 and Case 39/86 *Lair* [1988] ECR 3161 para 36. See F. Pennings, 'Inclusion and Exclusion of Persons and Benefits in the New Co-ordination Regulation', in M. Dougan and E. Spaventa (eds.), *Social Welfare and EU Law* (Oxford: Hart, 2005) 256.

their work in order to study rely on their potential future engagement with the market in order to secure access to welfare resources under market solidarity?

Wholly unemployed citizens, who have no continuous economic connection with the state of (former) employment, have no right to benefits from that state on the basis of their previous employment.[68] It is the state of residence, instead, which must provide such benefits on the basis of the social link that connects the citizen to the state. Partially unemployed frontier workers, who retain links to the employment market in the state of employment for example by continuing to work intermittently or on 'a part-time basis, while remaining available for work on a full-time basis',[69] on the other hand, can obtain unemployment benefits from their state of (partial) employment rather than the state of residence.[70] In other words, access to social benefits is again conditional upon continuous economic engagement with the labour market of that state.[71] This requirement has been confirmed by a Decision by the administrative commission for the coordination of social security systems, which distinguishes between wholly and partially unemployed workers (and thus determines the scope of market solidarity) on the basis of 'whether or not any contractual employment link exists or is maintained between the parties, and not on the duration of any temporary suspension of the workers' activity'.[72]

This answer may appear less obvious for migrant workers who are unemployed while undertaking education or vocational training. The argument to extend market solidarity to cover this category of migrants is that the migrant's education or retraining might be related to their economic engagement with the labour market,[73] or where the (involuntarily) unemployed worker pursues vocational training that adapts him to the changing demands on the labour market.[74] In such circumstances, after all, the temporary economic inactivity can be seen as bolstering the mutually advantageous nature of the interaction between migrant worker and host state's society that underlies market solidarity, the assumption being that such worker will

[68] Case C-258/04 *Ioannidis* [2005] ECR I-8275 para 31; *Collins* para 63, and Case C-444/98 *De Laat* [2001] ECR I-2229 para 37. See also M. Dougan, 'The Court helps those who help themselves...The legal status of migrant work-seekers under Community law in the light of the *Collins* judgment' (2005) 1 European Journal of Social Security 15.

[69] *De Laat* para 37.

[70] Article 65 of Regulation 883/2004.

[71] See also Case C-43/99 *Leclere* [2001] ECR I-4265 paras 58–9.

[72] Decision U3, OJ C106/45, 2010.

[73] Article 7 (3) (d) of Directive 2004/38.

[74] Case C-413/01 *Ninni-Orasche* [2003] ECR I-1027 and Case C-158/07 *Förster* [2008] ECR I-8507. See also T. Hartley, 'Equal Treatment in Education', in N. Green, T. Hartley, and J. Usher (eds.), *The Legal Foundations of the Single European Market* (Oxford: OUP, 1991) 183.

make a (more efficient) return in the labour force of the host state after completion of the programme of tertiary education. Initially, in its decisions in *Lair* and *Brown*, the Court seemed sympathetic to the idea that migrant students derived a right to equal treatment under market solidarity, as long as the degree was a continuation of previous employment.[75] More recently, in *Ninni-Orasche* and *Förster*, however, the Court appeared to reject this possibility,[76] even if in the meantime the Union legislator had codified this extension of market solidarity.[77] The latter case dealt with a German national who had enrolled on a course to become a primary school teacher and a course on educational theory, both at the Hogeschool Amsterdam. She had a number of jobs in the first few years as a student, which qualified her as a 'worker', and she was consequently eligible for the *studiefinanciering* (Dutch student grants). From October 2002 until June 2003, Förster completed a paid work placement in a Dutch school providing secondary education to pupils with behavioural and/or psychiatric problems, after which she did not take up another job until July 2004.[78] Förster claimed that since she was attending a vocational course that directly related to her previous employment, she still maintained her economic relationship with the Dutch labour market and should be entitled to receive *studiefinanciering*.[79] AG Mazak forcefully argued in favour of such interpretation:

> In applying the criterion of continuity, it should also be borne in mind that, as the Court has already alluded in *Lair*, continuous careers are less common in today's working environment than was formerly the case. In particular, younger people at the beginning of their professional lives are, for a number of reasons, often expected or even forced by the conditions in the job markets to show flexibility with their education and training as well as their first steps in employment. The requirement of continuity should therefore not be interpreted too strictly, in order to avoid excluding a substantial part of working students from the benefits of their rights as Community workers despite the fact that they have already been economically active and have entered the employment market of the host Member State.[80]

The Court declined Mazak's invitation to reconstruct the extent to which market solidarity can still trigger equal access to social benefits once the

[75] *Lair* para 37; Case 197/86 *Brown* [1988] ECR 3205 paras 27–8; and Hartley, 'Equal Treatment in Education', 185.

[76] *Ninni-Orasche* paras 43–4.

[77] See Article 7 of Directive 2004/38.

[78] Opinion of AG Mazak in *Förster* paras 21–8.

[79] Opinion of AG Mazak in *Förster* paras 76–90.

[80] Opinion of AG Mazak in *Förster* para 85.

migrant has stopped being economically active. Instead, it structured market solidarity as a sort of 'all-or-nothing': when a continuous economic link to the labour market exists, migrant citizens have full right to equal treatment; but when they are no longer employed, they lose all such entitlements. At the same time, this general trend that can be traced in the rulings in *Ninni-Orasche* and *Förster* sits uneasily with the approach taken by the Court in cases such as *Trojani*, where the qualification of a migrant as 'worker' primarily depended on a job being '*capable* of being regarded as [a]normal part of the labour market'; and with recent cases such as *Saint Prix*, where the Court held that a pregnant migrant worker, who temporarily stopped employment, could nevertheless be qualified as a worker.[81]

All in all, then, the first expression of market solidarity sees to extending domestic structures that protect the worker from the risks of, or reward him or her for engagement with, market interactions to include economically active mobile EU citizens. It seems that economic engagement in the host state alone, without further conditions, entitles such citizens to access welfare resources in their state of employment, even if increasingly the Court is faced with issues of coordination in situations where migrant workers also derive entitlements from their state of residence.

3.3 Insulating Market Solidarity from the Internal Market, or Insulating the Internal Market from Market Solidarity?

The development of market solidarity in the EU is more complex and contested when it comes to the regulation of the interaction between 'capital' and 'labour' on the internal market. The power relationship between these two is asymmetrically skewed in favour of the former. National political processes have since long infused norms of market solidarity in this economic interaction between capital and labour—in order to protect both the individual worker and the collectivity 'labour' from the potential for economic exploitation. In other words, the political process has historically been indispensable in ensuring that the economic interactions in the workplace conform to an idea of justice. The dynamics of the integrated European market,

[81] *Saint Prix* paras 39–44.

and in particular the undercurrents of mutual recognition and regulatory competition, however, risk undercutting the capacity of national political systems normatively to embed the relationship between 'capital' and 'labour', thereby liberating the former from the constraints of market solidarity and potentially subjecting the worker to unjust working conditions. It is in order to mitigate this structural effect—which an integrated market with decentralized regulatory norms almost inevitably engenders[82]—that social competences in policy fields directly linked to the regulation of the internal market have progressively been transferred to the Union.[83] This has led to the formulation of transnational forms of market solidarity, whereby the Union legislator and the Court are forced to think about the appropriate normative balance in the economic interaction between labour and capital on the transnational market. It appears that while the Union legislator is sensitive to the need to insulate *domestic* notions of market solidarity by way of transnational legal norms, rather than expose them to the dynamics of the internal market, the Court has not fully grasped the nature of market solidarity, which has led to the emergence of transnational ideas of market solidarity that are distinctly light on 'solidarity' and heavy on 'market'.

At the time of the signing of the Treaty of Rome it was expected that market solidarity would be included in the functioning of the internal market by way of domestic political processes.[84] The Ohlin Report,[85] compiled in the run-up to the negotiations, supported a model of economic integration that heavily relied on Ricardo's theory of comparative advantage, insisting on the free mobility of goods, services and factors of production.[86] This would not affect the capacity of Member States to ensure fairness on the market, given

[82] F. De Witte, 'EU Law, Politics and the Social Question' (2013) 14 GLJ 591–2; and F. von Hayek, *The Constitution of Liberty* (Chicago: University of Chicago Press, 1978) 184–5.

[83] See, for an overview of the gradual transfer of competences, D. Damjanovic and B. De Witte, 'Welfare Integration through EU Law: The Overall Picture in the Light of the Lisbon Treaty', in U. Neergaard, R. Nielsen, and L. Roseberry (eds.), *Integrating Welfare Functions into EU Law* (Copenhagen: DJOF, 2009) 67.

[84] See C. Barnard, 'EU Social Policy: From Employment Law to Labour Market Reform', in P. Craig and G. De Búrca (eds.), *The Evolution of EU Law* (Oxford: OUP, 2011) 642ff.; K. Lenaerts and P. Foubert, 'Social Rights in the Case-Law of the ECJ' (2001) 28 LIEI 267.

[85] International Labour Organization, Social Aspects of European Economic Co-operation. Report by Group of Experts ('Ohlin Report') (1956) 74 International Labour Review 99–123. See also D. Ashiagbor, 'Unravelling the Embedded Liberal Bargain: Labour and Social Welfare Law in the Context of EU Market Integration' (2013) 19 ELJ 307.

[86] See also S. Simitis and A. Lyon-Caen, 'Community Labour Law: A Critical Introduction to its History', in: P. Davies, A. Lyon-Caen, S. Sciarra, and S. Simitis (eds.), *European Community Labour Law: Principles and Perspectives*' (Oxford: Clarendon, 1996) 5ff.

that labour demand would grow where labour costs were the lowest, thereby facilitating an autonomous process of gradual levelling-up of social standards throughout Europe.[87] In other words, the internal market itself would generate fairness and market solidarity. This would be sufficient guarantee that the functioning of the internal market would not lead to challenges to the political capacity of the Member States to correct the market and embed demands of solidarity between labour and capital,[88] especially 'when account is taken of the strength of the trade union movement in European countries and of the sympathy of European governments for social aspirations'.[89]

Until the completion of the internal market in the early 1990s, any challenge to the norms of market solidarity by way of the internal market resulted primarily from the effect of increased competition on the worker's job security. The first labour law measures enacted on the European level can be seen as a recognition of this problem,[90] and were aimed at protecting the worker in case of business restructuring and thereby alleviating the hardship suffered by workers that resulted from the functioning of the internal market. As such, directives were enacted harmonizing workers' rights in case of collective redundancies,[91] transfer of undertaking,[92] or the insolvency of the employer.[93] These measures sought not only to protect the rights of individual workers but also to ensure 'fair competition' between companies, so that the 'casualties' of the internal market would not be dictated by differences between regulatory regimes.[94]

[87] Ohlin Report, 101 and 111–12.

[88] S. Giubboni, *Social Rights and Market Freedom in the European Constitution: A Labour Law Perspective* (Cambridge: CUP, 2006) 54–6. C. Barnard and S. Deakin, 'Market Access and Regulatory Competition', in C. Barnard and J. Scott (eds.), *The Law of the Single Market: Unpacking the Premises* (Oxford: Hart, 2002).

[89] Report by a Group of ILO Experts, 'Social Aspects of European Economic Co-operation' (Geneva, International Labour Office 1956) para 210.

[90] M. Shanks, 'The Social Policy of the European Communities' (1977) 14 CML Rev 377, who speaks of the 'political backlash' that would occur if capital was allowed to exploit the internal market.

[91] Directive 75/129/EEC on collective redundancies, amended by Council Directive 92/56/EEC, consolidated by Council Directive 98/59/EC; and Council Directive 80/987/EEC on acquired rights, amended by Council Directive 2002/74/EC.

[92] Directive 77/187/EEC on transfers of undertakings, amended by Council Directive 98/50/EC, consolidated by Council Directive 2001/23/EC.

[93] Council Directive 80/987/EEC on acquired rights, amended by Council Directive 2002/74/EC.

[94] See text in (1974) 1 European Industrial Relations Review 18; see also B. Bercusson, *European Labour Law* (Cambridge: CUP, 2009) 114, and B. Wedderburn, *Labour Law and*

In the early 1990s, however, this paradigm changed. After the completion of the single market, the capacity of the Member States to include norms of market solidarity in the functioning of the transnational market has been significantly limited by the processes of mutual recognition and regulatory competition. These last two terms relate to the (perceived) negative effects of free movement of factors of production on the integrated internal market on the capacity and political willingness of Member States to enforce their perception of justice on market participants. In response, the Union legislator's focus has gradually shifted from the harmonization of labour law towards the insulation of the capacity of *national* political processes to express market solidarity from the potentially distorting effects of mutual recognition and regulatory competition. The perceived threat of mutual recognition arises from the way in which it displaces political authority in the host state. Simply put: can service providers send out their workers to a host state with the retention of the laws applicable in the home state? The area of minimum wages provides the most politically sensitive and socially divisive example of the potential subversive effect of mutual recognition. National legislation setting out the minimum to be paid for a certain work is central to market solidarity, in that it directly ensures that workers are not exploited and are appropriately rewarded for their participation in the market. The level of minimum wages, however, differs radically within the European Union, making harmonization pointless, and mutual recognition potentially socially subversive.[95] After all, if a Bulgarian worker is 12(!) times less expensive than a Luxembourger worker, how can a company employing the latter ever possibly win a tender, assuming that both workers provide a service of comparable quality?[96] And maybe more importantly, when this tender is for a job within the Luxembourg territory, what capacity does the Luxembourg state have to ensure that its perception of worker protection and market solidarity is not undercut?[97] Properly understood, then, the threat of mutual recognition lies in the displacement of the exact political authority that is required to enforce ideas of market solidarity.

Freedom (London: Lawrence & Wishart, 1995) 397; G. Mancini, 'Labour Law and Community Law' (1985) 20 The Irish Jurist 1, 2, and 12.

95 S. Schmidt, 'When Efficiency Results in Redistribution: The Conflict over the Single Services Market' (2009) 32 West European Politics 855–6.

96 <http://epp.eurostat.ec.europa.eu/statistics_explained/index.php/Minimum_wage_statistics>, accessed February 2015.

97 A. Saydé, 'One Law, Two Competitions: An Enquiry into the Contradictions of Free Movement Law' (2011) 13 CYELS 370.

At the same time, the 'ghost' of regulatory competition made its entrance. It was feared that the increased ease of capital movement might be incompatible with the decision to leave the power to socialize the market within national political structures. Whereas the Ohlin Report had stressed that differences in labour standards throughout Europe were immaterial for competition as they reflected the relative competitiveness of Member States, the logic of mutual recognition entails that labour standards started to directly affect their competitiveness, as it highlighted that labour standards impose an indirect cost on production.[98] In consequence of the fact that capital is much more mobile and adaptive to dynamic competition than labour,[99] yet its presence on the national level vital to prevent the immense social cost of high unemployment, Member States, no longer able to use currency fluctuation to mitigate this effect,[100] could start to internalize concerns about their competitiveness in the political determination of labour standards.[101] In this view, the process of market integration would produce game-theoretical incentives for Member States to compete to attract capital by limiting indirect costs, such as labour regulations, for 'threat of exit' by capital,[102] thereby relinquishing their obligations of justice towards the workers in favour of courting transnationally mobile capital.[103]

The 'ghosts' of mutual recognition and regulatory competition, with their potential to limit the Member States' capacity and willingness to enforce domestic notions of market solidarity,[104] have focused the attention of the Union legislator on new regulatory techniques. Full harmonization of all labour standards proved too difficult politically, due

98 Bercusson, *European Labour Law*, 133; Schmidt, 'When Efficiency Results in Redistribution', 852.

99 See Case C-212/97 *Centros* [1999] ECR I-1459; S. Deakin, 'Legal Diversity and Regulatory Competition: Which Model for Europe?' (2006) 12 ELJ 448–50. See also H. Collins, *The European Civil Code: The Way Forward* (Cambridge: CUP, 2008) 38.

100 S. Deakin and F. Wilkinson, 'Rights vs. Efficiency? The Economic Case for Transnational Labour Standards' (1994) 23 Industrial Law Journal 296.

101 See W. Streeck, 'Citizenship Under Regime Competition: The Case of the "European Works Councils"' (1997) 5 EIoP No. 3, who traces this effect back to the work of Adam Smith.

102 Deakin and Wilkinson, 'Rights vs. Efficiency?', 295–6. See also M. Piore, 'Labor Standards and Business Strategies', in S. Hersenberg and J. Perez-Lopez (eds.), *Labor Standards and Development in the Global Economy* (Washington, DC: US Department of Labor, 1990).

103 F. De Witte, 'EU Law, Politics and the Social Question' (2013) 14 GLJ 590ff.

104 Giubboni, *Social Rights and Market Freedom*, 82; F. Scharpf, 'The Asymmetry of European Integration, or Why the EU Cannot be a 'Social Market Economy' (2010) 8 Socio-economic Review 222–4.

to the divergence of national legal techniques and political incentives, and economically undesirable, given that certain labour rights—such as minimum wages—reflect, and are therefore inextricably tied to, national (or sectoral) rates of productivity.[105] Moreover, full harmonization was not *necessary*. The objective of this second wave of labour legislation was, after all, not to protect workers' rights per se, but to insulate the political authority on the national level from the disruptive effects of regulatory competition and mutual recognition. Rather than prescribing the standard of worker protection to be implemented throughout Europe, then, two new legal techniques were introduced. Within the fields of labour law that are unrelated to rates of productivity, intervention on the European level aimed at establishing 'minimum standards below which nobody should be allowed to fall, but on the basis of which those [Member States] who can afford to do so should build their own more ambitious systems'.[106] In other words, it was thought that Member States would be less inclined to pursue regulatory competition,[107] and companies would be restrained from exploiting the logic of mutual recognition to force the workforce to accept lower standards of protection, if a 'floor of rights' could be agreed. The minimum standards set by harmonization measures are thus not really meant to serve as a new, default, transnational level of protection, but to induce 'second order effects'. By coupling regulation on the transnational level with the reaffirmation of national self-regulation,[108] and indeed encouraging Member States to set higher levels of labour protection,[109] the Union legislator managed simultaneously to prevent the threat of regulatory competition described above and to reinforce the capacity of the national political process normatively to embed the relationship between 'labour' and 'capital' in accordance with domestic understandings of market solidarity. Much of the recent labour and company law regulation on the European level had adopted this approach, from the Directive on information and consultation[110] and the Framework on Parental

[105] See also Deakin and Wilkinson, 'Rights vs. Efficiency?', 292 and 302–3.

[106] Shanks, 'The Social Policy of the European Communities', 380.

[107] Deakin and Wilkinson, 'Rights vs. Efficiency?', 289.

[108] Barnard and Deakin, 'Market Access and Regulatory Competition', 219.

[109] S. Deakin, 'Labour Law as Market Regulation: The Economic Foundations of European Social Policy', in P. Davies, A. Lyon-Caen, S. Sciarra, and S. Simitis (eds.), *European Community Labour Law: Principles and Perspectives* (Oxford: Clarendon, 1996) 87.

[110] See Articles 1 (1) and 9 (3) and (4) of Directive 2002/14/EC on information and consultation of employees.

Leave[111] to directives on part-time work,[112] fixed-term work,[113] temporary agency work,[114] working hours,[115] and the protection of pregnant workers.[116] All these measures set 'floors of rights', from which upward deviation is explicitly encouraged, so that national conceptions of market solidarity are not undercut by the dynamics of the internal market.

A similar logic applies to the role of the social partners on the European level. A tiered system of social partners has been created, whereby the exercise of the social dialogue on the European level is not meant to replace national equivalents, or create new norms that bind all Member States, but merely to supplement the functioning of the social partners on the national level by insulating the latter from the potentially disruptive effects of the internal market. In other words, the role of norm-setting on the European level is to empower, rather than replace, the social dialogue on the national level. Directives dealing with issues such as parental leave,[117] part-time[118] and fixed-time work,[119] all adopted on the basis of the social dialogue on the Union level,[120] emphasize this by explicitly allowing more favourable provisions to be negotiated by the social partners on the *national* level, thus leaving the latter in charge of the final substantive decision.[121] The Court indeed acknowledges this tiered structure and seems to grant wide discretion to national social partners in implementing such directives.[122] Rights to participation in the workplace, as well as rights to information and consultation, have been adopted using the same tiered approach, whereby

[111] See Clauses 1, 3, and 8 (1) attached to Directive 2010/18/EU implementing the revised Framework Agreement on parental leave.

[112] See Clauses 2 (2) and 6 (1) attached to Directive 97/81/EC on part-time work.

[113] See Clause 8 (1) attached to Directive 1999/70/EC on fixed-time work.

[114] See Article 9 of Directive 2008/104 on temporary agency work.

[115] See Article 15 of Directive 2003/88 on working time.

[116] See Recitals 5 and 22 and Article 1 (3) of Directive 92/85 on the protection of pregnant workers.

[117] See Directive 2010/18/EU implementing the revised Framework Agreement on parental leave.

[118] See Directive 97/81/EC on part-time work.

[119] See Directive 1999/70/EC on fixed-time work.

[120] Evolved into Article 155 TFEU now: 'should management and labour so desire, the dialogue between them at labour level may lead to contractual relations, including agreements. Agreements concluded at Union level shall be implemented either in accordance with the procedures and practices specific to management and labour (...) or (...) by a Council decision on a proposal from the Commission'.

[121] See recitals 11 and 12, and Clauses 1 (1) and 8 (1) of the new Framework Agreement as implemented by Directive 2010/18.

[122] See Case C-45/09 *Rosenbladt* [2010] ECR I-9391 paras 67–9.

transnational standards serve to insulate the capacity of national actors to impose standards of market solidarity.[123]

This tiered model of market solidarity is much more unstable where divisive issues are concerned. This is particularly so in the areas of minimum wages and collective action—the implementation of which is very disparate on the national level. Without being able to rely on transnational legislative standards to define the appropriate balance between labour and capital concerning minimum wage or collective action on the internal market, the Court has had to define the substance of market solidarity itself. As will be discussed, the Court has made the conceptual mistake of trying to define an autonomous transnational standard of market solidarity rather than using transnational legal mechanisms as a method to insulate domestic conceptions of market solidarity. The result is that the Court exposes labour rights to the pressures of mutual recognition and regulatory competition that are implicit in the functioning of the internal market, rather than protecting labour rights from such processes.

The area of minimum wages is a good example. Given the disparity between Member States,[124] no substantive level could possible effectively promote its objective—the prevention of the exploitation of the worker—in all Member States simultaneously. The cases *Seco*, *Rush Portuguesa*, and *Van der Elst*[125] all dealt with workers from 'low-wage countries' who were temporarily posted to work in 'high-wage countries'. In these cases, the Court first reiterated that while host Member States could not prevent access of service providers and their workers to their territory, they could nevertheless impose domestic labour law regulations: '[Union] law does not preclude Member States from extending their legislation, or collective labour agreements entered into by both sides of industry relating to minimum wages, to any person who is employed, even temporarily, within their territory, no matter in which country the employer is established.'[126] The Court later

[123] See Article 1 (1) of Directive 2002/14 and Recital 18, Articles 6 and 7, and Annex I of the Recast Directive 2009/38. Recitals 7 and 9-10 of Directive 2009/38. See also Case C-176/12 *AMS* EU:C:2014:2, where the Court denies the direct applicability of these norms in the Charter (i.e. they remain contingent on national legislation).

[124] See <http://epp.eurostat.ec.europa.eu/statistics_explained/index.php/Minimum_wage_statistics>, accessed February 2015.

[125] Joined Cases 62/81 and 63/81 *Seco* [1982] ECR 223, Case C-113/89 *Rush Portuguesa* [1990] ECR I-1417, and Case C-43/93*Van Der Elst* [1994] ECR I-3803.

[126] *Van Der Elst* para 23.

nuanced this stance, only allowing host Member States to impose norms of market solidarity which prevented the actual exploitation of workers, to the exclusion of double burdens and administrative requirements which make the provision of services less attractive without increasing the protection offered to workers.[127] Simply put, the Court reversed the idea of mutual recognition and took working conditions, including minimum rates of pay, 'out of competition'[128] in so far as such conditions differed between Member States. The task of elaborating the criteria of justice in the relationship between workers and employers on the internal market, then, is delegated to the national political arena.

The Posted Workers' Directive ('PWD') was adopted in order to codify these rulings and add transparency in case of the transnational provision of services. The PWD does not harmonize labour standards,[129] but rather arbitrates to what extent local labour standards of the host Member State govern the employment relationship, and to what extent home state labour standards may be 'imported'. Its Article 3 lays down a number of areas in which host Member States are allowed to insulate their own conceptions of fairness. These cover the fields most sensitive to direct competition, such as maximum hours, minimum paid holiday, minimum wage, health and safety, and non-discrimination. Two mechanisms ensure that Member States do not abuse this prerogative to frustrate the right to movement that service providers derive from the Treaty.[130] First, the PWD requires transparency of the content of the applicable law,[131] which must be imposed by law, be laid down in a collective agreement that has been declared universally applicable,[132] or mirror the collective agreements that are generally applicable to similar undertakings in the host state's territory.[133] This focus on transparency can

[127] See V. Hatzopoulos and T. U. Do, 'The Case Law of the ECJ Concerning the Free Provision of Services: 2000–2005' (2006) 43 CML Rev 972.

[128] Bercusson, *European Labour Law*, 358.

[129] Article 3 (1) (c) and (a) of Directive 96/71 on the Posting of Workers.

[130] See, most recently, Case C-515/08 *Santos Palhota* [2010] ECR I-9133 para 35.

[131] See recitals 5 and 6, as well as Article 4 of Directive 96/71 on the Posting of Workers, and in particular Article 4 (3), which requires Member States to set up bodies 'to make the information on the terms and conditions of employment referred to in Article 3 generally applicable'. See also Case C-165/98 *Mazzoleni* [2001] ECR I-2189 paras 35–6 and *Santos Palhota* paras 29–44 for an overview of the case law. See C. Kilpatrick, 'Laval's Regulatory Conundrum: Collective Standard-Setting and the Court's New Approach to Posted Workers' (2009) 34 ELRev 850.

[132] Article 3 (1) of Directive 96/71 on the Posting of Workers.

[133] Article 3 (8) of Directive 96/71 on the Posting of Workers. See also P. Davies, 'Posted Workers: Single Market or Protection of National Labour Law Systems?' (1997) 34 CML Rev. 571ff.

be seen as expression of the principle of non-discrimination on the basis of nationality.[134] Second, as Article 3 (7) PWD indicates, Member States may—in conformity with the case law of the Court (at the time)—impose higher standards only when they add to the protection of labour: 'paragraphs 1 to 6 shall not prevent application of terms and conditions of employment *which are more favourable to workers*'.[135]

On first reading, then, the PWD seems to be another instrument to ensure market solidarity.[136] It reappropriates the capacity of Member States to determine the 'just' economic interaction on the internal market and insulates that capacity from pressures that arise from direct competition between 'home' service providers and those from low-wage Member States.[137] This assumption, however, has suffered a fatal blow. In a series of cases that came before it in the mid-2000s, the Court has redefined the purpose and nature of the PWD. Cases such as *Laval*, *Rüffert*, and *Commission* v *Luxembourg*[138] dealt with mobile service providers seeking exemption from locally applicable rules on the basis that they infringed their freedom to provide services. At its core, the cases asked in the light of which objective the provisions of the PWD should be interpreted: is the PWD an instrument to prevent the subversive effects of direct competition on national conceptions of market solidarity, or a narrow exception to the logic of mutual recognition and the principle of home state control?[139] The Court chose the latter, arguing that the objective of the PWD was the protection of the 'interests of employers and their personnel [by laying down] the terms and conditions governing the employment relationship where an undertaking established in one Member State posts workers on a temporary basis to the territory of another Member State'.[140]

[134] See also, explicitly, Case C-260/04 *Commission* v *Italy* [2007] ECR I-7083 para 24.

[135] Article 3 (7), emphasis added. Also explicitly repeated in recital 17 of the preamble to Directive 96/71 on the Posting of Workers.

[136] See e.g. S. Deakin, 'Regulatory Competition after Laval' (2008) CBR Working Paper 15–16; C. Barnard, 'The UK and Posted Workers: The Effect of *Commission v Luxembourg* on the Territorial Application of British Labour Law' (2009) 38 ILJ 126; P. Davies, 'Market Integration and Social Policy in the Court of Justice' (1995) 24 ILJ 49; Kilpatrick, 'Laval's Regulatory Conundrum', 848; N. Reich, 'Free Movement v. Social Rights in an Enlarged Union—The Laval and Viking Cases before the ECJ' (2008) 9 GLJ 141.

[137] Davies, 'Posted Workers', 577–91.

[138] Case C-319/06 *Commission* v *Luxembourg* [2008] ECR I-4323; Case C-346/06 *Rüffert* [2008] ECR I-1989; Case C-341/05 *Laval* [2005] ECR I-11767.

[139] See also Case C-60/03 *Wolff & Müller* [2004] ECR I-9553 para 42.

[140] See *Laval* para 58.

The equation of the interests of employers and their personnel is, of course, already remarkable in the light of the (at least partially) opposed objective in entering into the employment contract.[141] Given that the PWD must—if it is to be in the interest of the employer that sends out his workers to work in another Member State—be an exception to the logic of mutual recognition, the Court then moved to interpret the norms elaborated in Article 3 PWD restrictively,[142] even to the extent that they become senseless. The term 'more favourable conditions' laid down in Article 3 (7) PWD, for example, was reinterpreted to refer to more favourable rules in the home state.[143] Article 3 (10) PWD, which allows host Member States to impose higher labour standards to protect public policy objectives of that state, was interpreted equally restrictively.[144] As a consequence, the PWD 'cannot be interpreted as allowing the host Member State to make the provision of services in its territory conditional on the observance of terms and conditions of employment which go beyond the mandatory rules for minimum protection'.[145]

In other words, any imposition of labour law beyond the areas defined in Article 3 (1) PWD, as well as any imposition beyond the minimum standards set, is automatically regarded as a restriction to the freedom to provide services.[146] Rather than a floor of rights, like other recent labour law directives, then, Article 3 (1) PWD provides a ceiling of rights, limiting the

[141] The 'logic' of the Court's ruling seems to be that any work is advantageous for workers, rather than work remunerated in accordance to standards of fairness. See also Case C-202/11 *Las* EU:C:2013:239 paras 22–3 and 31.

[142] *Laval* para 59.

[143] *Laval* paras 80–1. Which is—of course—completely counterintuitive as it presupposes that the provision of services would be imported into states where domestic competitors are cheaper.

[144] See also P. Davies, 'Case Note on Case C-346/06 *Ruffert*' (2008) 37 ILJ 293. As Barnard has argued, it is very difficult to imagine how any labour legislation, especially areas left out of Article 3 (1), such as the basic right to a written contract, rights to unfair dismissal, redundancy payments, 'living wages', and family rights, could pass the very high threshold of being a response to 'a genuine and sufficiently serious threat to a fundamental interest of society', as required by the Court in order to be considered to fall within the public policy exception. C. Barnard, 'The UK and Posted Workers: The Effect of *Commission* v *Luxembourg* on the Territorial Application of British Labour Law' (2009) 38 ILJ 126–9. See Case C-319/06 *Commission* v *Luxembourg* [2008] ECR I-4323 para 50.

[145] *Laval* para 80 and *Rüffert* para 33.

[146] *Laval* para 80 and *Rüffert* para 33. Indeed, in *Rüffert* the Court did not even test the imposition in the light of the Treaty. It simply assumed that a measure that goes beyond the 'nucleus' falls foul not only of the PWD but also of Article 56 TFEU. See also Davies, 'Case Note on Case C-346/06 *Ruffert*', 293.

scope of rules that may detract from the most effective (ab)use of the logic of mutual recognition and the potential of free movement.[147]

This interpretation of the PWD conflicts with the trend in EU labour law seeking to insulate the Member States' autonomy to ensure market solidarity.[148] A demand of transparency in the imposition of labour conditions on foreign service providers, for example, would have done exactly that without allowing the host Member States to protect their own industries.[149] Instead, the Court chose the exact opposite solution: it now insulates free movement *from* market solidarity, and actually mandates competition below the level of working conditions considered acceptable in the host state—in at least two different ways.[150] First, it essentially rules out that workers, whether domestic or foreign, are paid more than the minimum required, even for jobs that would normally fetch more due to the danger, timing, location, or prestige of the project.[151] It creates downward competitive pressure on wages and increases the number of workers who live on, or below, the minimum level of income meant to prevent commodification.[152] Second, the Court's interpretation of the PWD disbalances the domestic relation between 'labour' and 'capital'. By limiting the measures to be applied to foreign service providers to the areas covered by Article 3 (1) PWD alone, the Court has excluded entitlements such as the right to a written contract,[153] the protection against unfair dismissal, redundancy payments, living wages,

[147] Deakin, 'Regulatory Competition after Laval', 21–2. See also the Enforcement Directive on Posted Workers, Directive 2014/67, OJ 2014, L159/11.

[148] Cf. Case C-60/03 *Wolff & Müller* [2004] ECR I-9553 para 40.

[149] As the Court did in Case C-260/04 *Commission* v *Italy* [2007] ECR I-7083 para 24.

[150] Deakin, 'Regulatory Competition after Laval', 15. See also Kilpatrick, 'Laval's Regulatory Conundrum', 856, who shows that this has far-reaching consequences for cases of public procurement, where Member States must accept tenders below the standard of rights that it seeks to protect. A third challenge originates from the very narrow procedural interpretation of Article 3. See *Rüffert* paras 28–9.

[151] Kilpatrick, 'Laval's Regulatory Conundrum', 852, in combination with *Laval* para 70. Consider e.g. the difference between the UK minimum wage of £6.50 per hour and the living wage in London of £9.15, below which life in London becomes too expensive to live a normal life (figures correct for November 2014).

[152] See also *Rüffert*. In a public tender, the Land Niedersachsen had stipulated that whoever won the contract could not impose on its workers labour standards below the collectively agreed threshold. The subcontractor, who employed Polish nationals, got away with paying half the amount on the ground that the collective agreement was not declared universally applicable by the German state (nor could it, in fact, as a result of its federal structure). Cf. Schmidt, 'When Efficiency Results in Redistribution, 854–7.

[153] See e.g. Case C-202/11 *Las* EU:C:2013:239 para 31.

and family rights. This creates internal downward pressure on such rights in Member States, as it puts national workers in direct competition not only (and legitimately) with the qualities and productivity of foreign workers, but also with the level of labour regulation in the home state of those workers. This indicated the very limited conception of market solidarity in the case law of the Court: workers are entitled to only a limited range of basic entitlements in return for their engagement on the internal market.

The Court has—in the very same cases—made a similar conceptual mistake when it comes to rights to collective bargaining and collective action. Again, rather than understanding the transnational elaboration of such rights as an instrument to insulate the development of market solidarity on the national level, it has attempted to decide on the exact nature of market solidarity itself—and has thereby directly exposed the concept of market solidarity to the asymmetric power advantage that capital derives from the dynamics of the internal market. The right to collective action, even if it does not fall within the competences of the Union,[154] is protected by the CFR: 'Workers and employers, or their respective organisations, have, in accordance with Union law and national laws and practices, the right to negotiate and conclude collective agreements at the appropriate levels and, in cases of conflicts of interest, to take collective action to defend their interests, including strike action'.[155] In the light of the lack of legislative competences to elaborate on the transnational exercise of such rights, it appears that the inclusion in the CFR was meant to insulate the exercise of such rights on the national level rather than create a novel and autonomous right on the transnational level: '[t]he modalities and limits for the exercise of collective action, including strike action, come under national laws and practices, including the question of whether it may be carried out in parallel in several Member States.'[156] The defensive attitude by Member States in rejecting the legislative elaboration of transnational rights to collective action and collective bargaining is informed in part by the sensitive and highly politicized

[154] See Article 153 (3) TFEU, and Article 1, and recital 22, of Directive 96/71 on the Posting of Workers. Articles 1 (6), 1 (7), and 16 (3) of Directive 2006/123. See also Article 2 of Regulation 2679/98.

[155] See Article 28 of the Charter of Fundamental Rights. As a reflection also of their incorporation in the ILO Conventions, the European Social Charter, and simply by virtue of the fact that all Member States recognize such rights. See *Laval* para 90.

[156] See the Official Explanations relating to the Charter of Fundamental Rights (2007/C 303/02)10. See also Article 1(2) of the Protocol on the Application of the Charter of Fundamental Rights attached to the Treaty of Lisbon.

nature of such rights, but mainly by the apparent incapacity of the Union to reproduce the preconditions for their effective exercise.[157] None of these considerations, however, prevented the Court, in *Viking* and *Laval*, from interpreting the recognition of rights to collective action on the European level so as to require the exact opposite: namely the imposition of *transnational limits* on its *national exercise*. Both cases dealt with collective action that was directed against companies exercising their free movement rights. The assessment of the Court in both cases is relatively similar. First it argued that 'although the right to take collective action must (...) be recognised as a fundamental right which forms an integral part of the general principles of Community law the observance of which the Court ensures, the exercise of that right may none the less be subject to certain restrictions'.[158] Then, the Court continued, such restrictions cannot only flow from the national legislator (in accordance with their political perception of the required bargaining balance between labour and capital), but also from the EU legal order: 'it must therefore be examined whether the fact that a Member State's trade unions may take collective action (...) constitutes a restriction on the freedom to provide services, and, if so, whether it can be justified'.[159] In other words, the free movement provisions can directly limit the right to collective action and collective bargaining[160] as protected by national (constitutional) provisions. Rather than insulating national labour law, then, EU law exposes such rights to the dynamics of free movement. The first flaw in the Court's approach, in other words, is that it misread the tiered nature of market solidarity in the EU, and manoeuvred itself into a position where it could no longer defer the decision on the content of market solidarity to the national level or the political process, but had itself to define the normative content of a distinct and autonomous European form of market solidarity. This approach is diametrically opposed to the approach to delegation favoured by the Union legislator in creating the norms of transnational market solidarity, and leads the Court into answering a quintessentially political question, for which it is ill equipped.

[157] See, for reasons why national parliaments are sceptical, F. Fabbrini and K. Granat, 'Yellow Card but No Foul: The Role of National Parliaments under the Subsidiarity Protocol and the Commission Proposal for an EU Regulation of the Right to Strike' (2013) 50 CML Rev 115. See also B. Wedderburn, 'Multi-national Enterprise and National Labour Law', in B. Wedderburn, *Labour Law and Freedom* (London: Lawrence & Wishart 1995) 243.

[158] *Laval* para 91; *Viking* para 44.

[159] *Laval* para 96; *Viking* para 47.

[160] Case C-271/08 *Commission* v *Germany* [2010] ECR I-7091 paras 38–44.

In setting the balance between free movement and rights to collective action, the Court arguably made two further mistakes. The first and most crucial one was to interpret the role of trade unions akin to public actors.[161] It argued that the

> freedom to provide services would be compromised if the abolition of State barriers could be neutralised by obstacles resulting from the exercise, by associations or organisations not governed by public law, of their legal autonomy.[162]
>
> Article [49 TFEU] must be interpreted as meaning that, in circumstances such as those in the main proceedings, it may be relied on by a private undertaking against a trade union or an association of trade unions.[163]

In other words, the free movement provisions are horizontally applicable. Not only the state, but also trade unions may not restrict the regulatory movement of capital. While this finding is theoretically compatible with the rulings in *Bosman* or *Walrave*,[164] in which the Court extended the scope of the free movement provisions to cover regulatory bodies exercising (de facto) public power, its extension to trade unions constitutes a significant misreading of the nature of market solidarity.[165] As already described, such rights are explicitly meant to protect the autonomy of the social partners by setting out the markers within which the parties are allowed to negotiate.[166] Inexplicably, however, the Court transfers the obligation to determine these markers between which both parties may pursue and defend their interests onto the trade unions. After all, by allowing the free movement rights to be invoked against trade unions, the exercise of collective action can no longer be justified by self-interest, but by public policy requirements only.[167] This completely reverses the logic of struggle and autonomy. While capital can act out of complete self-interest, the weaker of both parties must take the legitimate interest of the stronger into account within the negotiation process! This questionable outcome is the result of the Court's oversight

[161] L. Azoulai, 'The Court of Justice and the Social Market Economy: The Emergence of an Ideal and the Conditions for its Realisation' (2008) 45 CML Rev 1350.

[162] *Viking* para 57.

[163] *Viking* para 61. In *Laval* the Court simply bypasses this question, see *Laval* paras 98–9.

[164] Case 36/74 *Walrave and Kock* [1974] ECR 1405; and Case C-415/93 *Bosman* [1995] ECR I-4921.

[165] D. Ashiagbor, 'Collective Labour Rights and the European Social Model' (2009) 3 Law & Ethics of Human Rights 222.

[166] C. Offe, 'The European Model of "Social" Capitalism: Can it Survive European Integration?' in Miller (ed.), *Worlds of Capitalism*, 160.

[167] H. Schepel, 'Constitutionalising the Market, Marketising the Constitution, and to Tell the Difference: On the Horizontal Application of the Free Movement Provisions in EU

of three central characteristics of market solidarity: first, the existence of a systemic bargaining asymmetry between labour and capital in favour of the latter, which needs to be balanced out to allow for a just interaction between the two; second, the crucial role of 'the political' in the establishment and maintenance of a more symmetrical interaction between the two parties,[168] achieved by insulating the autonomy of collective labour structures;[169] and third, the notion that rights to collective action serve not only as a tool for social dialogue, but also, and primarily, for social struggle.

After recognizing the horizontal effect of the freedoms, the Court limited the rights to collective action even further. Given that trade unions are now forced to justify their actions on grounds of public policy, the Court argued, it could take such action only if it was clear that it was aimed at protecting workers,[170] whose jobs or conditions of employment were under serious threat,[171] and then only when the trade union had exhausted any other means at its disposal.[172] This interpretation significantly limits the exercise of the right to collective action[173] and opens up the possibility for claims for damages by employers for 'disproportionate' strike action, which has already led to a significant curtailing of the exercise of the right to strike.[174] The legality of collective action, of course, cannot logically be contingent on its impact on capital, for that is exactly its objective. The more successfully the right to strike is employed, and the more capital is affected, the more likely it is to move towards the wishes of labour. The weapon of a strike ensures

Law' (2012) 18 ELJ 177; C. Barnard, 'EU Social Policy: From Employment Law to Labour Market Reform', in P. Craig and G. De Búrca (eds.), *The Evolution of EU Law* (Oxford: OUP, 2011) 667.

[168] See G. Orlandini, 'Right to Strike, Transnational Collective Action and European Law: Time to Move on? (2007) 8 Jean Monnet Working Paper 16-18. See also Case C-112/00 *Schmidberger* [2003] ECR I-5659, and Case C-265/95 *Commission v France* [1997] ECR I-6959 para 34, where the Court still humbly held that it is 'not for the Community institutions to act in place of the Member States and to prescribe for them the measures which they must adopt and effectively apply in order to safeguard [the exercise of free movement]'.

[169] This is stranger still given that in its previous case law the Court had indeed recognized both that the obligations of accommodating free movement were imposed on the Member States rather than private parties, and that the Member States retained a wider margin of appreciation in assessing the legality of the exercise of fundamental rights. See *Schmidberger* paras 60 and 93. See also Streeck, 'Citizenship Under Regime Competition', 3.

[170] *Viking* para 80; *Laval* paras 106–7. [171] *Viking* paras 81–3.

[172] Ibid. para 87. [173] See also Ashiagbor, 256–8.

[174] British Airways threatened their employees with a claim of £100 million per day if strike action was carried out, after which the trade unions cancelled their planned collective action. M. Rocca, 'Enemy at the (Flood)gates' (on file with author). See also K. Apps, 'Damages Claims against Trade Unions after *Viking* and *Laval*' (2009) 34 ELRev 141, and, for an account

the symmetry of bargaining power between labour and capital not only at the end of the bargaining process, but constitutes a lever throughout. The Court, by limiting its use and threat to situations in which all other options are exhausted, undermines its effect, and, simultaneously, the autonomy and bargaining power of labour in its struggle for better working conditions.[175] In fact, the Court's ruling has been severely criticized by the monitoring bodies of the ILO and ESC, stating 'the doctrine that is being articulated in these ECJ judgments is likely to have a significant restrictive effect on the exercise of the right to strike in practice in a manner contrary to the Convention'.[176]

If we compare the Court's approach in matters of minimum wage, posted workers, and the right to collective action with how the Union legislator has generally developed its norms of market solidarity, we notice a direct discrepancy. While in most aspects of labour law the tiered nature of market solidarity is increasingly visible—where Union legislation serves to insulate the norms of market solidarity on the national level *against* the dynamics of the internal market[177]—the Court has completely reversed that logic in the areas discussed above. Rather than taking working conditions 'out of competition'—and thereby protecting the worker from exploitation—the Court in fact mandates competition on the basis of working conditions. These rulings have indeed not only liberated capital from national constraints imposed in order to protect labour, but also allowed capital to exploit the additional bargaining advantage that it derives from the dynamics of the internal market. The Court has not understood that it is structurally incapable of making such normative assessments,[178]

of damages in the *Laval* case, U. Bernitz and N. Reich, 'Case Note on Case A 268/04, The Labour Court, Judgment No. 89/09, *Laval*' (2011) 48 CML Rev 611.

[175] C. Offe, 'The European Model of "Social" Capitalism: Can it Survive European Integration?', in Miller (ed.), *Worlds of Capitalism*, 160.

[176] International Labour Conference, 99th Session, 209; 2013 Report of the Committee of Experts on the Application of Conventions and Recommendations 178; Complaint No. 85/2012 Swedish Trade Union Confederation v Sweden.

[177] The legislator is keenly aware of this. See e.g. Green Paper: 'Modernising Labour Law to Meet the Challenges of the 21st Century' COM (2006) 708 final 6: 'Responsibilities for safeguarding working conditions and improving the quality of work in the Member States primarily rests on national legislation and on the efficacy of the enforcement and control measures on the national level. At the EU level, the social *acquis* supports and complements the actions of the Member States in this sphere.'

[178] Due to the lack of a supporting political sphere, its particular institutional role, and the different welfarist traditions that it has to contend with. See D. Ashiagbor, 'Unravelling the

nor has it grasped the *structure* of market solidarity or construed any *substantive* notion of market solidarity beyond the remarkable assertion that justice requires that capital be protected from the bargaining power of labour. This is potentially highly problematic for both the development of the internal market and the stability of market solidarity on the national level, which are a result of decades of political struggle—only to be outdone by a Court trying to figure out what a 'social market economy' entails.[179] It paints the picture of an internal market whereby free movement hollows out national understandings of market solidarity, which is 'unfair' to its participants and wherein the mediating function of market solidarity, stabilizing market interactions, is all but lost. In addition, the substantive re-regulation of such assessments of market solidarity by the Union legislator is deeply problematic—due to the lack of institutional politicization[180] and Member State resistance.[181]

3.4 The Right to Cross-Border Healthcare as Market Solidarity

Market solidarity can also be found beyond its 'natural habitat' of embedding the relationship between workers and their employers. The third way in which the logic of market solidarity manifests itself in EU law is in the area of healthcare. Free movement law, here, has been interpreted so as to allow patients to enforce the conditions of the healthcare contract that they have entered into with their Member State. Implicitly, what this tells us is that EU law understands healthcare to be based on a (fictitious) market contract between the patient and the public insurance structures, whereby

Embedded Liberal Bargain: Labour and Social Welfare Law in the Context of EU Market Integration' (2013) 19 ELJ 307; M. Hopner and A. Schafer, 'Polanyi in Brussels? Embeddedness and the Three Dimensions of European Economic Integration' MPIfG Discussion Paper 10/8.

[179] Blauberger shows that while, generally, Member States attempt to 'legislate around' ECJ case law, this is very difficult in the area of labour law due to domestic veto players. See M. Blauberger, 'With Luxembourg in Mind...the Remaking of National Policies in the Face of ECJ Jurisprudence' (2012) 19 JEPP 109.

[180] M. Dawson and F. De Witte, 'From Balance to Conflict: A New Constitution for Europe' (2015) 20 ELJ forthcoming.

[181] F. Fabbrini and K. Granat, 'Yellow Card but No Foul: The Role of National Parliaments under the Subsidiarity Protocol and the Commission Proposal for an EU Regulation of the Right to Strike' (2013) 50 CML Rev 115.

the latter insure the former against a set number of risks in return for a set contribution—whether levied directly by the insurer or through general taxation. It is, then, the economic relationship between the patient and his or her state of insurance (or state of 'affiliation', in technical terms) that creates a commitment of market solidarity that can be enforced through free movement law. In other words, when a public insurance scheme defaults on its contractual obligations, patients can access cross-border healthcare with retention of their right to reimbursement.

European states generally provide for universal, permanent, and adequate access to a wide range of high-quality treatment options for its citizens. In the light of the high (and still rising) costs of maintaining a system of healthcare (in 2007, the EU-27 spent €967 billion p.a. on healthcare),[182] such systems operate on the logic of compulsory (semi-public) collective insurance, through which citizens insure themselves and each other against physical harm. The costs of such schemes are generally borne by the state (and thus its citizens), even if it often asks for contributions by individual participants or their employers.[183] To some extent, then, healthcare is based on the market interaction between the patient and his or her state of affiliation (that is, the state in which he or she is covered for healthcare costs). The individual derives a *contractual right to healthcare* in return for his or her participation in the collective healthcare insurance schemes in that state: citizens insure themselves against a set number of injuries or diseases, and can, in return, access the treatment options required to prevent or cure such injuries and diseases. In order to ensure the financial stability and continuity of the systems of collective healthcare, Member States impose internal and external limitations on the individual's right to treatment. Internally, it generally limits the list of treatments that it funds, refusing to reimburse, for example, cosmetic treatments or dentistry.[184] The external limitation to the individual right to healthcare consists of the refusal to subsidise treatment for patients who are not affiliated to their healthcare scheme, and the refusal to subsidise treatments that affiliated patients undergo abroad. In an attempt to ensure that Member States meet their part of the bargain, and in order to protect

[182] See Commission Impact Assessment for the Directive on Cross-border Healthcare, SEC (2008) 2163, 9.

[183] See Van der Mei, *Free Movement of Persons*, 223–4, for an explanation of the different regulatory styles used by the different Member States.

[184] The Dutch, for example, recently excluded physiotherapy, professional help to stop smoking, and most non-pathological mental illnesses from compulsory reimbursement schemes. See, for an in-depth and exhaustive study of how the Member States fund, structure,

citizens from a breach of their contractual right to healthcare, however, the Court has extrapolated from market solidarity a sort of contractual liability. Whenever a state cannot, physically, provide a treatment for which it has insured its affiliated patients, market solidarity allows for the enforcement of the 'healthcare contract' by granting such patients the right to obtain the treatment in another Member State with the retention of reimbursement schemes in the state of insurance.

This contractual liability on the part of the Member States can be traced back to the very beginning of the regulation of cross-border healthcare. Article 22 (2) of Regulation 1408/71 was arguably aimed at the exact situation where Member States 'default' on their healthcare obligations. It stated that Member States must reimburse healthcare abroad where 'treatment in question is among the benefits provided for' by the legislation of the state of affiliation and such treatment cannot be given 'within the time *normally necessary* for obtaining treatment in the Member State of residence'. The term 'time normally necessary' thus seems to allow, in particular in the light of the autonomy which Member States retain to decide on their basket of healthcare, for waiting lists that inevitably arise in access to finite resources.[185] The right under market solidarity to enforce a healthcare contract by way of free movement only appears to cover instances where treatment 'cannot physically be provided' or is 'materially and technically impossible', rather than extending to instances where medical need warrants quick treatment.[186] After all, the contractual obligation that Member States enter into is to provide the treatments listed, not to ensure a healthcare system that is the most effective in the EU. The state of affiliation breaches its obligations under market solidarity only when it is simply incapable of providing a treatment for which it has agreed to insure its citizens in the first place.[187] Only in such circumstances, then, does market solidarity extend the contractual right to healthcare to cover the whole of the Union and allow the patient to seek, and be reimbursed for, treatment abroad.

On first sight, this exception appears quite unproblematic. Why would a Member State insure its citizens for a treatment that it cannot provide when it remains free to exclude certain treatments from its basket of

and order their systems of healthcare, a EP working paper: 'Healthcare Systems in the EU: A Comparative Study' (SACO 101 EN).

185 Van der Mei, *Free Movement of Persons within the European Community*, 256 and 305.

186 Opinion of AG Saggio in Case C-368/98 *Vanbraekel* [2001] ECR I-5363 para 13. See also Opinion of AG Villalón in Case C-173/09 *Elchinov* [2010] ECR I-8889 para 1.

187 See explicitly Case C-268/13 *Petru* [nyr].

healthcare?[188] The reality is a bit more complex than that. Many Member States list the treatments against which they insure their citizens in very general terms, either in order to keep up with technological developments in medicine, to convince all citizens to 'buy into' an insurance scheme, or simply to prevent bureaucratic hassle.[189] Such wide definitions of the precise basket of healthcare that affiliated patients may access at the expense of the state have provided fertile grounds for litigation as to the extent of the contractual obligation on states under market solidarity. *Peerbooms* is a good example of such a case. The case dealt with a comatose Dutch national whose doctor advised that he undergo intensive therapy using neurostimulation, which was, however, not available in the Netherlands.[190] Mr Peerbooms was instead transferred to an Austrian hospital where he was treated using neurostimulation, and eventually, awoke from his coma. Upon return to the Netherlands he claimed that the cost of treatment should be reimbursed by the Dutch state. The Dutch state, however, argued that such treatment fell outside the basket of healthcare provided and would, therefore, not be reimbursed. The Dutch legislation that defines the content of compulsory insurance schemes does not, however, offer an exhaustive list of all subsidised treatments but rather covers all treatments that are considered medically 'necessary' and 'normal in professional circles'.[191] Accordingly, the question to be answered, in order to assess whether Peerbooms had a right to be reimbursed on the basis that the Netherlands could not, physically, provide a treatment for which it had contractually undertaken to insure him, was whether neurostimulation was indeed both 'necessary' and 'normal'.

The Court implicitly acknowledges the concept of market solidarity by emphasizing that EU law allows for the enforcement of the state's contractual healthcare obligations:

> [Union] law cannot in principle have the effect of requiring a Member State to extend the list of medical services paid for by its social insurance system.

[188] *Elchinov* para 58.

[189] C. Newdick, 'Citizenship, Free Movement and Health Care: Cementing Individual Rights by Corroding Social Solidarity' (2006) 43 CML Rev 1662.

[190] Neurostimulation was used on an experimental basis in two hospitals in the Netherlands, which, however, required patients to be under 25. Peerbooms was 35 years old at the time of the accident.

[191] Case C-157/99 *Geraets-Smits and Peerbooms* [2001] ECR I-5473 paras 10, 91. Article 10 (a) of the current Dutch Zorgverzekeringswet still uses the same conditions: 'geneeskundige zorg (...) zoals die door huisartsen en verloskundigen placht te geschieden'.

> [However], a scheme of prior authorization cannot legitimise discretionary decisions taken by the national authorities. Therefore, in order for a prior administrative authorisation scheme to be justified (...) it must, in any event, be based on objective, non-discriminatory criteria which are known in advance, in such a way as to circumscribe the exercise of the national authorities' discretion, so that it is not used arbitrarily.[192]

In other words, whether or not patients have a right to enforce their contractual right to healthcare throughout the Union depends on the terms of the contractual relationship between the affiliated patient and the healthcare administration.[193] The Court then looked at the *content* of this contractual obligation: how must the terms 'normal' and 'necessary' of the Dutch healthcare contract be interpreted? It argues that the term 'normal' must take account not only of what is considered 'normal' by Dutch scientists, but also of international scientific opinions.[194] This way the Court ensures that Dutch patients can actually access treatments that are generally considered to fall within the scope of their healthcare insurance, rather than solely those that are actually available within the Dutch territory.[195] In interpreting the term medically 'necessary', the Court does not look for *medical* necessity—as it does under communitarian solidarity[196]—but rather whether the cross-border movement was necessary. In its ruling, the Court highlights that treatment abroad is always considered 'necessary'—and must therefore be reimbursed—when the 'treatment covered by the national insurance system *cannot* be provided by a contracted establishment'.[197] In the more recent *Petru* case, the Court makes this link even more explicit, arguing that 'the lack of medication and of medical supplies and infrastructure can, in the same way as the lack of specific equipment or particular expertise, make it impossible for the (...) treatment to be provided in the Member State of residence',[198] and highlighting that 'whether that is indeed impossible must be determined by reference to all the hospital establishments in the Member State of residence that are capable of providing the treatment in question'.[199] Read

[192] *Geraets-Smits and Peerbooms* paras 86 and 90.

[193] *Petru* paras 30–2.

[194] *Geraets-Smits and Peerbooms* paras 94–7.

[195] See, also explicitly, *Elchinov*, where the Court argued that the fact that a certain treatment cannot be provided on the territory of a state does not justify a presumption that it is not covered in that state's lists of treatments.

[196] See Chapter 4.

[197] *Geraets-Smits and Peerbooms*, my emphasis.

[198] *Petru* para 33.

[199] *Petru* para 34.

together, this seems to suggest that whenever a treatment option can be construed to fall within the basket of healthcare in the state of affiliation, but cannot be provided on its territory, the patient has a right to access, and be reimbursed for, that treatment in another state. The ruling of the Court in *Elchinov* seems to confirm this reading:

> it is for each Member State to decide which medical benefits are reimbursed by its own social security system (...) [However], where the list of medical benefits reimbursed does not expressly and precisely specify the treatment method applied but defines types of treatment (...) prior authorisation cannot be refused on the ground that such a treatment method is not available in the Member State of residence of the insured person, since such a ground, if it were accepted, would imply a restriction on the scope of the second subparagraph of Article 22(2) of Regulation No 1408/71.[200]

Market solidarity thus serves as a tool for patients to enforce access to the basket of healthcare that they are insured for under the terms of collective insurance schemes by way of free movement. Logically, then, and as accepted by the Union legislator in Article 35 of Regulation 883/2004,[201] the right to reimbursement under market solidarity covers the full cost of the treatment obtained abroad. It would indeed be strange if patients are made to pay for the inadequacies of the insurance scheme in their state of affiliation. Patient mobility under market solidarity is thus financially neutral for the patient,[202] while it can in theory be either advantageous or disadvantageous for the healthcare institution in the state of affiliation, depending on how the costs of treatment abroad compare to the costs of the treatment at home.

Situations in which patients are able to invoke a claim under market solidarity to obtain reimbursement for treatment which their state of affiliation cannot provide remain, however, very exceptional. Empirical research suggests that the unmet need of healthcare is very limited within the European Union,[203] and the situations in which such a clear incongruity between the treatments that are insured and those actually offered exists are likely to be

200 *Elchinov* paras 59 and 62. Article 22 (2) of Regulation 1408/71 is now replaced by Article 20 of Regulation 883/2004.

201 Article 35 reads: 'the benefits in kind provided by the institution of a Member State on behalf of the institution of another Member State under this Chapter shall give rise to full reimbursement'.

202 Opinion of AG Colomer in Case C-56/01 *Inizan* [2003] ECR I-12403 para 29.

203 Commission Impact Assessment for the Directive on Cross-border Healthcare SEC (2008) 2163, 68.

even smaller. Rather, the contractual nature of market solidarity highlights that this exception to the principle of territoriality is generally meant to help Member States meet their contractual healthcare obligations. Research shows that Member States use these provisions to make up for the lack of specialization or financial and technological resources required to treat rare diseases,[204] or to balance out a mismatch between the supply and demand of healthcare services among neighbouring states.[205] In such cases, Member States use cross-border healthcare, and the economic nature of their relationship with insured patients, as vehicles to meet the healthcare needs of their affiliated citizens that they—for whatever reason—are not capable of meeting themselves.

3.5 Conclusion

Market solidarity sees to the development of norms of justice in interactions between market actors. It tells us something about how economic relationships across borders change the way we think about justice. The purpose of market solidarity is to stabilize such interactions and, more specifically, to protect the weaker parties in the market from exploitation on the basis of asymmetric economic power. This chapter has discussed three different ways in which market solidarity has been incorporated in the functioning

[204] Malta and Luxemburg, for example, simply outsource treatment of such patients to other systems, which frees up resources for other treatments. Likewise, it allows less rich Member States to offer treatment options that are (for the moment) unavailable at home. See also Opinion of AG Villalón in *Elchinov* para 72: 'a system such as the Bulgarian system, which seeks to offer a very advanced list of treatment that is paid for by the fund, benefits from the knowledge and technology of other Member States which have the technical resources to which Bulgaria aspires. If a Member State wishes to be at the cutting edge of medical treatment (which naturally takes time), European Union law allows its citizens to receive in another Member State treatment which the former State wishes to make available domestically, although not at present in a position to do so.'

[205] Commission Impact Assessment for the Directive on Cross-border Healthcare, SEC (2008) 2163, 42: 'Belgium has had larger patient flows for planned care than most other Member States, in particular with Dutch patients being treated in Flanders through contracts between Dutch health insurers and Belgian providers. In this case study, the researchers consider that as well as being convenient for patients, this is more efficient for both the Dutch insurers (providing care that is faster and cheaper, as well as being perceived as technologically advanced and of high quality) and the Belgian providers (helping to overcome overcapacity in the acute hospital sector by treating patients from abroad).'

of the transnational market. In each of these three cases, the possibility of free movement alters our commitments to justice—either by forcing us to rethink which actors deserve access to welfare benefits on the basis of their economic engagement within a particular polity; by asking us to elaborate how justice constrains (or not) the interaction between labour and capital on the internal market; or by highlighting that the exercise of free movement itself might serve to enforce domestic obligations of justice. The Union legislator is keenly aware of these demands of market solidarity—unsurprising given that the primary site for the development of norms of market solidarity has always been the political arena. The Court, on the other hand, struggles at times to understand both the structure and substance of transnational market solidarity. Given the peculiar institutional structure of the Union, however, the effect of the Court's case law on the national structures that are meant to implement market solidarity is deeply pervasive and extremely difficult to revert.

4

Communitarian Solidarity

The European Union does not only create new types of economic links between its citizens; it also puts them in a social relationship—both on the European level, in the sense that all EU citizens are part of the incipient and ill-defined European polity, and on the national level, where citizens of different nationalities engage with each other through a whole range of social interactions. Communitarian solidarity seeks to articulate the obligations of justice that follow from such social interaction, both on the European level and within the nation state. Communitarian solidarity in the EU does not see to the production of a catalogue of substantive rights for all EU citizens, nor does it seek to mirror the role of national citizenship in reflecting the normative quality of a polity.[1] Rather, it seeks to reassess national conceptions of belonging, and asks Member States to rethink who the members of their 'community of care' are—not based on lazy ideas of nationality, ancestral lineage, or ethnic belonging, but on conceptually more sophisticated ideas such as reciprocity deriving from the social relationship between a migrant citizen and the host state polity (section 4.1). In essence, communitarian solidarity serves as a procedural mechanism through which domestic citizenship is structurally 'opened up' to include the associative social commitments that bind the migrant citizen to the host state polity.

As such, communitarian solidarity requires different things depending on the degree of social integration of mobile citizens within the host state polity, but also depending on the nature and social function of a

[1] See F. De Witte, 'Union Citizenship and Constrained Democracy', in A. P. Van der Mei and M. De Visser (eds.), *Twenty Years Treaty on European Union: Reflections from Maastricht* (Antwerp: Intersentia, 2013).

particular welfare good. In simple terms, the more integrated the mobile EU citizen and the more fundamental the welfare entitlement, the easier the mobile EU citizen will receive access to welfare resources in the host state. The child of an economically inactive migrant, in other words, can freely access primary education from the day of arrival, but may have to reside in the host state for a number of years before being able to access student benefits. Communitarian solidarity, in other words, attempts to tease out which *specific* associative connections between individuals is constitutive of a particular welfare benefit (section 4.2). In doing so, it prevents welfare entitlements from being extended to those who do not 'deserve' them, while remaining sensitive to legitimate claims by EU citizens. This chapter will discuss the two outer edges of this obligation on Member States under communitarian solidarity. At the one extreme we can discern a number of fundamental social rights, such as primary education, primary healthcare, and minimum subsistence benefits. It will be argued that such rights can be accessed by every EU citizen, in whichever state he or she happens to reside—without any further requirements (section 4.3). At the other extreme we will discuss student benefits. The question to what extent mobile citizens can access such benefits in the host state requires the Court to break down the complex structures of reciprocity and solidarity that sustain these benefits, which may include a mix between economic and social engagement with a host society, as well as prior and future commitments. As such, when exactly a mobile student meets these ill-defined criteria is not easy to assess. The Court has developed a procedural mechanism through which to assess Member State policies, and, despite many challenges and certain inconsistencies, the Court seems more and more comfortable in taking up this role (section 4.4).

Communitarian solidarity, then, is a sophisticated instrument that forces Member States to think of their 'communities of care' as something that is porous, and as something that is connected to more complex commitments of social engagement and social interaction than simply carrying the nationality of a Member State. In elaborating the commitments of communitarian solidarity it seems that the Court is led by the desire to force Member States to undertake this exercise of opening up their national citizenships, rather than to elaborate a range of normative commitments that supranational communitarian solidarity would require all Member States to converge around.

4.1 The Normative Premise and Legal Structure of Communitarian Solidarity

An individual derives rights and entitlements not only by virtue of his or her role as an economic actor in society, but also simply by virtue of being a citizen, that is, being part of a polity and society. The type of interactions that citizens have with each other within a certain society engender obligations and rights—much like the way in which market transactions do.[2] As Brunkhorst has argued, the self-constitution and constant reproduction of society by the individual citizens' engagement and interaction automatically generate claims of solidarity.[3] In its extreme, these norms, typically referred to as communitarian solidarity, can be understood as the normative texture of a society: they express the moral commitments binding a certain group of people in a certain place in time on a certain territory. Communitarian solidarity is thus both social and relational and speaks to the commitments between citizens who are engaged in the creation, elaboration, and reproduction of a certain community that reflects communal norms, values, and modes of interaction. As Rosanvallon explains, such interaction within society 'usually manifest[s] itself in unspoken forms of civility that nevertheless generate a diffuse kind of knowledge. Fleeting exchanges complement the sense that one has of living alongside others, which helps to develop an egalitarian ethos'.[4] The rights that an individual derives simply by virtue of his or her role as a participant in a certain social process—that is, on the basis of communitarian solidarity—are wide-ranging. Marshall famously made a distinction between economic rights (the right to engage in labour, to own property), political rights (the right to vote and stand in elections), and social rights (such as access to distributive programmes).[5] In general terms, such rights reflect the need to protect the individual's autonomy, in the private and the public sphere. Such rights are understood as allowing polities to operate functionally and bolster public authority: they clarify the relationship between citizens, the polity, and coercive power. As such, the guarantees of

[2] See section 3.1.

[3] H. Brunkhorst, *Solidarity: From Civic Friendship to a Global Legal Community* (Cambridge, Mass.: MIT, 2005).

[4] P. Rosanvallon, *The Society of Equals* (Princeton, NJ: Harvard University Press, 2013) 288.

[5] T. H. Marshall, *Citizenship and Social Class* (London: Pluto, 1992).

access to political voice, public goods, and resources required to live a free, dignified, and autonomous life are usually tied to an individual's status as a member of a political community. Historically speaking, nationality and citizenship have been used as proxies to define the personal scope of rights under communitarian solidarity. In other words, only citizens that could demonstrate long-term membership of a certain political project could derive economic, political, and social rights. The purpose of such proxies, as Thomas has identified, is to reflect a certain attachment to a polity that cannot easily be reproduced. As such, citizenship or nationality are, first of all, about blood, about a deep-rooted sense of belonging and heritage.[6] Second, citizenship results from, and expresses, a cultural identity. It is thought to be premised on a shared language, cultural heritage, historical trajectory, and primary socialization;[7] it fosters a sense of belonging through symbolic identification[8] with a national 'community of fate'.[9] A third conception of citizenship centres on the political and moral values that exist within a polity.[10] It is premised on identification with, and commitment to, core values that command authority, and inform behaviour and social interactions within a community.[11] Fourth, citizenship is based on a contractarian notion of reciprocity,[12] in which every citizen undertakes certain obligations towards the community and derives commensurate rights from that community. This highly complex and multifaceted understanding of who 'belongs' to a certain community makes its extrapolation to the transnational arena highly difficult.

The crucial connection between citizenship as *status* and citizenship as *entitlement* also explains the closed nature of national welfare systems, and seems to make intuitive sense. A Spanish citizen who has always lived and worked in Madrid has a different connection to the Spanish citizenry and political community than his Estonian neighbour who only just moved to Madrid. Given that it is exactly this connection, however—formalized by criteria of social

[6] E. Thomas, 'Who Belongs?: Competing Conceptions of Political Membership' (2002) 5 European Journal of Social Theory 329.

[7] Ibid. 330.

[8] S. Žižek, 'Eastern Europe's Republic of Gilead', in C. Mouffe (ed.), *Dimensions of Radical Democracy: Pluralism, Citizenship, Community* (London: Verso, 1992) 194–6.

[9] D. Millar, *On Nationality* (Oxford: OUP, 1997) 22–7 and 184–5.

[10] Thomas, 'Who Belongs?', 332.

[11] A. Follesdal, 'Union Citizenship: Unpacking the Beast of Burden' (2001) 20 Law and Philosophy 326.

[12] A. Sangiovanni, 'Global Justice, Reciprocity and the State' (2007) 35 Philosophy & Public Affairs 19ff.; Thomas, 'Who Belongs?', 333.

belonging, collective engagement, and diffuse solidarity—that defines an individual's claim to redistributive resources under communitarian solidarity, it is not surprising that the latter cannot make the same (welfare) demands towards the Spanish state as the former. The big question, then, for the development of communitarian solidarity on the European level, is to what extent Member States are still allowed to rely on proxies such as nationality or citizenship in order to define the categories of individuals that can access welfare resources in that state, given that such proxies are unable to reflect the social commitments (and the rights and entitlements that follow from such commitments) of non-national residents in the host state. In other words, EU law needs to take account not only of the economic interaction across borders, but also the way in which citizens—of different nationalities—stand in *social* relationship with each other.

In her opinion in *Ruiz Zambrano*, AG Sharpston seemed to suggest that Union citizenship could replace national citizenship as the proxy for access to a range of rights. She compared the Court's interpretation of the notion of Union citizenship with its landmark ruling in *Van Gend and Loos*, in which it defined the autonomous nature of the European legal order and drew the citizens closer to the functioning of the integration project.[13] Union citizenship, in her view, could serve as an instrument for another paradigmatic shift in our conception of the integration process, leading the way towards a fully fledged political community with autonomous justice claims and popular legitimacy attached to its membership. Union citizenship alone, in this logic, would guarantee all citizens a range of political, social, and economic rights. As the *BverfG* highlighted, in the same ruling where it implicitly denied the existence of a European *demos*, Union citizenship indeed reflects 'the nucleus of a European solidarity'.[14] The creation of the European polity, with its European 'citizens' as subjects, simply presupposes a (minimal) degree of horizontal identification among these citizens. Even if in an incipient, ill-defined, and functionally differentiated form, norms of communitarian solidarity govern the interaction between citizens and the public authority in the European Union.[15] As the progressive development of the polity of Europe, as well as the establishment of a range of European political

[13] Opinion of AG Sharpston in Case C-34/09 *Ruiz Zambrano* [2011] ECR I-1177 para 68 with reference to Case 26/62 *Van Gend en Loos* [1963] ECR 1.

[14] See *Lisbon* ruling of BverfG, 2 BvE 2/08 of 30.6.2009 para 395.

[15] D. Held, 'Between the State and Civil Society: Citizenship', in G. Andrews (ed.), *Citizenship* (London: Lawrence & Wishart, 1991) 19.

solidarities[16] and fundamental rights[17] demonstrates, there are indeed some identity ties, interpersonal links, and normative commitments that bind 'all Europeans' and spatially transcend the nation state's territory. The common identity that 'all Europeans' derive from Union citizenship entails a shared commitment to each other's needs, suffering, misery, happiness, and ambitions, just as (if clearly not to the same extent as) it does on the national level.[18] This normative commitment to citizen well-being and social justice is buttressed by its clear codification in the centre of Europe's constitutional objectives.[19] There is simply 'something' intangible attached to the status of the individual citizen in the European project. The intangible and dynamic nature of this 'something' makes its definition in terms of legally enforceable rights extremely difficult and highly contentious.

Indeed, there is no reason why Union citizenship *could* not serve the purpose of elaborating a catalogue of supranational communitarian rights for all Union citizens. At this moment in time, however, hardly anyone is seriously arguing that Union citizenship should challenge or even replace the conception of membership and the communitarian bounds of solidarity that are attached to citizenship on the national level.[20] In other words, the creation of a transnational political community does not mean that transnational communitarian solidarity will create a number of social entitlements that all its 500 million citizens can access. The elaboration of Union citizenship was in fact primarily seen as a political statement, and as an attempt to legitimize the deepening of the integration project, rather than as ascribing a certain normative vision or solidaristic rights to Europe as a political community. As the *BverfG* emphasized in its *Lisbon* ruling, Union citizenship is clearly secondary to national citizenship, and its establishment did not create a European *demos*.[21] This can be deduced from the wording of

[16] See, for examples of this political solidarity, the commitments in the area of external action (Articles 24 and 31 TEU), immigration and asylum (Article 80 TFEU), energy security policy (Articles 194 and 122 TFEU), and in the event of a terrorist attack (see Article 222 TFEU).

[17] See Charter of Fundamental Rights, 2010/C 83/02.

[18] See also Interim Evaluation of the Europe for Citizens Programme (Ecroy, 2011) 67, where it is argued that 'approximately 80% of participants (...) felt more solidarity with their fellow Europeans than in the previous survey'.

[19] Articles 2 and 3 TFEU.

[20] See e.g. T. Faist, 'Social Citizenship in the European Union: Nested Membership' (2001) 39 JCMS 51. See also *Lisbon* ruling of BverfG para 263.

[21] *Lisbon* ruling of BverfG paras 347–50.

Article 20 TFEU ('citizenship of the Union shall be additional to and not replace national citizenship'), from the fact that the Member States retain the autonomy to decide who qualifies as a Union citizen,[22] and from the fact that Union law explicitly protects communitarian rights granted under national citizenship from erosion by virtue of rights granted under Union citizenship.[23] Transnational communitarian solidarity is not, then, a reflection of the normative texture of the European polity, in the way that its national counterpart is often perceived.[24]

In fact, the way in which the Court understands norms of communitarian solidarity in the EU is not as a substantive form of solidarity that entitles all European citizens to certain rights within their own state or in their host state. Rather, it has understood communitarian solidarity as reflecting the social links between citizens (regardless of their nationality). Simple residence in a host state, in other words, comes with a range of rights and entitlements that reflect the social relational commitments that the migrant has with the host polity. As already argued it is, after all, the daily, quotidian social interaction between citizens and their communal reproduction of social norms within a certain territory that generate commitments of solidarity and that warrant access to welfare rights and entitlements. Simply residing on a particular territory and engaging in such interactions comes with rights based on communitarian solidarity. European Union law, in other words, ensures that the social engagement by mobile EU citizens in a host state is taken into account in the allocation of welfare rights and entitlements. The exact nature, strength, and extent of such rights and entitlements, as will be argued further, depend primarily on the exact nature, strength, and extent of the migrant's social interactions in the host polity.

This has—as will be discussed—forced Member States to rethink which exact social commitments warrant access to which social benefits. It can no longer lazily rely on ideas of nationality or national citizenship as defining who falls within their national 'community of care', and who can therefore derive social rights. Instead, Member States may only bar mobile EU citizens

[22] Case C-369/90 *Micheletti* [1992] ECR I-4239, and for an overview of excluded citizens, G.-R. De Groot, 'Towards a European Nationality Law', in H. Schneider (ed.), *Migration, Integration and Citizenship: A Challenge for Europe's Future* (Maastricht: Forum Maastricht, 2005), i.

[23] See Article 21 TFEU and Articles 1 to Directive 90/364, Directives 90/365 and 93/96, and Article 8 (4) of Directive 2004/38.

[24] R. Bauböck, 'The Three Levels of Citizenship within the European Union' (2014) 15 GLJ 751.

from access to social benefits if such citizens do not meet the criteria of reciprocity that are specific to a certain social entitlement. Once mobile citizens meet such criteria on account of the nature and strength of their social interaction in the host state polity, they become part of the national 'community of care' and can access its redistributive programmes. Communitarian solidarity on the European level, then, stretches notions of national community, reformulates criteria for inclusion, and is fluid: it behaves differently depending on the specific social function of a certain benefit, and the specific relationship between the migrant and the host state. While transnational communitarian solidarity, then, does not have significant normative substance, it is a very powerful procedural instrument in opening up national citizenship and infusing it with the cosmopolitan norms and relational commitments that permeate the process of European integration.[25]

4.2 Procedural Citizenship: Expanding Communitarian Obligations

The first case that explicitly discussed the rights that Union citizens accrue simply because of their residence in a host Member State was *Martinez Sala*. The case dealt with a Spanish national who had lived in Germany since the age of 12. Between 1976 and 1989 she had been in and out of jobs in Germany. In 1993, just after her child was born, she applied for child-raising allowance, which was denied by the Bavarian administration on the ground that she possessed neither German nationality nor a residence permit.[26] In its assessment, the Court came up with a novelty—Martìnez Sala had the right not to be discriminated against on the basis of nationality simply because she was an EU citizen lawfully residing on the territory of another Member State,[27] a right previously reserved for economically active EU citizens: 'in the sphere of application of the Treaty and in the absence of any justification, such unequal treatment constitutes discrimination prohibited

[25] See chapter 1; D. Kostakopoulou, 'European Union Citizenship: Writing the Future', (2007) 13 ELJ 623; S. Giubboni, 'European Citizenship and Social Rights in time of Crisis' (2014) 15 GLJ 935.

[26] This was a correct assessment of the factual situation, as the German authorities had not renewed her residence permit since 1984, but merely certified that she had applied for an extension, which allowed her to stay in Germany legally.

[27] Case C-85/96 *Martinez Sala* [1998] ECR I-261 para 61.

by Article [18 of the TFEU]'. This vast extension of the scope of the principle of non-discrimination and, by implication, far-reaching intrusion into national systems of social redistribution was justified by reference to the notion of Union citizenship: 'Citizenship of the Union is destined to be the fundamental status of nationals of the Member States, enabling those who find themselves in the same situation to receive the same treatment in law irrespective of their nationality, subject to such exceptions as are expressly provided for.'[28] This should not, it is argued, be interpreted to mean that Union citizenship alone allows for full equal treatment of all resident Union citizens in respect of all social benefits. Redistribution on the national level still presupposes 'support by strong social and symbolic ties of generalised reciprocity and diffuse solidarity',[29] which cannot automatically extend to all mobile Union citizens without causing the problematic distributive asymmetries discussed in Chapter 2. Rather, as highlighted by AG Colomer, the Court's demand of equal treatment cannot be seen in isolation from the fact that Martìnez Sala had lived practically her whole life in Germany,[30] and could therefore reasonably be regarded as 'deserving' the childcare benefits on account of her social engagement with German society. Such intuitive judgments as to the way in which EU law restructures domestic redistributive commitments to account for the social links between migrant and host state society may be pragmatic, but remain unsatisfactory for lack of normative elaboration and conceptual clarity.

Starting from its rulings in *D'Hoop* and *Collins*, therefore, the Court came up with a procedural test that serves to incorporate the social commitments entered into by migrants in a host state into the assessment of whether or not they 'deserve' welfare benefits in their host state. The Court demands that Member States draft eligibility criteria in such a way that they reflect only the social function and nature of a particular welfare entitlement. As summarized by AG Geelhoed, 'depending on the nature of the benefits concerned, the Member States may lay down such objective conditions as are necessary to ensure that the benefit is provided to persons who have a sufficient link with its territory'.[31] This obligation not to use nationality as a

[28] Case C-184/99 *Grzelczyk* [2001] ECR I-6193 paras 30–1; Case C-148/02 *Garcia Avello* [2003] ECR I-11613 paras 22–3; Case C-209/03 *Bidar* [2005] ECR I-2119 para 31; and Case C-50/06 *Commission* v *Netherlands* [2007] ECR I-9705 para 32.

[29] Faist, 'Social Citizenship in the European Union', 46.

[30] Opinion of AG Colomer in Case C-138/02 *Collins* [2004] ECR I-2703 para 65.

[31] *Bidar* para 33.

criterion for eligibility, but rather the specific connection that is constitutive of a particular welfare benefit, helps the Court to integrate migrant citizens within domestic welfare arrangements. This procedural test of communitarian solidarity is divided into two parts. First, the Court will analyse the precise function and nature of a particular social benefit, and assess which exact social commitment it reflects: 'The genuine link required between the [migrant] claiming the benefit and the host Member State need not be fixed in a uniform manner for all benefits, but should be established according to the constitutive elements of the benefit in question, including its nature and purpose or purposes.'[32] Once the type of social commitment that underlies a certain welfare benefit has been established, all migrants who can reproduce this same commitment must be granted equal access. Eligibility criteria that are not indicative of the nature and function of the benefit are in principle invalidated for breach of communitarian solidarity.[33] This requirement of contextualization of the migrant within the norms of reciprocity that underlie a welfare entitlement serves—as the Court has recently for the first time picked up on—simultaneously to reflect the migrant's social commitment to the host state and to protect the sustainability of those entitlements: 'the necessity of establishing a genuine and sufficient connection between the claimant and the competent Member State enables that State to satisfy itself that the economic cost of paying the benefit at issue (…) does not become unreasonable'.[34] As a consequence of this requirement of contextualization, communitarian solidarity is a differentiated type of solidarity: it demands different things depending not only on the depth and nature of the migrant's social integration in the host state, but also on the type of entitlements, in the light of their precise social function. To put it differently, communitarian solidarity extends the size of national sharing communities in accordance with the social function of a particular welfare good. In very general terms, this means that economically *in*active migrant EU citizens can access benefits whose function is to prevent human need or that are inextricably linked to territorial objectives from the moment they reside in the host state.

[32] Case C-75/11 *Commission* v *Austria* EU:C:2012:605 para 63.

[33] See, explicitly, Case C-503/09 *Stewart* [2011] ECR I-6497 paras 95–100; AG Mazak in Case C-158/07 *Förster* [2008] ECR I-8507 para 129: 'the criterion used must still be indicative of the degree of integration into society'. See also C. O'Brien, 'Real Links, Abstract Rights and False Alarms: The Relationship between the ECJ's "Real Link" Case Law and National Solidarity' (2008) 33 ELRev 653.

[34] *Stewart* para 103.

On the other hand, they do not derive an automatic and immediate right to welfare entitlements in the host state that reflect certain prior social commitments, whether in the form of personal insurance (such as pensions) or more intangible socio-cultural attachment (student grants). Communitarian solidarity, in other words, does not entitle mobile EU citizens to all welfare benefits in the host state, but only to those specific benefits that the nature of their *specific* interactions with the host state society warrants.

At times the assessment of the precise rights of migrants on the basis of their social engagement in the host state (society) is relatively simple to make; at other times this exercise is next to impossible. The reciprocal commitments that underlie childcare benefits, for example, are easy to break down. In *Geven* and *Hartmann*, AG Geelhoed and the Court highlighted that they 'constitute an instrument of national family policy intended to encourage the birth-rate in that country'[35] that 'the legislature's motive is also the underlying idea that raising a child in Germany makes a contribution to the future political, economic and social existence of society in that country',[36] and that '[the policy serves to] promote childbirth with a view to guaranteeing a certain degree of stability in the demographic composition of [the Member States'] populations'. [37] The function and nature of childcare benefits, in other words, is decisively territorial; and migrants can thus meet the social commitments that it reflects simply by having or raising a child in Germany. As Geelhoed concludes, childcare benefits must then be extended to all residents:

> [t]here can be no doubt that the Member States are wholly justified in pursuing policies aimed at promoting childbirth with a view to guaranteeing a certain degree of stability in the demographic composition of their populations. By their very nature such policies must ensure that measures taken are aimed at the persons resident on their national territories. (...) It would therefore seem that a residence requirement is appropriate to ensure that the child-raising allowance is provided to persons who belong to the Member State's national population, which, of course, includes not only German nationals, but all persons lawfully resident in Germany irrespective of their nationality.[38]

[35] Case C-213/05 *Geven* [2007] ECR I-6347 para 21; Opinion of AG Geelhoed in *Geven* para 29.

[36] Opinion of AG Geelhoed in Case C-212/05 *Hartmann* [2007] ECR I-6303 para 66. See also Case C-212/05 *Hartmann* [2007] ECR I-6303 para 32.

[37] Opinion of AG Geelhoed in *Hartmann* para 69; Opinion of AG Geelhoed in *Geven* para 29.

[38] Opinion of AG Geelhoed in *Hartmann* para 69; Opinion of AG Geelhoed in *Geven* para 29.

As soon as a child—although this will logically include its parents—has established lawful residence in a host member state, family benefits must automatically be extended. The imposition of other conditions, such as an economic commitment or prior residence, is not allowed, for they require a connection between applicant and state which is not indicative of the social function of the benefits requested.[39] Under the rules of Regulation 883/2004 there is indeed no doubt that family benefits, which are defined as 'all benefits in kind or in cash intended to meet family expenses, excluding advances of maintenance payments and special childbirth and adoption allowances',[40] must be extended to cover *all* resident Union citizens.[41] While neither the Regulation itself nor the Court's case law explains the normative basis for this demand of completely equal treatment, it is likely to follow the logic set out above. Family benefits are almost all inextricably tied to the same demographic concerns highlighted above, and reflect a societal engagement of citizens to the maintenance of the polity, which logically extends to include all resident Union citizens.

As a result of the procedural logic of the test, the Court will invalidate criteria for access to welfare benefits in Member States when they fail to reflect the type of social commitment that underlies a certain welfare benefit. In such a case, after all, Member State legislation can never be sufficiently sensitive to the social commitments entered into by migrant EU citizens on its territory. In reference to the Belgian tideover allowance, for example, the Court held that 'the purpose (…) is to facilitate the transition from education to the labour market for young people, [and] the Court has held that it was legitimate for the national legislature to wish to ensure that there is a real link between the applicant for that allowance and the geographical employment market concerned'.[42] The eligibility criteria for access to tideover allowance, then, must be such that they include all citizens that have this real link to the geographical employment market, and can only exclude those citizens that do not. In *D'Hoop*, therefore, the Court invalidated Belgian legislation that made eligibility for tideover allowance conditional upon the applicant having completed secondary education on the Belgian territory:

[39] See also *Dano*, where Germany did not contest the payment of childcare benefits to economically inactive migrants. Case C-333/13 *Dano* [nyr].

[40] Article 1 (z) of Regulation 883/2004.

[41] See combined reading of Articles 11 (3)(e), 4, and 5 of Regulation 883/2004.

[42] Case C-367/11 *Prete* EU:C:2012:668 para 33; with reference to *Collins* paras 68–70; and Case C-224/98 *D'Hoop* [2002] ECR I-6191 para 38.

A single condition concerning the place where the diploma of completion of secondary education was obtained is too general and exclusive in nature. It unduly favours an element which is not necessarily representative of the real and effective degree of connection between the applicant for the tideover allowance and the geographic employment market, to the exclusion of all other representative elements.[43]

In other words, a criterion of completion of secondary education indeed includes within the personal scope of the tideover allowance a group of citizens that have a link to the geographical employment market, but also excludes a number of citizens that have such a link. In other words, the eligibility criteria do not accurately reflect the social commitments that migrant citizens may have with the Belgian state. The Belgian legislator changed its eligibility criteria to demand that the applicant had completed at least six years of education on the Belgian territory. This was challenged by Deborah Prete, who had been to school in France, and had moved to Belgium after her marriage to a Belgian national. Unsurprisingly, the Court was not impressed with the new eligibility criteria:

[EU law] precludes a national provision (...) which makes the right to a tideover allowance for the benefit of young people looking for their first job subject to the condition that the person concerned has completed at least six years' studies in an educational establishment of the host Member State, insofar as that condition prevents other representative factors liable to establish the existence of a real link between the person claiming the allowance and the geographical labour market concerned being taken into account.[44]

In its ruling, the Court mentioned a plethora of other factors that could demonstrate the real link between Deborah Prete and the Belgian employment market: she has actively been looking for work in Belgium,[45] she has resided in Belgium for two years,[46] she is married to a Belgian national,[47] and she had studied only just across the border in France,[48] meaning that her link to the Belgian employment market was already established. What the Court demands, then, seems to come very close to perfect legislation. It demands that Member States define their eligibility criteria in such a way that *all* citizens who, one way or another, demonstrate a link to the domestic employment market are included—be it through personal circumstances

[43] *D'Hoop* para 39.
[44] Case C-367/11 *Prete* EU:C:2012:668 para 52.
[45] Ibid. para 46.
[46] Ibid. para 47.
[47] Ibid. paras 48–50.
[48] Ibid. para 45.

(marriage), objective reasons (residence), past commitments (secondary education), or prospective commitments (active work-seeking). Imposing such demands of perfection might be inappropriate—even if it does ensure that national legislation takes account of the social connections between migrant citizen and host state polity. It appears, however, that this imposition of an obligation of perfection is partly the result of Belgium's particular legislation, which, unlike the eligibility criteria for jobseeker allowances in other Member States, does not focus primarily on residence and active job-seeking. As the Court held in other cases, such demands do not in principle violate the requirements of communitarian solidarity.[49]

Gottwald is a good example of a case where the Court takes a broader-brush approach while still staying true to the conceptual logic of communitarian solidarity. The case dealt with an Austrian law that granted free toll discs to disabled residents, but not disabled non-residents. Mr Gottwald, as a disabled German resident on holiday in Austria, was not exempted from toll duty. The Court first traced the function of this particular benefit, before it assessed whether or not the claim of residence was indeed indicative of that function:

> The measure at issue (...) is intended to promote the mobility and social integration of disabled persons who, because of their disability, cannot use public transport and who, as a consequence, depend on a private vehicle. Thus, that measure applies, as shown by the validity of the toll disc of one year, to persons who have to use the road network relatively frequently.[50]
>
> With regard to a measure such as that at issue in the main proceedings, intended to facilitate regular journeys in Austria by disabled persons with a view to their integration in national society, the place of residence or of ordinary residence then appears to be a criterion suitable to establish the existence of a connection between those persons and the society of the Member State concerned.[51]

What seems to underlie the Court's ruling, then, is not that the policy itself is inherently territorial (such as the demographic policies underlying child-raising benefits), but rather that its objective, to encourage the social integration of immobile citizens, requires that the applicant demonstrate (a presumption of) the willingness to actually integrate in that society. That is the citizens' part of the bargain. A criterion of residence, in other words, is indicative for such willingness to integrate; implying that the right to free

[49] *Collins*. [50] Case C-103/08 *Gottwald* [2009] ECR I-9117 para 31.
[51] Ibid. para 36.

toll-discs does not extend to people such as Mr Gottwald, who only spent a few days in Tyrol and cannot demonstrate a social commitment to the host state's society that is sufficiently robust.[52]

Most other entitlements—such as student grants, which will be discussed in depth below—are multidimensional, and attach as much (if not more) importance to past commitments as to future participation in society.[53] The communitarian obligations incumbent on Member States to extend such benefits to cover economically inactive migrants are much more difficult to define. The Court has used a whole range of different legal instruments to help it make such complex assessments. The proxies of 'real link' and 'degree of social integration', or the demand on national courts to take the personal circumstances of the individual into account, serve to contextualize ideas of communitarian solidarity within national reciprocal commitments. One of the main conceptual problems that the Court has had to face is whether or not to demand that Member States take an individual migrant's personal circumstances into account. The argument for doing so, of course, is that if communitarian solidarity is about teasing out whether or not a migrant meets abstract conditions of social integration, personal circumstances must play a central role. The fact that an applicant might have learned the language of the host state, might be married to a national of that state, or might have strong cultural or familial ties indicates degrees and gradations of social integration that blunter instruments, such as a fixed period of residence, cannot. Indeed, increasingly the Court looks at exactly such circumstances in order to establish the connection between an individual and the Member State issuing welfare entitlements.[54] The argument against including the individual's circumstances in assessments of the demand of communitarian solidarity is, however, equally convincing. As discussed already in reference to the *Prete* case, such assessment runs the risk of looking for *any* link between the individual and the Member State, rather than looking for the particular link that is central to the delivery of a certain welfare entitlement. Moreover, Member States are understandably uncomfortable with the obligation to take personal circumstances into account, for reasons of legal certainty, the

[52] See Opinion of AG Mazak in *Gottwald* para 10.

[53] O. Golynker, 'Case note on *Förster*' (2009) 46 CML Rev 2033. See also Opinion of AG Sharpston in Case C-542/09 *Commission* v *Netherlands* EU:C:2012:346 para 147.

[54] *Prete* paras 45–50; *Stewart* [2011] para 100; C-507/12 *Saint Prix* EU:C:2014:2007 para 42; Case C-523/11 and 585/11 *Prinz and Seeberger* EU:C:2013:524 para 38; Case C-20/12 *Giersch* EU:C:2013:411 para 81.

risk of endless litigation, administrative burdens, and added legislative complexity. Both the Court, in *Förster*, and the Union legislator, in Directive 2004/38, therefore seemed to exclude personal circumstances from being taken into account in assessing an individual's degree of social integration.[55] Instead, the legislator has opted for a temporal proxy. According to Directive 2004/38, such migrants have no rights to social entitlements in the first three months of their residence in the host state,[56] some rights after the first three months, and equal rights across the whole spectrum after five years.[57] This temporal axis seems unduly rigid. If the objective of the use of a proxy is to accommodate the social commitments that migrants have undertaken in the host state polity within national reciprocal commitments, length of residence cannot but be one of the criteria assessed, in combination with the nature and function of the welfare good and other personal circumstances of the migrant.[58] The temporal proxy simply assumes that a migrant is not socially integrated until the day before completing the five years of residence, and miraculously becomes socially integrated overnight. Society, and the social interactions that reproduce it, are simply more complex than that.

Whichever proxy is used, it is fair to say that it remains an 'intellectually impoverished substitute[s] for the sort of rigorous analysis of the meaning of social solidarity within Europe's multi-level welfare society'.[59] The absence of such rigorous analysis is caused by the absence of a sufficiently robust transnational political structure and by the Court's inability to describe the normative legal texture of Union citizenship. Such description would be, however, a tall order. Union citizenship and communitarian solidarity are in constant flux. They emerged in 1992, became really visible in 1998, and have since been constantly redefined.[60] At this moment in time, communitarian solidarity can perhaps best be defined as a normatively hollow but procedurally robust form of solidarity based on a commitment to equality.

[55] *Förster* para 54 and Article 24 (2) of Directive 2004/38. See, for the opposite view, Opinion of AG Mazak in *Förster* paras 129–30.

[56] Article 6 and 14 (1) of Directive 2004/38. See also C. Barnard, 'EU Citizenship and the Principle of Solidarity', in E. Spaventa and M. Dougan (eds.), *Social Welfare and EU Law* (Oxford: Hart, 2005) 166–75.

[57] Articles 16 and 24 (2) of Directive 2004/38, recently confirmed in *Dano*.

[58] See, explicitly, *Stewart* paras 95–100.

[59] M. Dougan and E. Spaventa, '"Wish you weren't here...": New Models of Social Solidarity in the European Union', in M. Dougan and E. Spaventa (eds.), '*Social Welfare and EU Law*' (Oxford: Hart 2005) 203–4.

[60] See, most recently, *Ruiz Zambrano* and Case C-256/11 *Dereci* EU:C:2011:734.

It demands that all Union citizens can access social entitlements in other states as soon as they can reproduce the reciprocal (social) commitments that underlie such entitlements. More than anything else, in fact, the problems encountered in assessing when exactly mobile citizens indeed reproduce such commitments is testament to the incredible reconfiguration of national communities of care undertaken in the name of transnational communitarian solidarity.

4.3 The Development of a Catalogue of Fundamental Social Rights

From the outset it appears that a claim on the basis of communitarian solidarity is strongest in respect of fundamental social entitlements, such as emergency healthcare, primary education, housing, or minimum subsistence allowance. Such goods are both foundational and fundamental to the capacity of citizens to live their lives with at least a minimum of autonomy and dignity, and are implicit in any social and political relationship between human beings. In other words, access to such primary social goods is not sustained by significant commitments of social integration in society, but simply reflects a basic commitment between participants in the same social process not to diminish each other's capacity to live his or her life with at least a minimal level of dignity and autonomy. As a result, each resident citizen derives a claim to access such basic social benefits under communitarian solidarity. The Court appears only half committed to this element of solidarity—insisting on the right to education and healthcare but not on the migrant's right to minimum subsistence benefits—most likely under the political pressure of Member States that fear their welfare model is under threat by 'welfare tourists'. It is remarkable that such ungrounded and tendentiously presented fear should prevail over a commitment to ensure basic levels of human dignity for citizens that are part of a Member State's society.

4.3.1 *The Right to Adequate and Timely Healthcare*

Communitarian solidarity offers all citizens a right to adequate and timely healthcare—a right that they can enforce against whichever state they reside in. Good health is of central importance for the individual's physical integrity and his capacity to live a 'good' life—or indeed *any* life.[61] Medical assistance such as prenatal care, emergency surgery, or treatment of infectious diseases is 'fundamental and foundational' for citizens even merely to survive, let alone to live a 'good life'.[62] It does not seem farfetched to argue, then, that individuals are reliant on access to certain treatments in order to exercise most other rights. The provision of basic and adequate primary healthcare, which should extend to cover (at the very least) treatment meant to 'avoid premature death and escapable morbidity',[63] such as the treatment of common diseases and injuries, the provision of essential drugs, immunization against infectious diseases, and basic maternity and childcare,[64] as well as a range of high-quality and adequate treatment options to prevent debilitating pain, constitutes, ultimately, a basic obligation on all types of social structuring—as recognized by national, European, and international law.[65] In other words, citizens undertake such obligations vis-à-vis all other participants in society.

Because of the fundamental and foundational nature of primary healthcare, migrant EU citizens automatically gain access to it in whichever state they find themselves. It is simply the migrants' role as part of society that justifies such entitlements. This extension is not really disputed, and was implicitly accepted in *Baumbast*. In that case, the Court discussed the requirement under Directive 2004/38 that economically inactive Union citizens who wish to reside in another Member State must obtain 'comprehensive sickness insurance'. This is meant to prevent 'unreasonable' burdens on the host state's welfare budget. Mr Baumbast, a German national residing in the UK,

[61] J. Ruger, *Health and Social Justice* (Oxford: OUP, 2009) 2–3.

[62] Article 7 (3) of the 1978 Alma Ata Declaration on Primary Health Care defines primary healthcare as including 'at least: education concerning prevailing health problems and the methods of preventing and controlling them; (...) maternal and child health care (...) immunization against the major infectious diseases; prevention and control of locally endemic diseases; appropriate treatment of common diseases and injuries; and provision of essential drugs'.

[63] Ruger, *Health and Social Justice*, ch. 4.

[64] See B. Toebes, 'The Right to Health as a Human Right in International Law', in A. Eide, C. Krause, and A. Rosas (eds.), *Economic, Cultural and Social Rights* (The Hague: Kluwer, 2001) 243ff. See also Regulation 1231/2010, which extends the application of Regulation 883/2004 to third-country nationals.

[65] On the national level (e.g. Article 23 of the Belgian constitution, Article 52 of the Bulgarian constitution), the European level (Article 35 CFR, Articles 11 and 13 of the European Social Charter) and the international level (1978 Alma Ata Declaration on Primary Health Care, or Article 12 of the International Covenant on Economic, Social and Cultural Rights). See also Toebes, 'The Right to Health as a Human Right', 243.

had his application for a residence permit rejected by the UK authorities on the ground that he was insured for all medical expenses except emergency treatment.[66] The Court, however, held that the absence of insurance covering emergency treatment could not as such impose an unreasonable burden on the public finances of the host state, and could therefore not serve as an excuse not to grant Mr Baumbast a residence permit.[67] Given that the British healthcare system operates on the basis that treatment is 'free at the point of use',[68] this finding entailed that Mr Baumbast could indeed demand that the UK shoulder the financial burden for his access to emergency treatment.[69] This was, in reality, already possible under UK healthcare legislation, and appears the norm in many Member States.[70] Even though the Court does not explicitly link the social function of emergency healthcare to the question of whether or not migrants can impose an unreasonable burden on the welfare state, *Baumbast* serves to strengthen the argument that even in Member States that operate on the basis of compulsory insurance, economically inactive migrant Union citizens have an enforceable right to be treated equally as nationals when they require emergency healthcare, simply on account of their medical need and status as a member of the host state's society.

This focus on medical need as a trigger for a state's obligation under communitarian solidarity also finds expression in the rights that patients can assert against their own Member State. As Article 35 CFR emphasizes, all Union citizens have a right to access 'preventive healthcare'. It appears that a minimum core of healthcare entitlements exists that each citizen can claim in whichever state he or she resides. Whenever the patient's state of affiliation cannot offer treatment to avert significant health risks for the patient, communitarian solidarity allows the patient to be treated abroad without losing the right to full reimbursement. Incapacity to provide adequate basic healthcare, in other words, is considered such an egregious violation of the communitarian duty that polities have vis-à-vis their resident citizens that EU law secures access to the healthcare appropriate to protect the patient's physical integrity. Note that the demand of healthcare here is based on the medical need of the patient—and not, as discussed in the previous chapter,

[66] Case C-413/99 *Baumbast* [2002] ECR I-7091 para 89.

[67] *Baumbast* para 93.

[68] See, for a useful summary of the nature of the NHS and its relation to EU law, Opinion of AG Geelhoed in Case C-372/04 *Watts* [2006] ECR I-4325.

[69] *Baumbast* paras 92–3.

[70] For an overview of the precise rights in each state: <http://ec.europa.eu/social/main.jsp?catId=858&langId=en>, accessed February 2015. See e.g. *Dano* para 26.

on the incapacity of a Member State to offer the range of treatments that it had promised its citizens.[71]

Two situations exist in which a state is unable to meet the basic healthcare needs of its citizens. First, an affiliated patient may urgently need treatment while temporarily abroad (a car accident on holiday, say). As the Court already held in *Cowan*, EU law guarantees its citizens 'protection from harm' while temporarily in another Member State.[72] Indeed, Article 19 of Regulation 883/2004 emphasizes that an insured person who falls ill when on the territory of another state 'shall be entitled to the benefits in kind which become necessary on medical grounds during [the] stay'.[73] The state providing the emergency treatment can then send the bill to the state of affiliation.[74] What exactly constitutes a medical necessity is not completely clear. Van der Mei has argued that it arises when, 'in the view of the doctor in the state of the visit, treatment cannot be postponed without endangering the life or health of the citizen concerned'.[75] This sounds very similar to Ruger's description of primary healthcare, meant to 'avoid premature death and escapable morbidity'.[76] Regulation 883/2004 adopts a slightly wider interpretation of medical necessity. The administrative commission on social security for migrant workers, whose task is to implement details of the cooperation between systems of social security, considers that:[77]

> The concept of 'necessary treatment' cannot be interpreted 'as meaning that [the benefit of that provision is] limited solely to cases where the treatment provided has become necessary due to sudden illness. In particular, the circumstance that the treatment necessitated by developments in the insured person's state of health during his temporary stay in another Member State may be linked to a pre-existent pathology of which he is aware, such as a chronic illness, does not mean that the conditions for the application of these provisions are not fulfilled.[78]
>
> In order to determine whether a benefit in kind meets the requirement [of necessity] only medical factors within the context of a temporary stay, taking into

[71] See section 3.4. [72] Case 186/87 *Cowan* [1989] ECR 159 para 17.

[73] Previously Article 22 (1)(a) of 1408/71. See *Baumbast* para 89 and Case C-512/08 *Commission* v *France* [2010] ECR I-8833 para 26.

[74] Article 19 of Regulation 883/2004.

[75] A. P. Van der Mei, *Free Movement of Persons* (Oxford: Hart, 2003) 252–3.

[76] See Ruger, *Health and Social Justice*, ch. 4.

[77] Case C-211/08 *Commission* v *Spain* [2010] ECR I-5267 para 9.

[78] Recital 7 of the preamble to Decision 194 of the Administrative Commission of the European Communities on Social Security for Migrant Workers (OJ 2004 L 104 127).

account the medical condition and past history of the person considered, shall be considered.[79]

When medical factors indicate a 'pressing need for intervention',[80] regardless of the patient's awareness that he or she could potentially require medical assistance while temporarily in another state,[81] the state of affiliation must refund the treatment undergone.

The second situation in which Member States are unable to meet the basic healthcare needs of their citizens is more contentious. In a number of rulings in the past 15 years, the Court has carved out a communitarian obligation on Member States to provide adequate healthcare within their territories. The normative justification for this obligation lies in the fundamental importance of health to the 'good life'. As AG Colomer put it, 'being a fundamental asset, health cannot be considered solely in terms of social expenditure and latent economic difficulties. (...) This right is perceived as a personal entitlement, unconnected to a person's relationship with social security'.[82] The Court and Union legislator have repeatedly emphasized the need for Member States to provide a system of 'safe, high-quality, efficient and quantitatively adequate healthcare',[83] on the basis of 'overarching values of universality, (...) equity and solidarity'.[84] Starting from its ruling in *Geraets-Smits and Peerbooms*, the Court has taken this to imply that whenever Member States cannot provide for such adequate healthcare within their territory, patients are allowed to seek, and be reimbursed for, treatment abroad. It carved out this right to extra-territorial healthcare in a subtle *a contrario* reasoning, stressing that Member States were only allowed to refuse reimbursement when 'the same or equally effective treatment can be obtained without undue delay at an establishment [in the state of affiliation]'.[85] In other

[79] Article 2 of exacting terms of Decision 194 of the Administrative Commission of the European Communities on Social Security for Migrant Workers (OJ 2004 L 104 127).

[80] Cf. C-206/94 *Paletta* [1996] ECR I-2357 para 20.

[81] *Commission* v *Spain*.

[82] Opinion of AG Colomer in Case C-444/05 *Stamatelaki* [2007] ECR I-3185 para 40, with reference to the Opinion of the European Economic and Social Committee on Healthcare (OJ 2003 C 234) 36.

[83] Recital 4 of Directive 2011/24. See also Article 35 of the Charter of Fundamental Rights, Article 12 of the International Covenant on Economic, Social and Cultural Rights, Article 11 of the European Social Charter.

[84] Recital 21 of Directive 2011/24. See also Council conclusions on common values and principles, 2006/C 146/01.

[85] Case C-157/99 *Geraets-Smits and Peerbooms* [2001] ECR I-5473 para 108. See Case C-173/09 *Elchinov* [2010] ECR I-8889 para 66 for the same *a contrario* reasoning.

words, when adequate treatment without undue delay cannot be guaranteed, Member States fail to meet their basic obligation towards their residents, and patients are to be reimbursed for the treatment obtained abroad.[86] It is clear that much of the practical relevance of communitarian solidarity in healthcare depends on how the terms 'effective treatment' and 'without undue delay' are interpreted. When does a Member State fail to provide adequate healthcare for its own citizens?

The Court has not explicitly discussed the concept of 'effective treatment'. The case in which it comes closest to defining the concept is *Elchinov*, which dealt with a Bulgarian national who suffered from a malignant oncological disease of the eye. The only treatment option offered by the Bulgarian healthcare fund with which he was affiliated was the removal of the eye.[87] Instead of opting for that procedure, Elchinov sough 'high-technology radiotherapy' in Germany (which cured the disease and allowed Elchinov to keep his eye) and he subsequently demanded that the costs be reimbursed by the Bulgarian healthcare fund.[88] Could Mr Elchinov base a claim to reimbursement on the fact that the treatment provided by Bulgaria was simply inadequate, or, more precisely, did not constitute 'effective treatment'? The Court argues that while in principle Elchinov cannot rely on EU law to obtain reimbursed treatment abroad when such treatment is not offered by his state of affiliation,[89] this may be different when 'the same or equally effective treatment'[90] is not available in that state. In making this assessment, the Court demands that account is taken only of the individual pathological condition of the patient, including the nature of the disease and the degree of pain.[91] In *Elchinov*, the Court found, without giving a real interpretation of the medical situation,

[86] Confusingly, the Court has couched such rights to adequate healthcare in both Regulation 1408/71 (now Regulation 883/2004) and Article 56 TFEU directly, while its language seems to suggest that it is in fact a citizenship right based on medical need alone, which could more convincingly be extrapolated from Article 21 TFEU and Article 35 CFR. Both approaches have been attacked in very dogmatic terms, but it is difficult to argue that such rights would not derive from the citizenship provisions anyway. See for critique, however, P. Cabral 'The Internal Market and the Right to Cross-Border Healthcare' (2004) 29 ELRev 677; Opinion of AG Colomer in *Geraets-Smits and Peerbooms*.

[87] Opinion of AG Villalón in *Elchinov* para 9.

[88] Arguably on the basis of market solidarity, as the Bulgarian insurer included 'high-technology radiotherapy for oncological and non-oncological treatment' in its basket but did not offer the treatment. See Opinion of AG Villalón in *Elchinov* para 9, and paras 59 and 62.

[89] See Case C-490/09 *Commission v Luxemburg* [2011] ECR I-247 para 32; Case C-385/99 *Müller-Fauré and Van Riet* [2003] ECR I-4509 para100; or *Elchinov* para 40.

[90] *Elchinov* para 65.

[91] *Elchinov* paras 66–7; Case C-268/13 *Petru* [nyr] para 30.

that given that the treatment options in Bulgaria were not as equally effective as those offered in Germany (an assessment made by the referring national court), Elchinov should be reimbursed for that treatment.[92] While the significance of *Elchinov* is difficult to gauge due to the conflation of different strands of case law, this individualized assessment, which looks at the healthcare needs of the citizen on the basis of his pathological condition alone, is consistent with the obligation under communitarian solidarity to provide for 'safe and high-quality' healthcare for all citizens. On this view, states have to reimburse treatment abroad that is vital for the patient's physical integrity but which cannot effectively be provided at home.

The Court recently further clarified its stance in these situations—even if it seems to conflate (as in much of its healthcare case law) the obligations under market solidarity and communitarian solidarity. The *Petru* case dealt with a Romanian national who suffered from a severe cardiovascular disease, and required open heart surgery. Prior to her operation she had stayed in a local Romanian hospital in Timişoara, and had noticed that the hospital lacked basic medical equipment such as painkillers, disinfectants, and sterile gauze, and that there was a significant shortage of hospital beds.[93] In the light of the risk of the operation and the absence of adequate medical resources in Timişoara, Ms Petru decided to undergo the operation in Germany, and reclaim the treatment costs from the Romanian healthcare provider on the basis that no adequate treatment was available at home. AG Villalón argues that—in case of structural and systemic indications that the healthcare system in a certain Member State cannot provide adequate treatment—patient mobility such as in the case of Ms Petru must only be refunded when this does not endanger the social security system underlying Romanian healthcare.[94] In other words, Villalón suggests that the obligation on Member States to ensure primary healthcare for its citizens is *conditional*, and that the absence of adequate healthcare is not per se a basic entitlement that Member States owe residents. This arguably misconstrues the obligations under communitarian solidarity. Such a view, first, glosses over the emergence of communitarian norms of solidarity in the EU—which consist of a core of basic entitlements that any citizen can avail him- or herself of—and, second, cannot possibly solve Villalón's concern (protecting Romania's immobile patients against loss

[92] *Elchinov* para 67. [93] Opinion of AG Villalón *Petru* para 6.
[94] Opinion of AG Villalón *Petru* para 38.

of medical resources). In fact, Villalón's insistence on a conditional obligation achieves the exact opposite: immobile Romanian patients remain faced with inadequate healthcare standards in their own country. The Court took a more nuanced view of the matter and imposed an unconditional obligation on Member States to provide for adequate healthcare for its nationals—at the risk of having to repay treatments abroad. It stresses that 'authorisation [to seek healthcare abroad] cannot be refused if the same or equally effective treatment cannot be given in good time in the Member State of residence of the person concerned',[95] which has to be assessed based on 'the patient's medical condition'[96] but also 'the lack of medication and of medical supplies and infrastructure'[97] in that Member State. In other words, the Court will protect the health of Union citizens against the inadequacy of the healthcare structures in their own Member State.

This leads us to the second variable in the Court's case law: the term 'undue delay'. The Court has discussed this most explicitly in *Watts*. In that case, Mrs Watts, a UK national, required a hip replacement. After the diagnosis had been made, however, she was to wait for over a year before such treatment could be offered within the UK, leaving her in 'constant pain' and unable to work.[98] Instead of waiting for a year, Watts opted to travel to France, where the treatment could be offered in a matter of weeks. Once back in the UK, she argued that she should be reimbursed by the NHS for the cost of treatment, given that treatment 'without undue delay' had not been available. The Court indicates that any assessment about whether the delay was medically acceptable or not must be made on the basis of the 'individual pathological condition of the patient'[99] alone, including the 'current state of health and the probable course of [the patient's] disease',[100] as well as of the 'degree of pain or the nature of the patient's disability' and 'his [or her] medical history'.[101] Where waiting times are too long or abnormal,[102] and thereby exacerbate medical need,[103] they 'restrict access to balanced, high-quality hospital

[95] *Petru* para 31. [96] *Petru* para 32. [97] *Petru* para 33.

[98] Opinion of AG Geelhoed in Case C-372/04 *Watts* [2006] ECR I-4325 paras 9 and 15, where the national court held that 12 months was 'clearly undue'.

[99] Opinion of AG Geelhoed in *Watts* para 87. See also *Müller-Fauré* para 92; *Elchinov* para 73; Case C-56/01 *Inizan* [2003] ECR I-12403 paras 42 and 44; *Watts* paras 56–7.

[100] *Elchinov* para 54.

[101] *Inizan* para 46; *Watts* para 62; *Elchinov* para 66; *Petru* para 32.

[102] In *Petru*, the Court explicitly referred to the GP's report suggesting that treatment needed to be carried out within three months. See *Petru* para 35.

[103] The referring national court in Watts had already established that the delay was 'undue'. See Opinion of AG Geelhoed in *Watts* para 15.

care',[104] and patients are allowed to 'queue jump' and demand that treatment abroad be funded by the state of affiliation. Medical necessity, in other words, trumps any financial or programmatic concern that underlies waiting lists.

In elaborating the exact conditions under which patients are allowed to seek treatment abroad to compensate for the failures of their own state's medical system, the Court is arguably (and intuitively) looking for instances that constitute an excessively egregious violation of the citizens' fundamental right to access safe and high-quality healthcare. Clearly, the fact that cosmetic surgery—as a rule—is not included in the list of refundable treatments, or that a waiting list might be in place for the removal of tonsils, cannot reasonably constitute a violation of a state's obligation to provide healthcare that is adequate to protect its citizens' physical integrity, whereas a waiting time of a year before a hip could be replaced, leaving the patient in 'constant pain', a refusal to treat malignant oncological disease of the eye (for which the only alternative domestic treatment is the removal of the eye!), or the absence of a basic medical infrastructure seems to constitute exactly that. Communitarian solidarity—that is, the commitments of justice that emerge by way of the social interaction between citizens and their communal elaboration of society—thus suggests that access to adequate primary healthcare automatically follows from the status of an individual as a member of society. Through its case law, then, the Court has made access to adequate healthcare a basic public social right that Union citizens derive by virtue of EU law,[105] and can be seen as some sort of institutionalized Hippocratic Oath.[106]

4.3.2 *The Right to Primary Education*

A second right that every EU citizen has simply on the basis of his or her social status as a participant in a particular national society is access to primary education. Again, the underlying rationale is that the provision of primary education is 'fundamental and foundational' for any individual's

[104] Opinion of AG Geelhoed in *Watts* para 84. See also *Watts* paras 63 and 70; *Müller-Fauré* para 92; and Van der Mei, *Free Movement of Persons*, 305.

[105] Contrast with the US approach, where the Supreme Court denied many patients a judicial remedy against the denial of healthcare by providers (*Aetna Health Inc* v *Davila*, 2004).

[106] The Hippocratic Oath reads like a cosmopolitan obligation on each polity. As defined in the Declaration of Geneva 1948: 'I solemnly pledge myself to consecrate my life to the service of humanity; (...) the health of my patient will be my first consideration; I will not permit considerations of religion, nationality, race, party politics or social standing to intervene between my duty and my patient (...)'.

capacity to have a good life, and constitutes a basic social commitment to ensure that fellow members of society can live a life of basic dignity and autonomy. Primary education is a vital procedural precondition for citizens to be 'free from need' (e.g. be able to read, write, and qualify for paid work) and 'free to aspire' (discover and pursue one's own preference as to what to do with the rest of one's life). As Terzi has argued, compulsory education 'is both fundamental and foundational to the capabilities necessary to well-being, and hence to lead a good life' and it therefore constitutes a 'fundamental entitlement',[107] which—in her opinion—extends to cover knowledge of, or ability in, literacy, numeracy, sociality and participation, learning dispositions, physical activities, science and technology, and practical reason.[108] Nussbaum more generally argues that compulsory education, as a prerequisite for the individual's freedom and social integration, should extend until 'the capability to make valued choices' is developed.[109] Primary education, in other words, helps develop the individual's identity and capacity for self-determination, enabling him or her to discover, and effectively pursue, his or her personal aspirations and ambitions. It enables individuals to be 'more free' by preparing them for the demands and possibilities of life and society, instils trust in processes of communication and cooperation, and fosters the transcendental appreciation of the nature and intensity of pain and happiness in other citizens. The general acceptance of education as pivotal in a person's capacity to live a 'good life' is reflected in the fact that the provision and consumption of education is compulsory until the pupil has reached a certain age, roughly about 16 in Europe.[110] The crucial nature of this minimum obligation on the state is underlined by its constitutional entrenchment in all Member States,[111] and its codification in international law as a human right: 'States Parties recognize the right of the child to education, and (...) shall, in particular make primary

[107] L. Terzi, 'The Capability to be Educated', in M. Walker and E. Unterhalter (eds.), *Amartya Sen's Capability Approach and Social Justice in Education* (Basingstoke: Palgrave, 2007) 24, 30–3.

[108] Ibid. 37–9.

[109] M. Nussbaum, 'Political Liberalism and Respect: A Response to Linda Barclay' (2003) 4 Nordic Journal of Philosophy 42.

[110] B. Peck, 'Compulsory Schooling in the Europe' (1995) 76 Phi Delta Kappan 616–22.

[111] See Article 14 of the Austrian Constitution, Article 24 of the Belgian Constitution, Article 53 of the Bulgarian Constitution, Article 66 of the Croatian Constitution, Articles 18 and 20 of the Cypriot Constitution, Articles 16 and 33 of the Czech Constitution, Article 76 of the Danish Constitution, Article 37 of the Estonian Constitution, Article 16 of the Finnish Constitution, Article 34 of the French Constitution (if only implicit), Articles 5 and 7 of the German Constitution, Article 16 of the Greek Constitution, Article 16 of the Hungarian Constitution, Article 42 of the Irish Constitution, Articles 33–4 of the Italian Constitution,

education compulsory and available free to all; encourage the development of different forms of secondary education, including general and vocational training'.[112] Likewise, the Charter of Fundamental Rights reads: 'Everyone has the right to education and to have access to vocational and continuing training. This right includes the possibility to receive free compulsory education.'[113] The vital nature of compulsory education for the very status of an individual as a 'free person' indicates that this obligation on the state includes *all* residents, whether nationals, Union citizens, third-country nationals, or even illegal immigrants.

The Court, in the cases of *Ibrahim* and *Teixeira*, has indeed accepted that access to primary and secondary education is a fundamental welfare entitlement that must therefore be extended to all resident EU citizens.[114] Both cases involved a child of migrant EU citizens, who had started primary education at the time when (one of) the parents were economically active in the host state, in this case the United Kingdom. After a number of years, such activity stopped. While the main questions in the cases dealt with the parent's right of residence as a corollary of the child's right to education,[115] the opinions by AG Kokott and AG Mazak, as well as the Court's ruling, discuss the basis upon which a Union citizen is entitled to access compulsory education in a host Member State once he or she is legally installed there.

In both cases, claims of equal access to primary education could not be premised on market solidarity. The economic activity of the parent, from which such right was derived in accordance with Article 12 of Regulation 1612/68, had, after all, stopped.[116] Both AG Mazak and AG Kokott—apparently convinced of the required outcome but unsure about a legal reasoning—appear in two (or even three) minds about the type of solidarity that the retention of the right to education notwithstanding the lack of economic activity would

Article 112 of the Latvian Constitution, Articles 40–1 of the Lithuanian Constitution, Article 23 of the Luxembourg Constitution, Articles 10–11 of the Maltese Constitution, Article 23 of the Dutch Constitution, Article 35 of the Polish Constitution, Articles 73–4 of the Portuguese Constitution, Article 32 of the Romanian Constitution, Article 42 of the Slovakian Constitution, Article 57 of the Slovenian Constitution, Article 27 of the Spanish Constitution, Articles 2 and 21 of the Swedish Constitution, and Article 2 of the British Human Rights Act.

[112] See e.g. Articles 13–14 of the International Covenant on Economic, Social and Cultural Rights, Articles 24 and 28 of the Convention on the Rights of the Child.

[113] See Article 14 CFR.

[114] Case C-480/08 *Teixeira* [2010] ECR I-1107; Case C-310/08 *Ibrahim* [2010] ECR I-1065.

[115] See C. O'Brien, 'Case Note on *Teixeira* and *Ibrahim*' (2011) 47 CML Rev. 203ff.

[116] Opinion of AG Kokott in *Teixeira* para 39; *Teixeira* para 49; Opinion of AG Mazak in *Ibrahim* para 34.

imply. AG Mazak's assessment seems stuck between the language of market solidarity and the logic of aspirational solidarity, focusing on the worker's aspirational right to movement:

> In my view, if the children of a Union citizen who is a former Community worker were effectively prevented from continuing their education in the host Member State on the basis that they had not attended school there for a some minimum duration, this may dissuade that citizen from exercising the rights to freedom of movement laid down in Article [45 TFEU] and would therefore create an obstacle to the effective exercise of that freedom.[117]

AG Kokott seems to follow Mazak's approach, albeit in clearer terms of market solidarity:

> A migrant worker would have far less incentive to exercise his right to freedom of movement if he could not be sure that his children could obtain an education in the host Member State and complete that education successfully.[118]

Yet, in the very same paragraph, Kokott moves towards an arguably much stronger and autonomous reason for extending the right to education beyond the period during which the parent of the child is economically active:

> If every interruption or cessation of the migrant worker's employment in the host Member State also resulted in the automatic loss of his children's right of residence and, accordingly, they were obliged to interrupt their education, there is a risk of disadvantage in relation to their educational and career development. The children might, in those circumstances, be compelled to continue their education abroad, which, in view of the differences between national education systems and the languages of instruction used, could lead to significant problems.[119]

The Court agrees with the outcome advocated by the two AGs, without explicitly discussing the moral basis for its demand of equal treatment. The rulings indicate that once a child has been 'installed' in the Member State (i.e. legally *entered* that state as a family member of a worker) and has started compulsory education in that Member State,[120] the right to equal access to such education behaves independently from the economic (in)activity of his parents: 'the right of children to equal treatment in access to education does not depend on the circumstance that their father or mother retains the status of migrant worker in the host Member State'.[121] In other words, and

[117] Opinion of AG Mazak in *Ibrahim* para 33.

[118] Opinion of AG Kokott in *Teixeira* para 44.

[119] Ibid.

[120] *Ibrahim* para 38; *Teixeira* para 45.

[121] *Ibrahim* paras 37, 39, and 45; and more explicitly *Teixeira* para 50.

as highlighted by the fact that the right to education for a child even comprises a right to residence for his primary carer,[122] the right to education is not premised on a degree of economic engagement with the host state, nor on a prior social link to that state's society, but instead constitutes an autonomous right attached to the status of a Union citizen who has legally entered another Member State.[123] Unlike in other aspects of welfare, the Court does not condition the equal treatment of Union citizens upon a criterion of social integration, which is a clear indication of its implicit acceptance that the mere status of legally resident Union citizen in a host Member State automatically implies equal access to core welfare entitlements such as compulsory education.

4.3.3 *The Right to Minimum Subsistence Benefits*

A third—and more contentious—entitlement that should be extended to all resident EU citizens is access to minimum subsistence benefits. Minimum subsistence benefits ensure that citizens have access to sufficient financial resources to obtain the bare minimum of commodities, such as shelter and food, required to live a dignified and autonomous life and, indeed, 'survive'. The delivery of such social goods, which are 'foundational and fundamental' for a citizen's capacity to live, is based on a basic moral demand that citizens, and by inference polities, must 'save' fellow humans in dire need. Any political system that is normatively premised on the alleviation of needs and the facilitation of aspirations of fellow citizens cannot but provide such guarantees of minimum dignity and autonomy to all citizens that make up society.[124] Even if organized within national spatial boundaries, then, the type of reciprocity that underlies it is very diffuse and not particularly parochial. It connects to the status of the applicant as a human being and his or her need rather than his or her status as a member of a certain political community. In consequence, it would seem that minimum subsistence entitlements must be extended to *all* legally resident Union citizens who fall below the level of resources set by the applicable national legislation. The European Convention on Social and Medical Assistance, to which 15 Member States are signatories,[125] already expresses this basic obligation:

> Each of the Contracting Parties undertakes to ensure that nationals of the other Contracting Parties who are lawfully present in any part of its territory to which

[122] *Ibrahim* paras 30–1; *Teixeira* paras 38–9.

[123] *Ibrahim* paras 48 and 56–8; *Teixeira* para 59.

[124] See section 1.1.

[125] Belgium, Demark, Estonia, France, Germany, Greece, Ireland, Italy, Luxembourg, Malta, Netherlands, Portugal, Spain, Sweden, and the United Kingdom are signatory states.

this Convention applies, and who are without sufficient resources, shall be entitled equally with its own nationals and on the same conditions to social and medical assistance.[126]

This approach seems to tie in with the Court's and legislator's decision in Article 70 (2) of Regulation 883/2004 to allocate the responsibility for the provision of special non-contributory social benefits which are meant to provide minimum subsistence income exclusively to the state of residence of the citizen.[127] That state is both under the obligation and in the position to assess the need of citizens and tailor access to social assistance mechanism to meet that need. Lawful residence, it would appear, is sufficient to establish a right to equal treatment in access to minimum subsistence benefits.[128]

In *Dano*, the Court had the chance to elaborate whether communitarian solidarity indeed demands that Member States take care of all lawfully resident EU citizens 'in need'.[129] The case dealt with a Romanian national, lawfully resident for three years in Germany, who claimed access to jobseeker's provision. According to the German legislation, such welfare entitlement was meant to ensure that applicants can live a life 'in keeping with human dignity', and covers costs such as housing and heating.[130] AG Wathelet argues that Germany does not have to extend such benefits to migrants such as Ms Dano, who 'did not enter Germany in order to seek employment and she is not trying to find a job there'[131] and who 'has not finished her high-school degree, cannot read German and has never worked in either Romania or Germany'.[132] The logic here (to the extent that one can be traced) seems to be that one of the preconditions for access to subsistence provision is either the willingness or the capacity to engage in the job market:

By refusing basic provisions benefits to persons who come to Germany solely in order to benefit from the social assistance system of that Member State and who do not seek in any way to integrate themselves into the labour market, the national legislation is consistent, in my view, with the EU legislature's intention. It serves to prevent persons exercising their right to free movement without intending to

[126] Article 1 of the European Convention of Social and Medical Assistance.

[127] See also Case C-299/05 *Commission* v *Parliament and Council* [2007] ECR I-8695.

[128] Case C-456/02 *Trojani* [2004] ECR I-7573 para 40ff.

[129] Case C-333/13 *Dano* [nyr].

[130] Opinion of AG Wathelet in *Dano* para 69.

[131] Opinion of AG Wathelet in *Dano* para 92.

[132] Opinion of AG Wathelet in *Dano* para 34.

integrate themselves from becoming a burden on the social assistance system (...) In other words, it serves to prevent abuse and a certain form of 'benefit tourism'.[133]

Wathelet seems to confuse the case law of the Court on this point, suggesting that the need to integrate in the labour market is required before welfare entitlements need to be extended to economically inactive migrants. While that seems a correct interpretation of the demands of communitarian solidarity for benefits that seek to empower citizens to access the labour market, and that might be contingent on a number of applications per month, or on the obligation to accept suitable employment, it is *not* the case for entitlements which (despite being formally classified as jobseeker allowances) have the explicit objective of ensuring that citizens can live 'decent' lives with at least a minimum of dignity and autonomy. Access to such rights depends on a certain degree of social integration—demonstrated by a daily, quotidian, engagement with the host state polity—and not economic integration.

The Court took a slightly more nuanced view. It appreciated that despite the formal qualification of the benefit as 'jobseeker provision', its function was to ensure a basic safety net to prevent abject destitution of citizens. It then assessed the question head on: can economically inactive migrants claim minimum subsistence allowance in the host state? The Court's answer is slightly circular, and creates tensions with several aspects of its previous case law.[134] The Court argues that economically inactive EU citizens derive a right to equal treatment only as long as they meet the conditions for residence in the host state, which include, according to Article 7 (1) of Directive 2004/38, the need to have 'sufficient resources for themselves and family members' not to become a burden on the welfare system of the host state.[135] Dano's request to receive minimum subsistence allowance, the Court seems to reason, demonstrates that she no longer meets this requirement of sufficient resources, and can therefore not have a right to residence in Germany, let alone a right to equal treatment to welfare benefits.[136] The fact that Dano and her son were 'materially supported' by her sister for three years, and

[133] Opinion of AG Wathelet in *Dano* para 131.

[134] On the question whether or not resources need to be 'personal' (Case C-408/03 *Commission* v *Belgium* [2006] ECR I-2647); on the direct effect of Article 21 TFEU and the requirement of proportionality (*Baumbast* para 93); and on the case law that suggests that economically inactive migrants can derive welfare entitlements once 'installed' in a Member State, that is, once they legally entered the Member State (*Ibrahim* paras 48 and 56–8; *Teixeira* para 59).

[135] *Dano* para 69.

[136] *Dano* para 71

thus clearly—factually—*did* possess sufficient resources not to have become a burden on the German welfare state, was not taken into account.[137] This degree of logical confusion in the Court's ruling and glaring inconsistencies with previous case law seem to be premised on the Court's desire to reassure (certain) Member States that they indeed can prevent 'welfare tourism', whereby citizens supposedly move to a particular Member State exclusively to make use of its welfare resources.[138] The Court could hardly have been more explicit in its engagement with this political question when it argued that '[a] Member State must therefore have the possibility (...) of refusing to grant social benefits to economically inactive Union citizens who exercise their right to freedom of movement *solely* in order to obtain another Member State's social assistance although they do not have sufficient resources to claim a right of residence.'[139] This ruling, of course, raises as many questions as it answers, in particular relating to the question of whether the 'sufficient' resources need be personal; how the possible loss of resources after a few years of residence impacts on the migrant's right to equal treatment (given the evident social commitments built up during those years); what happened to the 'degree of financial solidarity with nationals of other Member States' that the Court discovered in *Grzelczyk*; and whether the migrant's objective and subjective intention in moving to the host state is determinative in assessing his or her subsequent right to equal treatment. [140]

Before *Dano*, it was clear that migrants who are in need of social assistance upon entry into the host state could be denied a right to residence (and equal treatment) under Article 8 (4) of Directive 2004/38. Citizens must already possess what is considered a minimum of resources to live a dignified and autonomous life in the host state before they can establish lawful residence. At the same time, the Court held that Member States may only take account of the level of resources at the time of entry into the Member State,[141] must include resources from family members or sponsors in the host state,[142] and subsequent loss of sufficient resources may not automatically lead to the expulsion of migrants from the host state.[143] Indeed, in the

[137] *Dano* paras 37 and 75. See, for a discussion of the illogical uses of the notion of 'unreasonable burden', A. Somek, 'Solidarity Decomposed: Being and Time in European Citizenship' (2007) 32 ELRev 795.

[138] Opinion of AG Wathelet in *Dano* para 117.

[139] *Dano* para 78, my emphasis.

[140] See, for an insightful study on the last point, A. Sayde, *Abuse of EU Law and Regulation of the Internal Market* (Oxford: Hart, 2014).

[141] *Grzelczyk*.

[142] See e.g. Case C-408/03 *Commission* v *Belgium* [2006] ECR I-2647.

[143] *Trojani*.

recent *Brey* case, the Court highlighted that the loss of sufficient resources after those initial three months might in fact give rise to access to social assistance benefits (widely construed), depending on the personal circumstances of the individual applicant,[144] even if it also highlighted that this right should be balanced against the need to protect the general stability and availability of welfare resources. The rulings in *Brey* and *Dano* stand in contrast with cases such as *Teixeira* and *Ibrahim*, where economically inactive EU citizens could, once legally installed (i.e. once they legally entered the Member State), derive a right to equal treatment in respect of those welfare entitlements that allow them to live a life with minimum levels of human dignity. The theory of communitarian solidarity would suggest that access to elementary subsistence benefits, such as at stake in *Dano*—which are premised on, and sustained by, a basic moral duty between citizens that stand in a social relationship to each other—must be extended to all legally resident citizens, regardless of economic status, nationality, or engagement with the labour market in the host state, in the same way as access to primary healthcare and primary education. It remains to be seen if the Court will interpret the exception to communitarian solidarity in *Dano* restrictively, allowing Member States to prevent only the most obvious cases of 'welfare tourism', or widely, as a general limitation upon the right to equal treatment for economically inactive EU citizens.

4.4 Student Benefits: A Reward or an Investment?

Completely at the other end of the spectrum of welfare entitlements we can find student benefits. Rather than reflecting a need to ensure that citizens live their lives with a minimum degree of dignity and autonomy, such benefits reflect much thicker social commitments towards social mobility between citizens, which are linked to complex commitments that simultaneously reflect past, prospective, social, and economic commitments. Before starting classes and lectures on free movement and citizenship I always ask my students to make an intuitive assessment of the allocation of the obligation to offer student benefits in this scenario: Ms X is a British national who has lived her whole life in Belgium, while her parents have

[144] See also Case C-140/12 *Brey* EU:C:2013:565 paras 65–77.

worked their whole lives in Luxembourg. X, once she completes her secondary education in Belgium, is applying to study at a British university. From which state—Belgium, Luxembourg, or the UK—should Ms X receive student benefits? Essentially, this is a question of communitarian solidarity: which exact type of commitment underlies access to student benefits? Remarkably, students—when given this hypothetical scenario—divide almost perfectly into three equally large groups. Intuitively, it seems each of the three Member States has *a* link to Ms X that *could* warrant access to student benefits. In fact, it seems that the three welfarist traditions that we find in Europe would also suggest a different answer.[145] Given that access to tertiary education is often tied up with temporary voluntary or compulsory withdrawal from the labour market, Member States will usually intervene to a greater or lesser extent to cover the temporary economic dependence of students in order to encourage wide and democratic access to such a system of tertiary education. This can take the form of financial grants or loans meant to cover tuition or registration fees, ensuring equal access, or grants to cover maintenance costs such as accommodation, books, transport, and living expenses. Idiosyncrasies in the institutional welfare make-up of Member States, however, entails that the precise scope, nature, duration, and level of such support mechanism differ widely between the different Member States.[146]

The social-democratic or *universalist* welfare traditions tend to see the (typically) 18-year-old student as an independent young adult who should receive financial assistance in order to facilitate his or her social mobility and pursuit of a chosen interest and profession.[147] In such a scenario, the most important factor is the *social* link that the student has with a certain polity. In our example, then, it would be Belgium that is obliged to offer student benefits to Ms X. The corporatist or conservative tradition, on the other hand, approaches the 18-year-old student as a dependent actor, whose access to student benefits follow from the past economic engagement of his parents within a certain

[145] Many thanks to Hendrik Skovgaard-Petersen for pointing this out to me.

[146] To see how the different Member States fit into this triptych, see N. Willemse and P. De Boer, 'Three Worlds of Educational Welfare State? A Comparative Study of Higher Education Across Welfare States' (2012) 22 Journal of European Social Policy 115; and O. Golynker, 'Student Loans: The European Concept of Social Justice According to *Bidar*' (2006) 31 ELRev 394.

[147] See G. Esping-Andersen, *The Three Worlds of Welfare* (Princeton: Princeton University Press, 1990) 169; H. Pechar and L. Andres, 'Higher-Education Policies and Welfare Regimes: International Comparative Perspectives' (2011) 24 Higher Education Policy 25.

society.[148] In our example, then, it would be Luxembourg that is asked to offer Ms X student benefits. Finally, in the liberal tradition, the 18-year-old is seen as an investor—as a rational market actor who chooses to pursue higher education in order to ensure a higher return on that investment in terms of future earnings. Student benefits, in turn, are dependent on a future economic contribution of the student to society.[149] This might be in the form of a student loan rather than a student grant, or as 'homecoming requirements', under which student loans are converted into grants only if the student, upon completion of the degree, is employed on the territory of a certain state for a number of years. In our example, that would entail that Ms X can demand student benefits from the UK.

All this leaves the Court in a difficult position—having to navigate its way between three different welfarist traditions, with three complete different ways of thinking about the role of the student. It also means that, in making an assessment under communitarian solidarity, it has to take account of a number of possible ties between the student and the different Member States: prior and prospective economic links, social and cultural links, the individual link between the student and the host state polity, and the derivative link between the student and his or her parents' state of employment. To make the job of the Court—assessing which specific link justifies access to student benefits—even more difficult, it has had to contend with an asymmetrical docket. The first wave of cases concerning student benefits challenged restrictions to student benefits in the students' host state (in our example, the UK). As such, cases such as *Bidar* and *Förster* focused on the question of when exactly a migrant student can demand that the state in which he or she studies offers him or her student benefits. The second wave of cases discussed the obligations on the students' home state (in our example, Belgium). To what extent does the link between a student and the state in which he or she grew up warrant access to student benefits despite the student being enrolled in university abroad? To be precise, it will be argued that such questions fall within the domain of aspirational solidarity, to be discussed in the next chapter.[150] Cases such as *Morgan and Bucher* and *Prinz and Seeberger* will nevertheless be discussed here, as they offer great insights into the exact link that is required between a prospective student and a Member State before

[148] See Esping-Andersen, *The Three Worlds of Welfare*, 168, Willemse and De Boer 'Three Worlds of Educational Welfare State?', 105.

[149] Esping-Andersen, *The Three Worlds of Welfare*, 167; Pechar and Andres, 'Higher-Education Policies and Welfare Regimes', 31.

[150] See section 5.3.

the former can claim student benefits. Finally, and most recently, the third wave in the case law of the Court has focused on claims towards the *state of employment* of the students' parents (in our scenario, Luxembourg). Cases such as *Commission* v *Netherlands* and *Giersch* discuss to what extent students can derive a right to student benefits from the state of employment of their parents, without there being any further link between the student and that Member State. The problem with this case-by-case analysis is that the Court has not approached the question of the allocation of the responsibility to offer student benefits as a question of communitarian solidarity. It has not engaged in an explicit analysis of which exact link is required before students can claim student benefits. Instead it has taken a case-by-case approach, first (as will be discussed below) invalidating rules in host states that do not take account of the social ties that the students builds up while studying; then invalidating rules in home states that do not take account of that link that the student has built up before studying; and finally invalidating rules in the state of the parent's employment, for not taking account of the economic and derivative link that students have with it. This makes the case law of the Court on access to student benefits conceptually and analytically difficult to grasp—if perhaps not the Court's fault. It is argued, however, that the Court should start thinking about this problem more holistically and in the light of communitarian solidarity, and define which *specific* tie between the student and a Member State warrants access to student benefits, rather than invalidating domestic legislation as it comes before it. The latter approach risks leading to situations whereby *any* tie between a polity and a student suffices for access to student benefits, making it impossible for the Member States to devise legislation that takes simultaneous account of all possible ties: employment history, family ties, cultural ties, residence, place of education, language skills.[151]

The first wave of cases discussed by the Court concern limitations for students seeking access to student benefits in their host state, that is, the state in which they pursue higher education but where they have not lived before. It seems that such students—in the absence of any further tie than their status as Union citizens—have limited claims to student benefits in the host state. Dougan summarizes thus:

> the shared identity which derives from common Union citizenship might well permit [migrant students] to make certain demands of financial solidarity

[151] See Opinion of AG Sharpston in Case C-359/13 *Martens* [nyr] para 103.

upon the host society, but it cannot necessarily entitle them to claim full membership of the political community, and thus establish a legitimate expectation of equal treatment with domestic students across the entire educational sphere.[152]

The Court discussed the matter in *Bidar*. Dany Bidar, a French national, moved to the United Kingdom in 1998 to live with his grandmother. He finished the final three years of his secondary education in the United Kingdom without having recourse to social assistance. In 2001 he enrolled in a course on economics at University College London. He applied for financial assistance to cover his tuition fees and for financial assistance to cover his maintenance costs. While the former was granted, the latter was denied in accordance with the Student Support Regulations 2001, which required a student to be 'settled' in the United Kingdom before he became eligible for such maintenance support. It was common ground, however, that nationals of other Member States could never, in their capacity as students, obtain the status of being 'settled' in the United Kingdom.[153] While this difference in treatment was, according to the Court, in principle incompatible with Bidar's status as an EU citizen,[154] it could be justified with reference to the need to extend benefits only to students who can reproduce the reciprocal commitments that underlie student grants. This precise requirement was the real issue in *Bidar*. The Court held that:

> In the case of assistance covering the maintenance costs of students, it is legitimate for a Member State to grant such assistance only to students who have demonstrated a certain degree of integration into the society of that State. (...) The existence of a certain degree of integration may be regarded as established by a finding that the student in question has resided in the host Member State for a certain length of time.[155]

In other words, the Court argued that the commitments that underlie access to student grants, which seem to be based in part on the financial efforts of the (parents of the) student, in part on the individual's social ties, and in part on the projected future contributions by the student to the state's society, can

[152] M. Dougan, 'Fees, Grants, Loans, and Dole Cheques: Who Covers the Costs ofMigrant Education within the EU?' (2005) 42 CML Rev 954.

[153] Case C-209/03 *Bidar* [2005] ECR I-2119 para 18.

[154] Ibid. para 31.

[155] Ibid. paras 57 and 59.

be distilled into a condition of social integration, which is demonstrated by previous residence. In consequence:

The additional condition [of being settled] prevents a student who is a national of a Member State and who is lawfully resident and has received a substantial part of his secondary education in the host Member State, and has consequently established a genuine link with the society of the latter State, from being able to pursue his studies under the same conditions as a student who is a national of that State and is in the same situation.[156]

Bidar, in other words, seems to tell us that full membership rights in the educational sphere are thus acquired when the student can prove a strong enough attachment to the host state, that is, when he is socially integrated in that state.[157] In *Bidar* the Court, without further elaboration, held that a requirement of three years of residence was acceptable as a test for such degree of integration.[158] The question of the factors to be taken into account when establishing the 'degree of integration' was again explicitly discussed in *Förster*. The Dutch *Hoge Raad*, clearly uncertain about the legality of a blanket five-year residence requirement, which excluded individual circumstances that could demonstrate the social integration of the citizen in the host state from being taken into account, specifically asked the Court 'which residence duration may be required' and whether individual factors that 'indicate a substantial degree of integration into the society of the host Member State' are to be taken into account.[159] AG Mazák's reasoning is very clear and convincing:

Member States are obviously allowed to some extent to apply general conditions which require no further individual assessment, such as the three years' residence requirement at issue in *Bidar*. However, the case-law of the Court also suggests that the condition imposed may not be so general in scope that it systematically excludes students, regardless of their actual degree of integration into society, from being able to pursue their studies under the same conditions as nationals of the host Member State. In other words, the criterion used must still be indicative of the degree of integration into society. (...) In my view, that is not the case with a five-year residence requirement, since it can reasonably be assumed that a number of students may have established a

[156] Ibid. para 62.

[157] Including all aspects of educational policy, such as the right to export student grants, or to be considered a 'national' in quota systems.

[158] *Bidar* para 60.

[159] Case C-158/07 *Förster* [2008] ECR I-8507, questions 3 (d) and 4 respectively.

substantial degree of integration into society well before the expiry of that period.[160]

Mazak is spot on—both in his emphasis on the procedural commitment to connect eligibility for student grants to the links of reciprocity that sustain them, and in his factual assessment that a residence requirement of five years seems to go beyond that. The Court was not convinced, however, and 'reasoned' that 'a condition of five years' continuous residence cannot be held to be excessive having regard, inter alia, to the requirements put forward with respect to the degree of integration of non-nationals in the host Member State'.[161] While this circular reasoning can hardly count as judicial reasoning, the Court seems to suggest that the decisive criterion for the allocation of the obligation to fund a mobile student lies with the Member State where the student has resided for a number of years prior to his access to university. Only after having resided for five years in a host state, after all, does the student become socially integrated 'enough' to claim such benefits against the host state.

This line of reasoning was largely followed by the Court in the second wave of cases—where students challenged the decision of their home state (typically, the state in which they grew up) not to offer student benefits to students who study abroad. As mentioned above, these cases really speak to the norms of aspirational solidarity which will be discussed in the following chapter,[162] but are discussed here as they offer interesting insights into the matter of the specific link that a student must demonstrate before being able to access student benefits. In *Morgan and Bucher*,[163] a German provision that entitled all German nationals to student maintenance support on condition that they enrol in educational establishments within Germany was challenged. Export of study grants was allowed only in very limited circumstances.[164] The case concerned two German nationals whose entitlement to student grants was revoked by virtue of their choice to register

[160] Opinion of AG Mazak in *Förster* paras 129 and 130.

[161] *Förster* para 54.

[162] See section 5.3.

[163] Joined Cases C-11/06 and 12/06 *Morgan and Bucher* [2007] ECR I-9161.

[164] See Article 5 (1) and (2) of the *BAfoG*, which allows export when the individual remains at his or her permanent residence in Germany and daily travels from there to the educational establishment abroad; or, in case the individual migrates to the host state when attendance at the new programme is beneficial for the student's degree, is with a recognized institution, and the programme attended abroad constitutes the continuation of the student's prior enrolment of at least one year with a German tertiary education establishment.

with foreign tertiary education establishments instead of with universities in Germany.[165] Coincidentally, in both cases, both Rhiannon Morgan and Iris Bucher enrolled for degrees (applied genetics and ergotherapy, respectively) that were not provided by German educational establishments.

Germany argued that it was allowed to limit student benefits to those who studied within Germany. Germany in fact relied on the ruling in *Bidar* to argue that it had to extend student benefits only to those students who could demonstrate a degree of social integration in the state. Students who chose to move abroad, as such, were no longer sufficiently socially integrated.[166] The reliance on *Bidar*, however, appears contradictory. In that case, after all, the Court emphasizes that the social nature of financial assistance is closely tied up with membership of a polity and complex retrospective dynamics of participation, rather than with current residence in the territory of that polity. While one could indeed imagine examples whereby a national loses social integration by virtue of having left the territory of his or her home state decades ago,[167] in the case of Rhiannon Morgan and Iris Bucher the welfare entitlements were denied solely on the basis of their choice to move abroad. Had they stayed within Germany there is no doubt that they would have been entitled to the financial benefits. It is unsurprising, then, that the Court rejected Germany's arguments, and accepted that the prior social link between the applicant and the Member State is decisive in allocating the responsibility to fund welfare benefits.

Years later, Laurence Prinz and Philipp Seeberger challenged the same rule, which had in the meantime been amended to allow the export of student benefits for those students who had resided in Germany in the three years prior to commencing the university degree.[168] Laurence Prinz, a German national, had resided for ten years with her family in Tunisia, where her father was employed for a German company. She returned to Germany for the last two and a half years of her secondary education, and then applied for a course in Business Management in Rotterdam. Philipp Seeberger, on

[165] One of the students decided to study applied genetics in Bristol (UK) and another ergotherapy in Heerlen (NL).

[166] *Morgan and Bucher* para 42.

[167] Although not necessarily. It does not seem discriminatory for Member States to assert that all their nationals are entitled to certain entitlements notwithstanding lack of integration. See K. Lenaerts and T. Heremans, 'Contours of a European Social Union in the Case-Law of the European Court of Justice' (2006) 2 European Constitutional Law Review 107; and Opinion of AG Mazak in *Förster* para 67.

[168] Joined Cases C-523/11 and 585/11 *Prinz and Seeberger* EU:C:2013:524 para 5.

the other hand, is a German national who grew up in Germany until the age of 12, then moved to Mallorca until the age of 22. He lived in Munich between October 2006 and September 2009, when he applied for a course in Economics at the university in Palma de Mallorca.[169] Both Prinz and Seeberger were denied access to student benefits for not meeting the requirement of having lived in Germany for three years. Both students, at the same time, argued that such a requirement violated EU law as it did not fully reflect their social integration into German society, and as such misconstrued their entitlements to student benefits.

While the Court accepts that Germany is entitled to limit the payment of student benefits to those students who can demonstrate a sufficient degree of integration into German society, it argues that the criterion used to gauge this degree of integration must 'not be too exclusive in nature or unduly favour one element which is not necessarily representative of the real and effective degree of connection between the claimant and this Member State, to the *exclusion of all other representative elements*'.[170] The Court then moves on to invalidate the German rule, arguing that while a period of residence of three years *may* be indicative of social integration, students can also be socially integrated without meeting this criterion, for example by virtue of their nationality, family ties, language skills, or other social factors.[171] In other words, what the Court essentially argues is that the type of reciprocity that underlies student benefits is more abstract than residence alone—it is based on more intangible socio-cultural ties between the individual and the polity, not solely, or necessarily, on residence. Young adults, in other words, derive a right to pursue their chosen career and receive help in their upward social mobility by virtue of their being part of a certain polity in social terms.

This conclusion was revised, or at least nuanced, in the recent *Commission v Netherlands* and *Giersch* cases. Both cases dealt with the question of whether students could claim benefits from the state of employment of their parents. In other words, they asked whether an economic and derivative link might suffice to claim access to welfare, even in the absence of a

[169] Ibid. paras 6–15. In Seeberger's case, some of the confusion arose from his alleged residence in Munich before his official registration, which would bring him over the '3-years hurdle'. This is immaterial for our assessment, however.

[170] Ibid. para 37. My emphasis. See also Case C-220/12 *Thiele Meneses* EU:C:2013:683 para 38.

[171] *Prinz and Seeberger* para 38. See also Opinion of AG Sharpston in *Prinz and Seeberger* para 95.

personal social link between the applicant student and the Member State. In *Commission* v *Netherlands*, a Dutch rule was challenged that offered student benefits to students studying abroad when they had lived at least three out of the six previous years in the Netherlands. This rule, according to the Netherlands, was meant to limit benefits to those who are likely, in the future, to enrich Dutch society by returning to work in the Netherlands upon completion of their degree. In other words, the Netherlands argued that the links of reciprocity required for access to student benefits were not based on prior social links, but on prospective *economic* links between the student and a certain polity. The criterion of 'three-out-of-six', in this sense, was meant to distil which students were likely to return to the Netherlands upon completion of their degree. In other words, the argument made by the Netherlands suggested that there was a strong link between the place where the student resides before studying, and the place where he will eventually work.[172] The Commission challenged this rule only in respect of the children of economically active migrants—arguing that such a criterion violates EU law for not taking account of the economic ties that link the student with the Dutch state.

Giersch involved a similar situation, in which a Luxembourg provision was challenged that made access to student benefits for studying abroad available solely for nationals and residents. Elodie Giersch and her fellow applicants were all nationals and residents of either Belgium or Germany. The link with Luxembourg that they all shared, however, was economic and derivative: their parents had worked in Luxembourg for between 23 and 32 years.[173] In other words, just as in *Commission* v *Netherlands*, the question was whether this derivative economic link alone would justify access to student benefits. In reality, Luxembourg argued, the criteria of nationality or residence are used to identify those students who are likely to settle in Luxembourg and participate in the Luxembourg economy and employment market *after* their degree. In other words, both the Dutch and Luxembourg claims are based on the assumption that the real link that warrants access to student benefits is not a past social link, as the previous cases discussed indicate, but a future

[172] Case C-542/09 *Commission* v *Netherlands* EU:C:2012:364. See also F. De Witte, 'Who Funds the Mobile Student? Shedding Some Light on the Normative Assumptions Underlying EU Free Movement Law' (2013) 50 CML Rev 203.

[173] Case C-20/12 *Giersch* EU:C:2013:411. See also S. O'Leary, 'The Curious Case of Frontier Workers and Study Finance: Giersch' (2014) 51 CML Rev 601.

economic link, which can be approximated by looking at the place in which the student resided *before* studying.

These two cases raise two questions. First is whether this requirement of a future economic link is indeed constitutive of the reciprocity that underlies access to student benefits. The Court, in both cases, like AG Mengozzi and AG Sharpston, seem to accept this. As such, access can be limited to students who are 'likely to use their experience abroad to enrich Netherlands society and (possibly) the Netherlands employment market'.[174] In other words, student benefits are not a reward for past social commitments to a polity, but an investment in the economy of that state. The second question is whether past economic commitment by the parents of the student are an indication that the students are likely to return to that Member State to work—or, conversely, whether only past residence or nationality can indicate such likelihood.[175] The Court, in both cases, in principle accepts the argument that the place of residence prior to the degree is likely to be the place in which the student will, after completion of the degree, access the employment market: 'students who are resident in Luxembourg when they are about to embark on their higher education studies may be more likely than non-residents to settle in Luxembourg and become integrated in the Luxembourg labour market after completing their studies, even if those studies were undertaken abroad'.[176] AG Mengozzi, while accepting this assumption, feels that Luxembourg should offer empirical evidence of this link before it is allowed to exclude non-resident children of frontier workers from student benefits,[177] while AG Sharpston is highly sceptical, suggesting that 'of course, [the student] may return to his previous Member State, but he may equally well remain where he studied or move on elsewhere'.[178] Simply put, she convincingly argues that 'it is not self-evident that past residence is a good way of predicting where students will reside and work in the future'.[179] In fact, the Court had come to that conclusion itself in *Prete*, where it argued that 'the knowledge acquired by a student in the course of his higher education does

[174] Opinion of AG Sharpston in *Commission* v *Netherlands* para 135; *Commission* v *Netherlands* para 77; Case *Giersch* paras 64–8; Opinion of AG Mengozzi in *Giersch* para 55.

[175] In addition, of course, it raised the question to what extent market solidarity can extend to cover the non-resident family members of the worker. See also section 3.2.

[176] *Giersch* para 67; *Commission* v *Netherlands* para 76.

[177] Opinion of AG Mengozzi in *Giersch* paras 58, 63–4. See also O'Leary, 'The Curious Case of Frontier Workers', 601, 611–12.

[178] Opinion of AG Sharpston in *Prinz and Seeberger* para 117.

[179] Opinion of AG Sharpston in *Commission* v *Netherlands* para 147.

not in general assign him to a particular geographic market'.[180] Despite this confusion, however, the Court does not accept the Dutch and Luxembourg provisions. Even though the Court in principle accepts that residence prior to starting a university degree is a good proxy for employment after the degree, it strikes down both the Dutch and Luxembourg provisions because they do not take into account that other factors, such as the durable economic participation of the parents of the student, or their proximity to the Member State that grants student benefits, may also be indicative of the place in which the student will eventually work.[181]

What these two cases seem to tell us is that the type of reciprocity that underlies access to student benefits is in fact not (only) a prior social one, as suggested by *Bidar*, *Förster*, *Morgan and Bucher*, and *Prinz and Seeberger*, but also a prospective economic one—whereby Member States must be able to extract a return upon their investment in the young student. This reading of the Court's recent case law is strengthened by the suggestion, made by the Court itself, that Member States might be allowed to condition access to student grants on a 'homecoming criterion', whereby students are obliged to work in the issuing Member State for a number of years after the completion of their degree.[182] This suggestion is, frankly speaking, bizarre, and Luxembourg has even declined to impose such a criterion since it thought that it would hamper the free movement of workers too much.[183] It also implies an understanding of the purpose of student benefits that is highly instrumental: they serve to enrich the Member State's own society and economy,[184] not the EU's society and economy, let alone the student's awareness, aspirations, or preferences. This seems very fundamentally at odds with most of its previous case law in the area of student grants and the case law on access to social entitlements,[185] as well as the way in which most Member States understand the role of student benefits: as an entitlement that allows young adults who are part of the socio-cultural fabric of their society to explore their potential, intellectual and vocational preferences.[186]

[180] *Prete* para 45.

[181] *Commission* v *Netherlands* para 86; *Giersch* paras 77–80.

[182] *Giersch* para 79.

[183] O'Leary, 'The Curious Case of Frontier Workers', 618. See also Opinion of AG Sharpston *Commission* v *Netherlands* para 139, who convincingly suggests that such a requirement would be unlawful.

[184] See, very explicitly, *Commission* v *Netherlands* para 77.

[185] See De Witte, 'Who Funds the Mobile Student?', 203.

[186] Willemse and De Boer, 'Three Worlds of Educational Welfare State?', 115.

The Court may have another opportunity soon to rethink its argumentation,[187] and it is argued that it should—not only by answering the particular factual situation that it is faced with, or even the policy objectives of the particular Member State, but by thinking more fundamentally about which specific link is required between a state and an individual student before the latter can demand access to student grants. That is, after all, the big promise of communitarian solidarity: forcing Member States to rethink who falls within their community of care on the basis of their social commitments within the state, *not* nudging Member States to adapt to a highly instrumental and liberal view of the role of the student, nor demanding that Member States prove a negative, in so far that legislation may only exclude those citizens who do not have *any* possible link with the territory of the state.[188] It appears that, in fact, a rule such as the one that will be discussed by the Court in the *Martens* case, whereby a Member State allows the export of student benefits for citizens who have resided on its territory for at least three out of the past six years, to the exclusion of other possible links, would be suitable,[189] in particular if the Court, after three years, shifts the obligation to the host state of the individual student. If, after all, the main demand of reciprocity is one of social integration into the fabric of society, it may be expected that the current threshold of five years before migrants can access benefits in the host state is too high.[190]

4.5 Conclusion

This chapter has discussed the emergence of communitarian solidarity. Communitarian solidarity articulates the commitments of justice that

[187] Case C-359/13 *Martens* [nyr].

[188] See e.g. Case C-220/12 *Thiele Meneses* EU:C:2013:683 para 50, where the Court comes very close to doing exactly that.

[189] This is not the view of AG Sharpston, who claims that the free movement of the *former* worker, the parent of a student, may suffice as a link in order to claim exportable student benefits. See AG Sharpston in *Martens* para 103.

[190] In *Martens*, moreover, which essentially challenges the same Dutch provision as discussed in *Commission* v *Netherlands*, but then from the perspective of economically inactive citizens, the Court will not have to contend with the added complexity of students having derivative rights by virtue of their economically active parents. Before the emergence of Union citizenship, after all, it was that status that was the premise for granting children of migrant workers access to student benefits in the state of employment of the parents. Perhaps the hangover of this practice explains the confused rulings of the Court in *Giersch* and *Commission* v *Netherlands*, which clearly broke with the *ethos* of earlier case law.

follow from the social relationships between European citizens. It was argued that its supranational development is inherently constrained in the light of the absence of a sufficiently thick political sphere in the EU that can elaborate its normative substance.[191] Instead, communitarian solidarity has developed as a *procedural* mechanism, through which Member States are forced to think about the social relationship between citizens in their society and which exact redistributive commitments follow from such relationships. This entails—as the Court has picked up—that the obligations on Member States differ depending on the nature and social function of a certain welfare good *and* on the nature and depth of the social integration of the migrant citizen in the host state society. As discussed, this entails that certain fundamental social rights must be extended to all resident EU citizens, whereas other entitlements only have to be extended after the migrant can demonstrate a significant degree of integration into the society of the host state. This process of rationalization of the social commitments between citizens in the European Union, and of teasing out the exact implications for the domestic 'community of care', is not easy. The fact that the Court's case law appears at times to be conceptually and analytically confused is perhaps understandable in this light, even if a more holistic and explicit engagement with that task might be preferred.

[191] D. Kochenov, 'The Right to Have What Rights? EU Citizenship in Need of Clarification' (2013) 19 ELJ 502.

5

Aspirational Solidarity

Polities grant their citizens specific rights not only on the basis of their roles as economic or societal actors, but also in accordance with the polity's specific aspirations. In the EU, that specific aspiration has always been to check the coercive capacity of the state in limiting available realizations of the 'good life'. This objective lies at the core of the Union's legitimacy and of its free movement rights, and at the same time explains the peculiar role of law and centrality of individual rights in the integration process.[1] European Union law, as such, can be seen as rationalizing the exercise and limits of public power. Aspirational solidarity tells us about the rights and obligations that follow from this shared political commitment. It suggests that Member States cannot prevent their own nationals or migrant EU citizens from accessing the instruments that make up a 'good life'—such as the labour market, public goods, or welfare benefits (section 5.1). Aspirational solidarity, however, is easily the most divisive type of solidarity, as it has the potential to skew the redistributive preferences of Member States, constrain many of the traditional instruments that Member States have used in order to manage their welfare models, and pit the interests and aspirations of individual citizens against each other. There are simply not enough jobs, hospital beds, and resources for unemployment benefits in the Member States to employ, cure, and sustain all the Union's citizens. As discussed above, then, EU law needs to be sensitive to its own limits: it should not inhibit the elaboration of associative commitments

[1] J. Weiler, 'Van Gend en Loos: The Individual as Subject and Object and the Dilemma of European Legitimacy' (2014) 12 ICON 94.

between citizens. Aspirational solidarity, then, is conditional. Its conditionality is entirely consequential and dependent on the factual circumstances: when the aspirations of individual citizens risk undermining the associative commitments between citizens, aspirational solidarity finds a limit.

This chapter discusses the obligations of, and limits to, aspirational solidarity in reference to three different types of welfare policy. The first way in which EU law checks the coercive capacity of the state in limiting the individual's aspirations is in employment market regulation. The Court has interpreted the obligations of non-discrimination (in particular on the basis of age) as implying that Member States may only limit access to the labour market in order to protect associative commitments between citizens in that state. Put somewhat less abstractly, this means that workers can *only* be forced off the labour market if the Member State can demonstrate that this contributes to the capacity of *all* citizens to live a 'good life' (section 5.2). Aspirational solidarity also suggests that Member States may not limit the individual's aspirations by making access to welfare benefits conditional on continuous residence in the state. In other words, citizens may export welfare benefits, and Member States may only limit this right in order to protect the sustainability of the associative commitments undertaken by citizens—that is, when allowing export would destabilize internal redistributive commitments (section 5.3). Finally, aspirational solidarity can also be traced in the Court's regulation of the right to cross-border access of public goods, such as university and hospitals. Yet again, Member States are in principle required to open up their universities or hospitals to migrant citizens: they cannot limit the citizens' aspirations and choices as to what constitutes a good life. And, yet again, the only limit to aspirational solidarity can be found where allowing access for migrants would undermine the associative commitments entered into by citizens in the host state (section 5.4). Aspirational solidarity, then, rationalizes the way in which Member States impact on the capacity of their citizens to make valued choices about how to live their lives, but at the same time remains sensitive to the commitments to justice and solidarity that citizens undertake collectively. Another way of saying this is that aspirational solidarity releases the individual from the constraints imposed by public authority, but not those imposed by fellow citizens in their elaboration of what justice requires.

5.1 Normative Premise and Legal Structure of Aspirational Solidarity

Every organization structures the role of the individual in accordance with the communal aspirations and objectives. This applies to book clubs, football teams, or terrorist organizations as much as it does to transnational integration projects. The EU grants individuals rights not only to protect their roles as economic agents or as members of society, but also as a reflection of its specific aspirations or objectives. Within the context of the integration process, these aspirations have always centred on the promise of providing a better life for the citizen, and its method has always been the limitation or rationalization of the way in which Member States and their national political systems limit the choices and opportunities of their citizens.

As highlighted in the first chapter,[2] the ability of individuals to choose how to live their lives, and how to prioritize the different possibilities that modern society offers, significantly adds to their capacity to live 'good lives'. This aspirational promise can be traced back to the start of the integration project, which served 'the essential purpose of constantly improving the living and working conditions of their people'. While originally this saw to the production of 'peace' and 'prosperity', increasingly the focus has shifted to the capacity of the EU to secure individual rather than communal objectives—to help individual citizens make something of their lives. This is partially due to its incomplete institutional structure, which makes the setting out of normative communal objectives very difficult, and partially due to its legal structure, that is premised on individual rights that can be asserted against public authorities in Europe.[3] Increasingly, however, the EU is appropriating the narrative of aspirational solidarity: that the EU offers its citizens a chance to improve their lives—both domestically and by making use of the free movement provisions. This adds not only the stability of the transnational project—as Breton argued, in a multi-level system of governance all levels must be relevant for the individual's experiences in life[4]—but also

[2] See section 1.1. A. Sen, *The Idea of Justice* (New York: Penguin, 2010) 235.

[3] Weiler, 'Van Gend en Loos', 94.

[4] R. Breton, 'Identification in Transnational Political Communities', in K. Knop, S. Ostryn, R. Simeon, and K. Dwinton (eds.), *Rethinking Federalism: Citizens, Markets, and Governments in a Changing World* (Vancouver: University of British Columbia Press, 1995) 42.

complements the task of the national welfare state in creating the preconditions for individuals to live 'good lives'.

Aspirational solidarity, as such, is a *negative* obligation. Its core understanding is that Member States (or any public authority, for that matter) should not deprive individuals of the possibility to make use of life's chances and to live their lives in accordance to their personal preferences. In other words, it controls the coercive capacity of the state in limiting available realizations of the 'good life'.[5] This primarily relates to the capacity of citizens to move across borders, but also to processes internal to the Member States, such as access to the employment market. Both free movement law and non-discrimination law can be read in the light of this negative obligation of aspirational solidarity: as rationalizing the limit and exercise of public power, and the Member States' capacity to impose a particular view of the 'good life' on its citizens.

There is a dark side to aspirational solidarity, however, which still sparks fierce legal and political debate.[6] For lack of a political structure that can mediate its effects, aspirational solidarity expands in accordance to its own logic and is insensitive to the limits of the national welfare structures with which it engages. It has been typified, somewhat gratuitously, as 'abusive' solidarity,[7] especially in socially sensitive areas such as labour law, healthcare, and education, where it is perceived as destabilizing national normative or redistributive decisions. As emphasized in Chapter 2, strong normative reasons exist to be sensitive to this dark side of aspirational solidarity, and to ensure that EU law in fact stabilizes rather than challenges national distributive arrangements.[8] It is argued that a coherent interpretation of the demands of aspirational solidarity *is* in fact sensitive to its potential negative effects. Properly understood, aspirational solidarity entails a conditional obligation to allow citizens to pursue their conception of the 'good life', not an absolute obligation to accommodate or stimulate this pursuit. In other words, the negative obligation on Member States not to encroach on citizens' choices

[5] H. Brunkhorst, *Solidarity: From Civic Friendship to a Global Legal Community* (Cambridge, Mass.: MIT, 2005) 125; M. Kumm, 'The Idea of Socratic Contestation and the Right to Justification: The Point of Rights-Based Proportionality Review' (2010) 4 Law & Ethics of Human Rights 157.

[6] See, for a well-known example, R. Herzog and L. Gerken, 'Stop the European Court of Justice', *Frankfurter Allgemeine Zeitung*, 8 September 2008.

[7] As argued e.g. in C-147/03 *Commission* v *Austria* [2005] ECR I-5969 or Case C-212/97 *Centros* [1999] ECR I-1459.

[8] See section 2.2.3.

can be rebutted with reference to the need to stabilize communal redistributive practices. Jeremy Waldron explains why justice requires such a limit to aspirational solidarity—which becomes evident once the issue is approached from the perspective of the different obligations of justice that 'insiders' and 'outsiders' are under.[9] While the former have certain (relational) duties of justice towards the other citizens with whom they stand in a particular political, social, or economic relationship, the latter do not. The latter, in fact, are only under an obligation not to undermine the commitments of justice in the Member State that they 'visit'.[10] This argument—and the limit to aspirational solidarity—is thus entirely consequentialist: 'the claim made in its behalf will be that everyone should recognize that there is value in justice being done, even when they are not those among whom it is being done in this particular instance. For that reason, [outsiders] should refrain from interfering with it'.[11] What this limit to aspirational solidarity means in practice will be discussed below with reference to the management of the employment market, and structures for education and healthcare. Much like the other solidarities, aspirational solidarity, then, forces Member States to undertake a rationalization exercise: the freedom of choice for individual citizens can only be limited if necessary to sustain a redistributive commitment that sees to all citizens.

The contours of aspirational solidarity can be traced in three domains. First, they can be traced in the Union's engagement with national employment policy. The way in which EU law has interpreted the prohibition on discrimination based on age, for example, forces Member States to rationalize the reasons for which and the way in which it excludes individuals from the employment market. The negative and conditional nature of the obligation under aspirational solidarity comes through very clearly in the Court's case law. Member States are in principle not allowed to limit access to the employment market for (groups of) citizens *unless* they can demonstrate particular adverse effects on other vulnerable groups in society *and* as long as the exclusion of the individual from the employment market does not cause

[9] J. Waldron, 'Special Ties and Natural Duties' (1993) 22 Philosophy and Public Affairs 3.

[10] See also P. Eleftheriadis, 'Citizenship and Obligation', in J. Dickson and P. Eleftheriadis (eds.), *Philosophical Foundations of European Union Law* (Oxford: OUP, 2012) 172. This distinction can even be traced in Kant's concept of hospitality—which is a negative right of *laissez-passer* and not one of *laissez-faire*. See J. Waldron, 'Cosmopolitan Norms', in S. Benhabib, *Another Cosmopolitanism* (Oxford: OUP, 2006) 88.

[11] Waldron, 'Special Ties and Natural Duties', 17.

particular hardship for the individual. Second, aspirational solidarity suggests that Member States may in principle not prevent the export of benefits by their own citizens. In *Morgan* and *Nerkowska* the Court has clarified that Member States must in principle allow 'their' citizens to export (financial) welfare entitlements.[12] In *Da Silva Martins* the Court even argued that EU law allows, as a general principle, for the export of benefits 'especially where those advantages represent the counterpart of contributions which [citizens] have paid'.[13] The logic here, again, is a negative and conditional one. Member States do not need to accommodate free movement, for example by levelling up entitlements to meet the level required in the host state,[14] but may simply not obstruct free movement or penalize its exercise. The justification for this demand of aspirational solidarity is not dissimilar to that employed in communitarian solidarity. Just as the latter allows citizens to access social entitlements in the *host* state that reflect their social integration there, the former allows citizens to retain access to social entitlements provided by their *home* state for which they still meet the conditions of reciprocity. The conditional obligation of aspirational solidarity means something different in respect of the host state to which a migrant moves. This is the third domain of aspirational solidarity that will be discussed. The absence of an absolute obligation under aspirational solidarity means that economically inactive migrants are in principle not eligible for financial entitlements in their host state until they are sufficiently integrated to be able to make a claim on the basis of communitarian solidarity. The aspirational commitment to allow citizens to make use of the opportunities generated by the rights to free movement does entail, however, a right to access the host state's public goods such as universities and hospitals. Such goods are in principle non-divisible and non-rival, and access by 'outsiders' normally neither limits access for 'insiders' nor substantially increases the costs of such public goods, which are by and large infrastructural. Aspirational solidarity, however, finds its limit where it undercuts stable access to welfare goods for immobile citizens.

The EU's aspirations have always centred on providing its citizens with the preconditions to live 'good lives', and this has to a large extent been achieved by limiting the coercive capacity of the state in determining what such a 'good life' presupposes. This section has highlighted the demands of solidarity that

[12] See Joined Cases C-11/06 and 12/06 *Morgan and Bucher* [2007] ECR I-9161 and Case 499/06 *Nerkowska* [2008] ECR I-3993.

[13] See Case C-388/09 *Da Silva Martins* [2011] ECR I-5737 para 74.

[14] Case C-76/05 *Schwarz* [2007] ECR I-6849 paras 78–80.

are implicit in such a commitment. Member States are, in simple terms, not allowed to impose any limit on the individual's access to the employment market, public goods, and welfare entitlements unless such a limit protects the associative commitments to justice that 'insiders' have entered into.

5.2 Access to the Employment Market and the 'Good Life'

The most important structure that offers citizens meaningful choices pertaining to the 'good life' is the employment market. Whether seen as a means to a 'good life' or as an end in itself, access to a stable job has the capacity radically to transform an individual's quality of life—in the good and the bad sense. This leaves the national regulation of access to the employment market with a problem. Given that not enough high-quality jobs exist for all citizens, Member States, in their management of the employment market, constantly need to devise mechanisms to ensure that all citizens have an equal chance to engage in that market—and that those who cannot have a job still manage to live their lives with the retention of basic levels of dignity and autonomy. This is a highly contested process, as it invariably pits one citizen's aspirations against everyone else's, something that is most clearly felt in respect of compulsory retirement schemes, which are primarily meant to encourage access to the employment market for young workers—a process that is necessary more than ever before in the EU.[15]

The importance of employment in the individual's aspirational pursuit of a 'good life' is evident. It adds meaning to the individual's life, is an instrument for self-determination, provides a context for social interaction, and generates the income necessary for the pursuit of other interests and desires.[16] Conversely, unemployment can be hugely damaging for the individual's capacity to live the life he or she desires. Lack of motivation, confidence, meaningful social context, and income can all lead to downward spirals in the capacity and willingness to work, and ultimately create traps of social

[15] Eurostat statistics for June 2014 set the percentage of youth unemployment at 56.3% in Greece, 53.5% in Spain, and 43.7% in Italy. See <http://epp.eurostat.ec.europa.eu/statistics_explained/index.php/Unemployment_statistics#Recent_developments_in_unemployment_at_a_European_and_Member_State_level>, accessed February 2015.

[16] See for a good analysis of the different ways in which employment contributes to the 'good life', P. Bachman, 'Social Needs, Development, Territories and Full Employment

exclusion. In addition, high figures of unemployment are damaging for more indirect reasons. High unemployment causes a massive strain on the welfare budget, given that states compensate for periods of non-participation of the individual in the employment market through their systems of social security—think of unemployment benefits or old-age pensions[17]—and it destabilizes normative standards such as working conditions, health and safety, minimum wages, and even the system of collective bargaining or collective action.[18] In consequence, the objective of full employment remains squarely at the centre of most Member States' employment policies, as it not only accommodates the aspirations of those within the labour market, but also finances the aspirations of those who are excluded. On the macro-economic level, states try to attain full employment by generating public sector jobs, funding vocational training courses aimed at the development of marketable skills, or providing for an attractive regulatory climate for investors. Nevertheless, as mentioned earlier, not enough (quality) jobs exist to satisfy the aspirations of all citizens, and Member States must therefore inevitably balance the aspirations of those who are in employment against the aspirations of the 'excluded' citizens in their management of the employment market.[19]

The most obvious way in which the European Union contributes to the individual's aspirations is by ensuring access to the labour market in other Member States.[20] Union law, however, also contributes to the aspirations of citizens regardless of their movement between different Member States. It does not set out to standardize retirement age or employment market regulation throughout the EU, but rather focuses on helping individuals overcome the two strongest exclusionary forces on the employment market: lack of marketable skills, and discrimination in access to the

Based on Solidarity', in R. Salais and R. Villeneuve, *Europe and the Politics of Capabilities* (Cambridge: CUP, 2004).

[17] N. Bernard, 'Between a Rock and a Soft Place: Internal Market Vs. Open Coordination', in M. Dougan and E. Spaventa (eds.), *EU Social Welfare Law* (Oxford: Hart, 2005) 279.

[18] C. Offe, 'The European Model of "Social" Capitalism: Can it Survive European Integration?', in M. Miller (ed.) *Worlds of Capitalism* (London: Routledge, 2005) 161 and 167 for a brilliant metaphor of a house.

[19] Dewhurst contests this narrative of offsetting retiring workers and young workers. See E. Dewhurst, 'Intergenerational Balance, Mandatory Retirement and Age Discrimination in Europe: How can the ECJ Better Support the National Courts in Finding a Balance between the Generations?' (2013) 50 CML Rev 1343.

[20] E. Muir, *EU Regulation of Access to Labour Markets* (Alphen aan den Rijn: Kluwer, 2012).

employment market.[21] The paradigm offered by the EU, both in its 'soft' and its 'hard' law, aims to ensure that all citizens have a shot at finding employment. At the same time, the Union stresses that Member States are allowed to encourage access to the employment market for certain groups of citizens, but this should not deprive the citizens who are excluded from pursuing their aspirations in the private sphere. The role of aspirational solidarity in labour law seems to require the rationalization of the impact that Member States' employment policies have on the lives of its citizens. To put it in blunt terms, Member States may limit a citizen's opportunity for work, but not his or her opportunity to live a 'good life'.

This entails a double focus: one the one hand it calls for the empowerment of the individual to find a job, while on the other hand it presupposes the existence of safety nets and mechanisms of social security to cater for the aspirations of those excluded. This double focus is visible in the 'soft law' approach through which the Union seeks to steer national employment policies towards more inclusive paradigms. The main instruments of the OMC approach, such as the flexicurity agenda, or the employment guidelines, clearly emphasize this aspirational orientation. One the one hand, they seek to enhance the individual's capabilities[22] and employment opportunities[23] by retraining workers, devising programmes of life-long learning, increasing the individual's adaptability, and promoting active labour policies that match skills with the demands of the labour market.[24] On the other hand, they encourage Member States to take care of their citizens beyond the workplace. The focus on the need to modernize welfare systems stems from a vision that strong social security safety nets are not the result, but in fact constitute a prerequisite for an open and inclusive employment market with high employment

[21] Offe, 'The European Model of "Social" Capitalism', 169.

[22] J. Browne, S. Deakin, and F. Wilkinson, 'Capabilities, Social Rights and European Market Integration', in R. Salais and R. Villeneuve (eds.), *Europe and the Politics of Capabilities* (Cambridge: CUP, 2004).

[23] See the four pathways in the Annex to 'Towards Common Principles of Flexicurity: More and Better Jobs', COM (2007) 359 final, and Council Conclusions on Flexicurity, adopted on 8 June 2009, see <http://www.consilium.europa.eu/uedocs/cms_data/docs/pressdata/en/lsa/108369.pdf>, accessed March 2015.

[24] See S. Deakin, 'The Capability Concept and the Evolution of European Social Policy', in M. Dougan and E. Spaventa (eds.), *Social Welfare and EU Law* (Oxford: Hart, 2005). See, for a critique on how the OMC has failed to incorporate the social aspects of employment policy, D. Ashiagbor, *The European Employment Strategy: Labour Market Regulation and New Governance* (Oxford: OUP, 2005).

numbers.[25] In other words, the flexicurity approach and the employment guidelines accept that not all the aspirations of all citizens can be met through the employment market. It stresses, however, that excluded citizens should not be left behind, but must be accommodated in social security structures that guarantee such citizens a basic income, either with a view to reinstating them as productive actors in the market or to mitigate the effect of unemployment on their capacity to live decent lives.[26] While research suggests that the OMC approach struggles to convince Member States to move beyond policy objectives that are already identified on the national level,[27] the renewed focus on direct supervision over employment market policies within the context of the excessive deficit procedure, macro-economic imbalance procedure, and country-specific recommendations linked to the European semester might well lead to a hardening of these policy preferences.[28]

One area of the regulation of the employment market has already seen the 'hardening' of this aspirational paradigm. Ever since the Treaty of Rome, the exclusion of certain (groups of) citizens from the employment market, or their discrimination within the market, has been perceived as both potentially frustrating the optimal functioning of the internal market[29] and as undermining the social aspirations and private autonomy of such citizens.[30] More recently, discrimination in access to the employment market has been

[25] 'Towards Common Principles of Flexicurity: More and Better Jobs', COM (2007) 359 final 7. See also <http://ec.europa.eu/eu2020/pdf/115346.pdf>, Council Presidency conclusions, 1, accessed February 2015. See also, explicitly, Council Conclusions on Flexicurity, adopted on 8 June 2009, see <http://www.consilium.europa.eu/uedocs/cms_data/docs/pressdata/en/lsa/108369.pdf>, 4, accessed March 2015. See, for a very detailed overview of the proposals, 'Modernising European Union Labour Law: Has the UK Anything to Gain?', HoL European Union Committee, 22nd Report of 2006–7.

[26] T. Wilthagen and F. Tros, 'The Concept of 'Flexicurity': A New Approach to Regulating Employment and Labour Markets' (2004) 10 European Review of Labour and Research 215–17.

[27] P. Copeland and B. Ter Haar, 'The (In)Effectiveness of the European Employment Strategy' (2013) 23 Journal of European Social Policy 21.

[28] Which raises significant concerns about democratic oversight. See M. Dawson and F. De Witte, 'Constitutional Balance in the EU after the Euro-crisis' (2013) 76 MLR 817.

[29] See C. Barnard, 'The Changing Scope of the Fundamental Principle of Equality?' (2001) 46 McGill Law Journal 955, and Case 43/75 *Defrenne II* para 9 where the Court argues that Article 119 EEC was meant to 'avoid a situation in which undertakings established in States which have actually implemented the principle of equal pay suffer a competitive disadvantage in intra-Community competition as compared with undertakings established in States which have not yet eliminated discrimination against women workers are regards pay'.

[30] See also Opinion of AG Maduro in Case C-303/06 *Coleman* [2008] ECR I-5603 paras 10–11. See Directive 76/207 on equal treatment of men and women and *Defrenne* paras 8–12.

highlighted as a cause for structural underemployment.[31] For both economic and social reasons, then, the Union has implemented measures ensuring the principle of non-discrimination on the basis of sex, race, religion or belief, age, disability, or sexual orientation in access to employment.[32] One area of regulation of the employment market in particular has seen much litigation.[33] Since the employment market cannot provide for sufficient quality jobs for all, discrimination on the basis of age, fostering access to the employment market for the young by excluding the old, is a widely used policy tool to ensure generational solidarity in the distribution of jobs—think of compulsory retirement. Such policies, however, are not only highly divisive and politicized, as they pit the aspirations of whole groups of citizens against each other, but also have an enormous distributive impact, both on the individual (promoting or curtailing access to stable income) and on the communal level (as exclusion is tied to welfare access).

Two mechanisms of employment market regulation in particular have been challenged by way of EU law. First litigants have challenged measures through which the state forces certain age groups off the employment market to make room for the younger generations through compulsory retirement schemes; and second, they have challenged fixed-time schemes, which make it easier for certain age groups to (re-)enter the employment market.[34] The approach taken by the Court in assessing the legality of such schemes implicitly draws its normative justification from the aspirational paradigm discussed above, whereby the management of access to the employment

[31] In 1997, as part of a wider socio-economic agenda, the Treaty basis for legislative activity in all areas of discrimination was introduced, which is now Article 19 TFEU. In the same year, the European Employment Strategy (EES) was unveiled. It laid down four pillars on the basis of which structural unemployment could be combated—one being the pillar of 'equal opportunities'.

[32] Directive 2000/43 and Directive 2000/78.

[33] The principle of non-discrimination on the basis of age was appropriated primarily by the 'grey lobby' to re-challenge national regulatory decisions. As such, the docket is asymmetric—with the exception of Case C-555/07 *Kücükdeveci* [2010] ECR I-365, all litigants have argued in favour of more favourable employment access for older workers.

[34] Case C-411/05 *Palacios de la Villa* [2007] ECR I-8531; Case C-45/09 *Rosenbladt* [2010] ECR I-9391; Joined Cases C-159/10 and C-160/10 *Fuchs and Kohler* [2011] ECR I-6919; Case C-388/07 *Age Concern* [2009] ECR I-1569; Case C-144/04 *Mangold* [2005] ECR I-9981; Case C-109/09 *Deutsche Lufthanse* [2011] ECR I-1309; Case C-341/08 *Petersen* [2010] ECR I-47; Joined Cases C-250/09 and C-268/09 *Georgiev* [2010] ECR I-11869; Case C-286/12 *Commission v Hungary* EU:C:2012:687; Case C-476/11 *Experian* EU:C:2013:590; Case C-447/09 *Prigge* [2011] ECR I-8003; Case C-555/07 *Kükükdeveci* [2010] ECR I-365; Case C-499/08 *Andersen* [2010] ECR I-9343.

market must be coordinated with access to social security, so that *all* citizens, one way or another, can live 'good lives'.[35] This wider reading of the principle of non-discrimination, which prevents the aspirations of individuals from being directly pitted against each other, is a smart way of taking the divisive 'sting' out of aspirational solidarity, and explains the seemingly haphazard distinction between instances in which the Court allows discrimination on the basis of age and instances where it does not. While Article 2 of Directive 2000/78 gives citizens a directly enforceable right not to be discriminated against based on age, Article 6 (1) of Directive 2000/78 indicates that Member States in principle retain a reasonable scope of discretion in differentiating on the basis of age within their employment policies: 'Member States may provide that differences of treatment on grounds of age shall not constitute discrimination, if, within the context of national law, they are objectively and reasonably justified by a legitimate aim, including legitimate employment policy, labour market and vocational training objectives, and if the means of achieving that aim are appropriate and necessary.'[36] This balance between, on the one hand, the individual right not to be forced off the labour market due to age, and, on the other, collective objectives in fostering access to the labour market is a delicate one—whereby slight legal changes might lead to radical decreases in paternalist control over the lifecycle, but also lead to downward pressure on labour rights, more difficulty in promoting access to the labour market for vulnerable groups, and dismissal of workers based not on their age but on their incapacity to perform their job properly.[37] Wisely, the Court has not undertaken a radical reorientation of the individual right of the worker to the detriment of the Member States' capacity to control access. Instead, it has used more sophisticated mechanisms to incorporate a concern for the individual's aspirations with collective employment policy aims.

The Court has generally been lenient in assessing national schemes of compulsory retirement, as long as such schemes consider their impact on the aspirations of those excluded from the employment market. Recitals 6 and 25,

[35] This same logic of rationalizing the excluding effects on national employment policies can be traced in the EU regulation of atypical work. See S. Peers, 'Equal Treatment of Atypical Workers: A New Frontier for EU Law?' (2013) 32 Yearbook of European Law 30.

[36] Article 6 (1) of Directive 2000/78.

[37] See, for a careful analysis in how US and EU policy differ in these regards, J. Suk, 'From Anti Discrimination to Equality: Stereotypes and the Life Cycle in the United States and Europe' (2011) 60 American Journal of Comparative Law 75.

as well as Article 6 (2) of Directive 2000/78, create a strong presumption that such schemes—even though they clearly limit access to the employment market for citizens over a certain age—do not constitute discrimination. The Court has, however, introduced two conditions that must be met by compulsory retirement legislation before it is in compliance with aspirational solidarity. First, its objective must be to actually help certain groups in accessing the employment market:[38] 'Encouragement of recruitment undoubtedly constitutes a legitimate aim of Member States' social or employment policy (…), in particular when the promotion of access of young people to a profession is involved. Consequently, encouragement of recruitment in higher education by means of the offer of posts as professors to younger people may constitute such a legitimate aim.'[39] In assessing national compulsory retirement schemes, however, the Court demands not only that the exclusion of older workers fosters access for younger workers, but also that the exclusion of the former is necessary, taking account of the 'actual situation in the labour market', including 'political, economic, social, demographic and/or budgetary considerations',[40] while it is for the national court to 'assess the probative value of the evidence adduced [in order to demonstrate this need] which may, inter alia, include statistical evidence'.[41] This requirement of specificity, which looks at the employment market in a certain sector[42] or even geographical region,[43] serves to ensure that the aspirations of those excluded from the employment market are not unnecessarily restricted.[44] In other words, aspirational solidarity prevents Member States from excluding more workers from the employment market than necessary—and in doing so rationalizes the coercive capacity of the state to limit the individual's potential to live a 'good life' while remaining sensitive to collective conditions of justice.

Once the need for a compulsory retirement scheme is established, the Court imposes a second, more substantive, requirement. This requirement—which

[38] *Petersen* paras 65–8; *Palacios de la Villa* para 65; *Rosenbladt* para 43. See also Opinion of AG Bot in *Georgiev* paras 30–1.

[39] *Georgiev* para 45.

[40] *Palacios de la Villa* para 69. See also Case C-45/09, *Rosenbladt* [2010] ECR I-9391, para 44.

[41] *Fuchs and Kohler* para 75.

[42] *Rosenbladt* para 49; Opinion of AG Bot in *Georgiev* para 35; *Georgiev* paras 46 and 51–2.

[43] *Petersen* paras 71–2.

[44] Ibid. paras 62 and 64. See, specifically, *Prigge* para 60, where the Court ruled that compulsory retirement of pilots over 60 on reasons of safety could not fall under Article 6 (1) as they were unrelated to employment policy objectives.

is essentially one of proportionality[45]—connects access to the employment market with the aspirations that individuals may have *beyond* the workplace. In this view, compulsory retirement must be accompanied by social security mechanisms that ensure that the individuals excluded can still live a decent life. In other words, forced exclusion from the employment market is allowed only if the state assumes responsibility for the well-being of individuals excluded:

> the measure cannot be regarded as unduly prejudicing the legitimate claims of workers subject to compulsory retirement because (...) the relevant legislation (...) also takes account of the fact that the persons concerned are entitled to financial compensation by way of a retirement pension (...) the level of which cannot be regarded as unreasonable.[46]
>
> [T]he decisive factor is that the professor has acquired a right to a retirement pension.[47]

Conversely, in cases where forced retirement causes particular hardship due to lack of sufficient income, individuals cannot be forced off the market, as this would result in a disproportionate limitation of their capacity to live a good life.[48] In other words, the coercive capacity of the state to limit an individual's aspirations finds an absolute limit where it directly leads to particular hardship. In *Rosenbladt*, for example, the Court held that:

> The automatic termination of employment contracts causes significant financial hardship to workers in the commercial cleaning sector in general and to Mrs. Rosenbladt in particular. As poorly paid part-time employment is a typical feature of this sector, the statutory old-age pension is not sufficient to meet the basic needs of workers. (...)
>
> [A]ccount must be taken both of the hardship [that compulsory retirement] may cause to the persons concerned and of the benefits derived from it by society in general and the individuals who make up society.[49]

[45] See, for a discussion of how this external element was introduced in the principle of proportionality, E. Muir, 'Enhancing the Effects of Community Law on National Employment Policies: the *Mangold* Case' (2006) 31 ELRev 886.

[46] *Palacios de la Villa* para 73. See also *Rosenbladt* para 48 and the Opinion of AG Bot in *Georgiev* [2010] ECR para 36, and *Georgiev* para 54.

[47] *Georgiev* para 63.

[48] The Court also seems to include an element of foreseeability in this assessment (i.e. workers must be able to plan their retirement and pension by knowing in advance when they will be asked to retire). See *Commission* v *Hungary* para 70.

[49] *Rosenbladt* paras 71–3.

This citation shows what the Court takes aspirational solidarity to mean in labour law: employment policy choices may limit the individual's capacity to work, but not his or her capacity to live a 'good life'. In other words, the Court's rationalization of the leeway that Member States dispose of does not challenge their legitimate assessments as to who should receive priority access to employment, but instead demands that such policies be objectively necessary and take account of their specific and precise impact on the aspirations of those excluded from the employment market.

This double requirement of rationalization explains why the Court, in *Mangold*, *Kücükdeveci*, and *Commission* v *Hungary*, found that certain national employment measures infringed obligations of transnational aspirational solidarity. In those cases, the national measures were invariably general in nature, did not contribute to fostering access for younger workers, and did not take account of the individual's aspirations beyond the workplace. In *Commission* v *Hungary*, for example, the lowering of the retirement age for judges from 70 to 62 violated both these conditions. On the one hand, it did not actually help create intergenerational justice in the Hungarian public sector (it simply sliced the eldest workers off, causing a one-off redistributive effect).[50] On the other hand, the drastic decrease of the retirement age did not take the personal circumstances of judges into account, in the sense that the loss of eight years of expected employment decreased their pensions by 30 per cent without affording them reasonable time to plan their economic and financial situations.[51] In *Mangold*, a German measure that lifted the prohibition on successive fixed-term contracts for all employees older than 52 was challenged. The measure's objective was to facilitate the inclusion of older workers in the labour force.[52] It was not, however, specific enough to show the necessity of the measure: 'such legislation takes the age of the worker concerned as the only criterion (...) regardless of any other consideration linked to the structure of the labour market in question or the personal situation of the person concerned'.[53] Moreover, given that the national measure also applies to workers already in employment, it has the potential to decrease significantly the aspirations of such workers without alleviating the ensuing hardship. Simply put, the risk exists that workers who would have had an open-ended contract now end up with fixed-term contracts. This

[50] *Commission* v *Hungary* paras 78–9.
[51] Ibid. para 70. [52] *Mangold*.
[53] See *Georgiev* paras 58–9, and the Opinion of AG Bot in *Georgiev* para 38.

constitutes a disproportionate limitation of such workers' aspirations since it 'leads to a situation in which the workers concerned [already in employment] (...) are in danger, during a substantial part of their working life, of being excluded from the benefit of stable employment which constitutes, according to the Court, a major element in the protection of workers'. [54]

In *Kücükdeveci* another German measure was challenged. The legislation at issue made the period of notice to be given to the employee dependent on the number of years that the employee had worked for the employer, discounting any years worked before the age of 25.[55] As a justification, Germany adduced that this would stimulate employers to hire more young workers, and that, since such workers would react more adequately to changing demands on the labour market, a degree of flexibility might be expected of them. The Court was convinced neither that the measure was necessary for its objective of encouraging companies to hire more young staff—indeed, it promotes their subsequent exclusion—nor that it took account of how the scheme affected the aspirations of more vulnerable individuals. Under the scheme, bluntly put, a cashier who started work at 16 suffers disproportionate hardship if compared to a lawyer who starts work at 25:

> The legislation is not appropriate (...) since it applies to all employees who joined the undertaking before the age of 25 (...) even if the person concerned has a long length of service in the undertaking at the time of dismissal. (. .) [I]t affects young people who enter active life early after little or no vocational training, but not those who start work later after a long period of training.[56]

At the same time, the Court accepts domestic legislation that carefully contextualizes the differences in treatment between workers of different ages within their specific needs. In *Experian*, for example, the Court explicitly lauded the Danish legislation that set higher pension contribution rates by both employer and employee for older employees. The logic here is that it allowed older workers to ensure adequate retirement savings even when entering the employment market relatively late, and to cover death, incapacity, or serious illness, which is 'statistically more likely for older workers', while at the same time allowing younger workers to retain a higher disposable income.[57] While this can be criticized for perpetuating quite traditional

[54] Ibid. See also Green Paper: 'Modernising Labour Law to Meet the Challenges of the 21st Century', COM (2006) 708 final 3.

[55] *Kücükdeveci* paras 10–11.

[56] *Kücükdeveci* paras 39–42.

[57] *Experian* paras 58, 64–5.

understandings of the lifecycle that might appear inappropriate in the pluralist society and differentiated employment market of today,[58] it does show that the Court is intuitively looking for instances where domestic legislators think through how differentiation on the basis of age will affect the specific circumstances of the employee.[59]

The Court's case law is far from incoherent when read from the perspective of aspirational solidarity.[60] While each and every employment policy has winners and losers, dictated by economic requirements and legitimized through the national political process, the Court's rationalization effort seems to focus on policies that produce no winners—that is, when a worker's exclusion from the employment market is neither compensated by social security measures, nor contributes to someone else's aspirations. This way of controlling the exercise of the coercive capacity of the state in limiting the individual's aspirations implies that Member States must take the interests of all citizens into account when devising employment policies.

5.3 Exporting Welfare Benefits and the 'Good Life'

Aspirational solidarity also suggests that, in principle, welfare entitlements can be exported. Member States may not deprive their citizens of the opportunities offered by free movement by making its exercise contingent on relinquishing the rights to welfare benefits. This conceptual leap was made in *D'Hoop* and *De Cuyper*, where the Court held that the rights to free movement for Union citizens entailed not only a prohibition of discrimination but also a prohibition on all restrictions to such movement.[61] This leap has

[58] D. Schiek, 'Age Discrimination before the ECJ—Conceptual and Theoretical Issues' (2011) 48 CML Rev 777; Suk, 'From Anti Discrimination to Equality', 75.

[59] In *Andersen*, however, the Court seemed less receptive, and imposed a requirement that—even if carefully differentiated on the basis of the different needs of different workers—workers may not be forced off simply because they have access to more than adequate pensions.

[60] See, for the opposite view, AG Kokott in *Andersen* paras 22–3 and 53–9; AG Trstenjak in *Rosenbladt* paras 87–95 and 167–71. Dewhurst suggest that the real fault line in the case law lies between general compulsory retirement schemes (where the Court is hands-off) and sectoral rules (where the Court is much more prescriptive). See E. Dewhurst, 'Intergenerational Balance, Mandatory Retirement and Age Discrimination in Europe: How Can the ECJ Better Support the National Courts in Finding a Balance between the Generations?' (2013) 50 CML Rev 1345.

[61] See Case C-244/98 *D'Hoop* [2002] ECR I-6191; and Case C-406/04 *De Cuyper* [2006] ECR I-6947.

promoted the aspirational right of Union citizens to make use of the possibilities and opportunities of free movement into an almost constitutional right.

> The opportunities offered by the Treaty in relation to freedom of movement for citizens of the Union could not be fully effective if a national of a Member State could be deterred from availing himself of them by obstacles placed in the way of his stay in another Member State by legislation of his Member State of origin penalising him for the mere fact that he has used those opportunities.[62]

This obligation under aspirational solidarity is a *negative* obligation. Member States must allow their citizens to export benefits, but are not obliged to increase such benefits to account, for example, for higher living costs in the host state. Moving to another state, in other words, is not necessarily financially neutral for the citizen, while it is neutral for the Member State of origin. Such a move may, to use the Court's terms, 'be more or less advantageous for the person concerned'.[63] The obligation under aspirational solidarity is also conditional. As discussed in Chapter 4, the sustainability of welfare resources presupposes that citizens can only access welfare benefits to the extent that they meet the conditions of reciprocity that are particular to a specific benefit.[64] The limit to aspirational solidarity in the context of the export of welfare benefits, then, mirrors the logic of communitarian solidarity discussed above. Member States may only impose eligibility criteria that are indicative of the nature and function of any particular social benefit. Citizens are allowed to export welfare benefits provided by their home state for which they still meet the conditions of reciprocity, regardless of their lack of residence. The extension of such benefits, after all, reflects the prior social or economic commitment of citizens to the polity and, as such, does not challenge the sustainability of welfare resources for the immobile citizens who have remained in the host state.[65] In contrast, welfare benefits that are inextricably connected to the territory of the state, or presuppose a continuous or future social or economic connection to that polity, can in principle not be exported. After all, the extension of such benefits might deprive immobile citizens from accessing them, as it stretches the bounds of reciprocity

[62] Case C-345/09 *Van Delft* [2010] ECR I-9879 para 97; see also Case C-208/07 *Chomier-Glisczinski* [2009] ECR I-6095 para 82.

[63] Joined Cases C-393/99 and 394/99 *Hervein and Others* [2002] ECR I-2829 paras 50–2; Case C-562/10 *Commission* v *Germany* EU:C:2012:442 para 57; and Opinion AG Trstenjak in Case C-562/10 *Commission* v *Germany* EU:C:2012:442 para 76.

[64] See section 4.2.

[65] See Case C-388/09 *Da Silva Martins* [2011] ECR I-5737 para 74.

beyond the extent to which they can be stably reproduced.[66] For benefits that cannot be easily classified as being either based on prior commitments or reflecting a prospective link, such as student benefits or unemployment benefits, the Court undertakes a more fluid assessment of their nature and function. The direct connection between the right to export social benefits and the nature and function of those benefits serves to ensure that the aspirations of those who wish to make use of their rights to free movement are bolstered without undercutting the stability of the entitlements of immobile citizens. In other words, rights under aspirational solidarity are conditional upon the continuous availability of entitlements to *all* citizens.

Article 7 of Regulation 883/2004, like its predecessor Regulation 1408/71, indeed allows for the export of most financial benefits,[67] such as sickness benefits, old-age benefits, disability benefits, and death grants.[68] This general waiving of residence criteria finds its justification in the nature of the benefits covered, and the reciprocal commitments that they express. Simply put, the nature of such risk-based benefits entails that entitlement is contingent on past contribution, and not continuous residence in, or social commitment to, a certain state.[69] Most social security benefits, for example, are funded by making individual contributions compulsory. The contribution and insurance record, then, give rise to financial entitlements in the event of hardship.[70] In other words, both the reason for entitlement and the height of cash benefits are tied to the insurance record of the individual citizen. The Court has articulated the assumptions that underlie this right to export risk-based benefits somewhat more explicitly. *Meints* dealt with a German resident who had worked in the Netherlands and had applied for a Dutch compensation scheme for agricultural workers whose contract of employment was terminated as a result of the setting aside of land belonging to their former employer.[71] The Court held that, since the benefit was 'dependent on the prior existence of the employment relationship' and is 'intrinsically linked to the recipient's objective status as [a] worker',[72] Meints could access the benefit regardless of his

[66] See more, section 2.3. [67] Article 10 of Regulation 1408/71.

[68] See e.g. Articles 21, 36, 43 of Regulation 883/2004.

[69] See also recital 16 to Regulation 883/2004.

[70] See, for the Court's definition, Case C-215/99 *Jauch* [2001] ECR I-1901 para 25: 'a benefit is regarded as a social security benefit where it is granted, without any individual and discretionary assessment of personal needs, to recipients on the basis of a statutorily defined position'. See also Case C-228/07 *Petersen* [2008] ECR I-6989 para 19.

[71] Case C-57/96 *Meints* [1997] ECR I-6689 para 22. [72] Ibid. para 41.

residence in Germany. In other words, the benefit reflected a past commitment, and present residence was immaterial for continuous access. This approach was confirmed in *Leclere*. The case dealt with a Belgian resident who had worked in Luxembourg, and, in that capacity, was a victim of an accident at work. As a result of his participation in Luxembourg social security schemes at the time of the accident, he received an invalidity pension from Luxembourg, regardless of his status as a non-resident.[73] The Court emphasized that a former worker continues to be entitled to 'certain advantages acquired by virtue of his [terminated] employment relationship', even if he cannot 'acquire new rights having no links with his former occupation'.[74] In *Da Silva Martins*, the Court even explicitly linked past contribution to the right to export, arguing that EU law allows, as a general principle, for the export of benefits 'especially where those advantages represent the counterpart of contributions which they have paid'.[75] Access to such benefits is dependent on the individual's past commitment in the form of his or her insurance record, and not on 'thicker', more abstract demands of belonging, or social or economic participation in that state. As such, then, their export cannot destabilize the capacity of *immobile* citizens to access redistributive resources.

Tas-Hagen is a good example of another type of benefit that reflects a past commitment and should thus be exportable. It dealt with Ms Tas-Hagen, who wished to export Dutch civilian war benefits to which she was entitled on account of health problems that had occurred during the Japanese occupation of Indonesia.[76] In other words, the question was whether the nature and function of such benefit might require continuous residence:

> [C]ompensatory allowances for former prisoners of war, who prove that they underwent a long period of captivity, are commonly acknowledged as constituting testimony of national gratitude for the hardships they endured (...) [I]t would appear legitimate for a Member State to grant also to civilians with whom it has a particular connection both at the time of the war events and thereafter ertain social benefits as an expression of national solidarity for the material andnon-material damage they suffered during the war.[77]

[73] Case C-43/99 *Leclere* [2001] ECR I-4265 para 15.

[74] Ibid paras 58–9. See also, for similar assessment, Case C-33/99 *Esmoris Cerdeiro-Pinedo Amado* [2001] ECR I-4265.

[75] *Da Silva Martins* para 74.

[76] See also Case C-499/06 *Nerkowska* [2008] ECR I-3993; which dealt with similar benefits for Polish citizens deported to Siberia.

[77] AG Kokott in Case C-192/05 *Tas-Hagen* [2006] ECR I-10451 para 59.

A criterion requiring residence cannot be considered a satisfactory indicator of the degree of connection of applicants to the Member State granting the [civilian war] benefit when it (...) lead[s] to different results for persons resident abroad whose degree of integration into the society of the Member State granting the benefit is in all respects comparable.[78]

The Court disallows residence requirements for social benefits whose social function is unrelated to the national territory, but is instead premised on past commitments or occurrences. In *Tas-Hagen*, clearly, the benefit was meant to compensate for the hardship suffered during the Japanese occupation of Indonesia. The only possible condition indicative of that function, of course, is that the applicant has indeed suffered such hardship, not that she continue to reside in the Netherlands.[79] In consequence, Ms Tas-Hagen was allowed to move to Spain with retention of her benefit. This is a good example of how aspirational solidarity functions: it limits the capacity of the Member States unreasonably to limit choices made by citizens.

The case in which the Court has been most explicit in the demand that Member States must allow for the export of benefits depending on the nature of that benefit is *Stewart*.[80] The case dealt with a British girl who suffers from Down's syndrome, and who moved to Spain with her parents. While in Spain, she had received disability living allowance from the UK, but was refused access to a short-term incapacity benefit on the ground that she did not reside in the UK.[81] The Court faced the question head on: is a criterion of residence constitutive of the reciprocity implicit in short-term incapacity benefits? The Court argues that even if it might be, so many other factors could affect that determination that residence alone is not a legitimate criterion for eligibility:

While the rules for applying that condition do not, in themselves, appear to be unreasonable, none the less that condition is too exclusive in nature. Indeed, by requiring specific periods of past presence in the competent Member State, the condition of past presence unduly favours an element which is not necessarily representative of the real and effective degree of connection between the claimant to short-term incapacity benefit in youth and that Member State, to the exclusion of all other representative elements. (...)

In fact, is not inconceivable that the existence of such a connection could be established from other representative elements, [such as] the relationship between

[78] Case C-192/05 *Tas-Hagen* [2006] ECR I-10451 para 38. See also *Nerkowska* para 43.

[79] See also Opinion of AG Maduro in *Nerkowska* paras 22–4.

[80] Case C-503/09 *Stewart* [2011] ECR I-6497.

[81] ibid para 18-21.

the claimant and the social security system of the competent Member State (...) the claimant's family circumstances (...) [or the fact that] the appellant, a United Kingdom national, has passed a significant part of her life in the United Kingdom.[82]

What the Court argues, then, is not necessarily that Stewart should be awarded the benefit, but rather that the imposition of a criterion of current residence is not sophisticated enough to capture the reciprocal commitments that underlie short-term incapacity benefits. The Court seems to suggest that access to such benefits should reflect a more general prior societal engagement with society, which means that their export cannot detract from their availability for immobile citizens, and they are therefore exportable. *Stewart* reflects a problem in the Court's case law that has already been referred to. In assessing the links of reciprocity that are indicative of complex benefits, such as short-term incapacity or student benefits, which include both prior and future commitments to a polity, the Court runs the risk of demanding that Member States accept *any* link—social or economic, prior or future, derivative or autonomous—as warranting export of the benefit in question. This, in turn, runs the risk of destabilizing the continuous provision of such welfare goods.

An example of welfare benefits that *cannot* be exported are minimum subsistence benefits. Such benefits do not involve prior insurance records or prior commitments, but rather membership of a particular society and personal need. The exportability of special non-contributory benefits is as such explicitly excluded by Regulation 883/2004. Article 70 (2) emphasizes that only residents can obtain such benefits. The Court's vast amount of case law on this provision is relatively coherent: as long as a benefit is (1) meant to provide for basic subsistence income and (2) is non-contributory, a criterion of residence is allowed.[83] In its case law, the Court gives little indication of the normative reason[84] for the prohibition of export beyond the fact that such benefits are 'closely tied to the socio-economic situation in the state of residence' of the applicant,[85] and are provided from public funds.[86] It seems that the non-exportability reflects the nature and function of such

[82] *Stewart* paras 95–101.

[83] Case C-299/05 *Commission* v *Parliament and Council* [2007] ECR I-8695; Case C-154/05 *Kersbergen* [2006] ECR I-6249 para 27, and Case C-537/09 *Bartlett* [2011] ECR I-3417.

[84] As opposed to practical concerns, which are also relevant, see F. Pennings, *European Social Security Law*, 5th edn. (Cambridge: Intersentia, 2010) 237–8.

[85] *Bartlett* para 38; Joined Cases C-419/05 and C-450/05 *Habelt* [2007] ECR I-11895 paras 78 and 81; *Kersbergen* para 33.

[86] *Kersbergen* para 37; Case C-215/99 *Jauch* [2001] ECR I-1901, paras 32–3.

benefits. They serve to liberate citizens from subsistence and allow them to live their lives with at least a minimum of autonomy and dignity by providing the basic level of resources necessary to ensure that they can survive in any given place.[87] These types of benefit are not returns upon investment through compulsory or voluntary insurance, but reflect a basic moral duty to 'save' fellow members of society—regardless of their nationality. Such a duty is incumbent on each political community in respect of all residents, and implicit in the associative connection between members of society.[88] In other words, the duty that underlies the provision of minimum subsistence allowances is territorial and such allowances are not exportable since by physically moving outside the confines of a certain political community, the citizens also move outside that community's obligation 'to save' (and into another's). In addition, the social function of these entitlements requires assessments of purchase power, inflation, and costs of primary goods such as housing, food, and electricity. In this light, only the state of residence of the citizen can actually 'save' him or her. The Court's continuous reference to the socio-economic situation of the place of residence is meant to reflect this logic: a benefit issued by the city of Bucharest, meant to ensure that a citizen can access primary goods, will not go very far in meeting that objective if the recipient lives in Stockholm. Likewise, an applicant for Swedish minimum subsistence allowance may nominally fall below the threshold at which he or she is entitled to such allowances, but if resident in Bucharest he or she may not actually find him- or herself in a position where he or she needs to be saved. In other words, citizens can demonstrate that they meet the preconditions of necessity that underlie access to minimum subsistence allowances only in respect of the state in which they reside. As a reflection of their nature and function, then, benefits that offer a minimum level of income cannot be exported.

Aspirational solidarity, as should be clear by now, serves to allocate responsibility for welfare resources between the home and the host state of a mobile citizen depending on his or her ties with the different states. The benefits for which this exercise is most difficult, as we saw in the previous chapter, are educational benefits, which involve both past commitments (which would suggest that they can be exported) and prospective commitments (which would suggest that they cannot be exported). As was discussed above, the Court does not

[87] Article 70 (2) of Regulation 883/2004.

[88] See also section 4.3.3, even if possibly undermined by Case C-333/13 *Dano* [nyr].

seem to have made up its mind about the precise type of commitment that warrants access to student benefits,[89] and generally allows for the export of benefits when the student has resided for a number of years in a state before deciding to study abroad. In *Prinz and Seeberger* and in *Morgan and Bucher*, the Court argued that the social ties that are built up in the years prior to starting university study are sufficiently strong to allow the export of student benefits.[90] Again, the obligations under aspirational solidarity are essentially negative. Member States must allow students to export their student benefits, but do not need to increase them to mirror higher living costs or tuition fees in other states.[91]

Healthcare entitlements—being based on insurance—can also be exported, be it in a slightly different form. Healthcare insurance is organized on a territorial basis, and, as such, a change in the state of residence also entails a change in the state of healthcare affiliation. Yet, healthcare entitlements can be exported from the state of affiliation in the sense that patients are simply allowed to choose to receive healthcare abroad without losing their right to be reimbursed by the state of affiliation.[92] Even if in practice very few patients even want to be treated abroad,[93] given that domestic healthcare systems, on the whole, produce satisfying results for citizens,[94] and in the light of 'linguistic barriers, geographic distance, the costs of staying abroad and lack of information about the kind of care provided',[95] the Court has clearly carved out a basic right for patients to export their right to treatment. Already in the late 1970s the Court first attempted to ensure the right for all Union citizens to be treated in whichever state they prefer. In the *Pierik* cases, the Court argued that Regulation 1408/71 offered citizens the unconditional 'opportunity' to seek healthcare abroad.

[89] See section 4.4.

[90] Joined Cases C-523/11 and 585/11 *Prinz and Seeberger* EU:C:2013:524; Joined Cases C-11/06 and 12/06 *Morgan and Bucher* [2007] ECR I-9161.

[91] As pointed out by the Court in Case C-76/05 *Schwarz* [2007] ECR I-6849.

[92] Even if it has been circumscribed in order to prevent distributive asymmetries from undermining the domestic provision of universal, adequate, and permanent access to a balanced range of high-quality healthcare. After all, one individual's exercise of cross-border healthcare should not deprive access to such care for other individuals. See section 5.4.

[93] A Commission study shows that just about 4% of patients receive treatment in another Member State, which impacts as little as 1% on national insurance schemes. Commission Impact Assessment for the Directive on Cross-border Healthcare, SEC (2008) 2163, 9.

[94] See, for statistical data on the unmet need for medical services in different Member States, Commission Impact Assessment for the Directive on Cross-border Healthcare, SEC (2008) 2163, 68.

[95] See P. Koutrakos, 'Healthcare as an Economic Service under EC Law', in M. Dougan and E. Spaventa (eds.), *Social Welfare and EU Law* (Oxford: Hart, 2005) 122, and Case C-385/99 *Müller-Fauré* [2003] ECR I-4509 para 95.

The Member States, however, evidently displeased with the Court's ruling, amended the Regulation to restrict the right to cross-border healthcare to cases where healthcare could not be offered 'at home'.[96] About two decades later the Court had another go, against the opinion of AG Colomer,[97] this time finding that the aspirational right to cross-border healthcare could be directly derived from Article 56 TFEU. In *Decker*, *Kohll*, and *Müller-Fauré*,[98] cases which all dealt with demands for reimbursement for medical services that could equally effectively have been provided on the territory of the state of affiliation, the Court acknowledged the right of patients to seek healthcare abroad out of choice rather than medical need as a new right to cross-border healthcare, which exists independently from[99] and in addition to the rights under Regulation 883/2004 and the right to timely healthcare under communitarian solidarity.[100] In other words, Member States may not limit the capacity of their citizens to choose where to undergo treatment.

Both the Court and the Union legislator have since cemented the aspirational right to seek treatment abroad with retention of reimbursement mechanisms. The Patients' Rights Directive 2011/24 clearly couches the right in aspirational terms,[101] as contributing to the individual's capacity to live a better life[102] by allowing him or her to choose healthcare that is cheaper, faster, better,[103] and closer to home,[104] or is simply his

[96] Case 182/78 *Pierik II* [1979] ECR 1977 para 17. See section 3.4.

[97] Opinion of AG Colomer in *Müller-Fauré* paras 56 and 61.

[98] Case C-158/96 *Kohll* [1998] ECR I-1931 paras 34–5; Case C-120/95 *Decker* [1998] ECR I-1831 paras 35–6.

[99] Recitals 28 and 31 of Directive 2011/24.

[100] Which also explains an apparent paradox in the Court's case law that some commentators have picked up. The Court had, on the one hand, held that the requirement of prior authorization under Regulation 883/2004 does *not* limit the right to free movement, but indeed facilitates it (see Case C-56/01 *Inizan* [2003] ECR I-12403 para 22), while that very same requirement is now held to be contrary to Article 56 TFEU. This, however, makes perfect sense: while a system of prior authorization in the Regulations does not limit the right to market solidarity (and indeed implements it), it does limit the right to aspirational solidarity which citizens derive from Article 56 TFEU directly.

[101] See, for information obligations and duty of care obligations, Opinion of AG Colomer in Case C-56/01 *Inizan* [2003] ECR I-12403 para 30.

[102] For example Opinion of AG Colomer in *Inizan* para 6: 'patients are entitled to benefit from scientific and medical advances achieved in other European states'.

[103] Consider the difference in survival rates for certain diseases. Survival rates for bladder cancer range from 47% in Poland and Estonia to 78% in Austria; and for breast cancer from 60% in Slovakia to 82.6% in Sweden. See Commission Impact Assessment for the Directive on Cross-border Healthcare, SEC (2008) 2163, 21, referring to ROCARE 3 SUMMARY: Annals of Oncology 14 (supplement 5): v128–v149, 2003.

[104] Recital 39 of Directive 2011/24.

or her 'preferred choice'.[105] In solidifying the *legal* aspirational right to cross-border healthcare, the Court has come up with a clever trick, which has now been codified in the PRD. It simply reversed the burden of proof for the actual exercise of cross-border healthcare: 'the Member State of affiliation shall ensure that costs incurred by an insured person who receives cross-border healthcare are reimbursed, if the healthcare in question is among the benefits to which the insured person is entitled in the Member State of affiliation'.[106] Rather than the patient having to argue why his or her treatment abroad should be reimbursed, the state of affiliation must now show that the patient's movement would cause (significant) problems for its capacity to sustain a system of high-quality healthcare—not simply that the same treatment was available 'at home'.[107] This limit reflects the conditional nature of aspirational solidarity. As such, the Member State of affiliation is obliged to reimburse the patient only up to the level that it would have granted in case the treatment had taken place 'at home' in order to prevent skewing the flow of resources to the detriment of immobile citizens.[108] The PRD now codifies this limit: 'the costs of cross-border healthcare shall be reimbursed or paid directly by the Member State of affiliation up to the level of costs that would have been assumed by the Member State of affiliation, had this healthcare been provided in its territory'.[109] At no point does the exercise of aspirational solidarity allow patients to ask for reimbursement of the *full* cost of treatment undergone in another Member State—which would potentially divert significant resources away from the domestic healthcare system,[110] and possibly lead to underfunded healthcare

[105] Commission Impact Assessment for the Directive on Cross-border Healthcare, SEC (2008) 2163, 8.

[106] See Article 7 and recital 38 of Directive 2011/24.

[107] The limits will be discussed in the following section.

[108] *Kohll* para 40. See also Case C-120/95 *Decker* [1998] ECR I-1831 paras 38–40; *Müller-Fauré* para 98: 'In any event, it should be borne in mind that it is for the Member States alone to determine the extent of the sickness cover available to insured persons, so that, when the insured go without prior authorisation to a Member State other than that in which their sickness fund is established to receive treatment there, they can claim reimbursement of the cost of the treatment given to them only within the limits of the cover provided by the sickness insurance scheme in the Member State of affiliation.'

[109] Article 7 (4) and recitals 4, 13 of Directive 2011/24.

[110] This argument is empirically tenuous, given that even a conservative estimate indicates that patient mobility would be financially beneficial for the Member States. See Commission Impact Assessment for the Directive on Cross-border Healthcare, SEC (2008) 2163, 34–6 and 55.

facilities in the state for the immobile citizens,[111] who tend to be the 'less vocal, and often already underempowered, categories of patients'.[112] In other words, cross-border healthcare is financially neutral for the state of affiliation—in contrast to situations under market and communitarian solidarity, where it is financially neutral for the patient—and cannot therefore possibly detract from the capacity of that state to provide universal access to high-quality healthcare. Any argument to that effect either has to assume that sick patients 'miraculously' recover if (threatened to be) treated in the state of affiliation, or, rather the opposite, die before they are treated. Only in these situations, after all, would the reimbursement of healthcare obtained abroad have financial implications for the state of affiliation.

One concern remains unaddressed by the Court. Above, it was argued that aspirational solidarity finds its limit where it skews national distributive or normative choices to the detriment of immobile citizens. In the field of healthcare, one such possibility still exists. While it has not been empirically demonstrated yet, it appears possible that the almost unconditional right to export healthcare funds could divert a more substantial part of the investment poured into healthcare from 'immobile treatments', such as cancer research, to more 'mobile treatments', such as kidney transplants or hip replacements, for which patients are more likely and able to seek treatment abroad.[113] If and when such a situation arises, the Court should carefully assess the extent to which political choices must be insulated from the dynamics of aspirational solidarity. That solidarity, after all, imposes a conditional obligation on Member States to allow the exercise of free movement, not a positive obligation to adapt distributive choices to facilitate such movement. The Court has indeed so far been quite consistent in its imposition of only negative and conditional obligations on the Member State for the export of healthcare entitlements. Member States are, for example, free to decide whether or not to reimburse patients for the travel and accommodation costs which they incur while seeking treatment. However, *if* they

[111] C. Newdick, 'Citizenship, Free Movement and Healthcare: Cementing Individual Rights by Corroding Social Solidarity' (2006) 43 CML Rev 1645ff.; S. Greer and T. Sokol, 'Rules for Rights: European Law, Health Care and Social Citizenship' (2014) 20 ELJ 79.

[112] C. Murphy, 'An Effective Right to Cross-Border Healthcare? On Patients, Primacy and Procedural Autonomy: Comment on *Elchinov*' (2011) 36 ELRev 555.

[113] C. Newdick, 'The European Court of Justice, Transnational Healthcare, and Social Citizenship—Accidental Death of a Concept?' (2009) 26 Wisconsin International Law Journal 844.

offer such refunds for treatment *within* the state of affiliation, they must also do so for treatment abroad.[114] Equally, it is completely acceptable for Member States to make reimbursement conditional on the patient consulting a GP before treatment is obtained,[115] or limit reimbursable healthcare to that obtained in public institutions,[116] as long as such rules apply regardless of the place of treatment.

Aspirational solidarity serves to limit the coercive capacity of the state. It ensures that Member States cannot make access to welfare benefits conditional on continuous residence of the individual on the territory of the state, but at the same time remains sensitive to the need to stabilize redistributive commitments between immobile citizens.

5.4 Public Goods and the 'Good Life'

Aspirational solidarity does not oblige host states to extend financial benefits to migrant citizens until they meet the conditions established in the previous chapters under market solidarity or communitarian solidarity. Migrant citizens that have not built up a sufficiently strong economic or social connection to the host state, in other words, have no right to benefits from the host state. Host states do, however, have an obligation to extend access to public goods to mobile EU citizens—an obligation that remains, however, conditional upon the state being able to offer adequate access to its public goods to its immobile citizens. Communal public goods such as libraries, water supplies, police service, public transport, roads, universities, parks, hospitals, museums, or the army are usually universal and non-divisible. Theoretically, granting unlimited access to indivisible public goods to 'outsiders' can generate externalities in which a certain group of consumers free-ride on the financial commitments of others or crowd 'insiders' out from accessing such public goods. [117] In practice, however, the non-divisible nature of public goods entails that it can absorb

[114] Case C-8/02 *Leichtle* [2004] ECR I-2641 para 48. [115] *Müller-Fauré* para 106.

[116] Opinion of AG Colomer in Case C-444/05 *Stamatelaki* [2007] ECR I-3185 paras 42 and 59; see also Case C-444/05 *Stamatelaki* [2007] ECR I-3185 paras 26 and 38.

[117] If citizens evaluate a certain claim by outsiders as 'unreasonable', they may be inclined to reduce their own (no longer reciprocated) commitments to communal sharing. See A. Falk and U. Fischbacher, 'A Theory of Reciprocity' (2001) CESifo WP No 457, 3–4 for a theoretical explanation and 5–19 for economic analysis.

access of economically inactive Union citizens such as students or tourists. The consumption of communal goods by 'outsiders' does not necessarily increase the cost of their provision (as most costs are structural), nor automatically decrease the capacity of 'insiders' to make use of them. One more person in the park, museum, university, or queue to receive a swine flu shot will not make much difference. In other words, access of migrant Union citizens to many non-divisible public goods is often inconsequential, and can therefore not be limited.[118] This may be different where mass access to a public good by mobile EU citizens entails that a Member State can no longer sustain normative commitment vis-à-vis its own, immobile, citizens. Ultimately, this limit to aspirational solidarity is premised on the understanding that in regard of non-divisible public goods, such as hospitals or universities, nationals and non-nationals are simply not fully equal, as the latter do not meet the reciprocal commitments to adequate healthcare or social mobility that underlies access to those public goods.[119] This consequentialist limit to aspirational solidarity prevents the aspirations of mobile Union citizens from being pitted against those of immobile citizens, and prevents 'the social bond which provides *all* persons *equal* access to the achievements of the functional system on which they are dependent [from being] torn'.[120]

In respect of healthcare, this limit to aspirational solidarity primarily results from the amount of planning that is required to sustain access to high-quality and adequate healthcare. The territorial nature through which healthcare is delivered serves to allow Member States structurally to predict the demand in medical services and match it on the supply side. To put it in simple terms, if Belgium knows that it needs to treat on average 500 patients with TB each year, it will ensure adequate access for roughly that number. If 500 extra patients from the Netherlands seek treatment for that disease in Belgium, the latter's capacity to treat its own Belgian patients, to which it has an obligation to offer adequate healthcare, comes under pressure. Likewise, if all Belgian patients seek treatment in the Netherlands, Belgium will have wasted precious personal, financial, infrastructural, and

[118] Such a limit was, after all, based on a consequentialist argument. See section 5.1.

[119] As such, positively discriminating for a Member State's own nationals seems allowed as their social relationship with their state is presumed by the very fact that they are nationals. See K. Lenaerts and T. Heremans, 'Contours of a European Social Union in the Case-Law of the European Court of Justice' (2006) 2 European Constitutional Law Review 107, and AG Mazak in Case C-158/07 *Förster* [2008] ECR I-8507 para 67.

[120] Brunkhorst, *Solidarity*, 91, emphasis added.

medical resources on providing unused TB treatment options, which may lead, potentially, to a decrease in investment on cost-intensive treatments; leaving 'immobile' patients in the state of affiliation with a qualitatively impoverished health service.[121] While empirically speaking these situations seem improbable, the recently adopted Patients' Rights Directive explicitly poses a limit to cross-border access to healthcare in these situations. Article 4 (3) of Directive 2011/24 now reads as a textbook example of the theoretical limits to aspirational solidarity:

> The principle of non-discrimination with regard to nationality shall be applied (...) without prejudice to the possibility for the Member State of treatment, where justified (...) by planning requirements relating to the aim of ensuring sufficient and permanent access to a balanced range of high-quality treatment in the Member State concerned or the wish to control costs and avoid, as far as possible, any waste of financial, technical and human resources, to adopt measures regarding access to treatment aimed at fulfilling its fundamental responsibility to ensure sufficient and permanent access to healthcare within its territory.

The infrastructural exception to aspirational solidarity has been interpreted quite narrowly by the Court, which requires that Member States objectively and empirically[122] demonstrate the existence and scope of infrastructural pressures,[123] that equally effective and timely treatment is indeed available at home,[124] and that a causal link exists between the exercise of free movement and the concerns of the quality of available healthcare.[125] All these requirements conform with the consequentialist logic of the limits to aspirational solidarity defined above.[126] In practice, and as codified by the PRD, it appears that this exception is meant primarily to protect such treatment as 'requires use of highly specialised and cost-intensive medical infrastructure

[121] See Opinion of AG Sharpston in Case C-512/08 *Commission* v *France* [2010] ECR I-8833 para 78.

[122] This argument appears quite tenuous and speculative, given that aspirational movement by patients is (at least) equally likely to lead to *more* efficient provision of healthcare for those patients who prefer to 'stay at home', by limiting waiting times and creating incentives for healthcare systems to provide high-quality care. See Commission Impact Assessment for the Directive on Cross-border Healthcare, SEC (2008) 2163, 44–5 and 63. Even a conservative estimate has shown that it would save €180 million (taking account of compliance costs), and allow 780,000 extra patients to be treated.

[123] See list used by France in *Commission* v *France* para 9; *Inizan* para 57. See also recital 44 of Directive 2011/24.

[124] Articles 8 (5) and (6) (d) of the PRD, and *Müller-Fauré* paras 89–92.

[125] *Müller-Fauré* paras 83–5.

[126] See section 5.1.

or medical equipment',[127] and the availability of which is more contingent on continuous investments and thus more sensitive to patient outflow.[128] Any assessment will therefore ultimately be based on the projected number of mobile patients together with the amount invested in a certain piece of technology, its operating costs, and whether or not it uses specialized equipment,[129] and not, as suggested in earlier case law and doctrine, on the somewhat simplistic distinction between hospital and non-hospital care.[130] The Commission's capacity to control the use of this exception by the Member States[131] has been bolstered significantly by the obligation on Member States to notify the Commission on the types of treatment that they consider should fall under this exception.[132] In the area of healthcare, then, the aspirational right to access healthcare in whichever state the patient prefers finds a limit when it threatens structural access to adequate and high-quality care for immobile patients.

The same logic applies to cross-border access to universities in the EU. While host Member States are not obliged to extend financial benefits to migrants who do not work (and have a right to benefits under market solidarity) or are not sufficiently integrated (and have a right to benefits under communitarian solidarity), they must allow access to their universities on equal terms for all EU citizens. The aspirational role of cross-border access to university is evident—both on the level of the individual student and the EU level. As the Sorbonne Declaration puts it: 'Universities were born in Europe, some three-quarters of a millennium ago (...) In those times, students and academics would freely circulate and rapidly disseminate knowledge throughout the continent. Nowadays, too many of our students still graduate without having had the benefit of a study period outside of national boundaries.'[133] In the 1980s, the Court had already latched on to the idea that aspirational solidarity allows students to access universities in other Member States. In *Gravier*, it argued that 'access to vocational training is

[127] Article 8 (2) of Directive 2011/24.

[128] e.g. Case C-157/99 *Geraets-Smits and Peerbooms* [2001] ECR I-5473 para 106, or *Müller-Fauré* paras 90–2.

[129] Opinion of AG Sharpston in *Commission* v *France* paras 79ff.

[130] *Commission* v *France* para 34. In *Müller-Fauré* the Court still made this sharp distinction.

[131] *Commission* v *France*; Case C-211/08 *Commission* v *Spain* [2010] ECR I-5267; Case C-490/09 *Commission* v *Luxemburg* [2011] ECR I-247.

[132] See Articles 8 (2) and 7 (11) of Directive 2011/24.

[133] Sorbonne Declaration, available at: http://www.bologna-berlin2003.de/pdf/Sorbonne_declaration.pdf. Interestingly, this process took place outside the Union framework, even if it

in particular likely to promote free movement of persons throughout the Community (...) by enabling them to complete their training to develop their particular talents in the Member State whose vocational training programmes include the special subject desired'.[134] In *Gravier* the Court explicitly highlights the enabling capacity of the use of Europe's regulatory diversity, allowing students to find the '*special* subject desired' in order to 'develop their *particular* talents'.[135] The fact that an obligation of aspirational solidarity exists, requiring Member States to allow access for foreign nationals on equal terms as home nationals, is not disputed anymore. As the Court put it, it covers 'the opportunity for students coming from other Member States to gain access to higher education, an opportunity which constitutes the very essence of the principle of freedom of movement for students'.[136]

Aspirational solidarity, however, is a conditional obligation: it can be rebutted if Member States can demonstrate that they can no longer offer adequate access to university for its own immobile citizens. These limits have been discussed primarily with reference to the Belgian and Austrian higher education policies. Both Member States have opted to provide complete free access for their nationals. Yet both are faced with a big neighbouring Member State (France and Germany, respectively), which has opted for a more restrictive access policy in, mostly, medical studies. Their imposition of such *numerus clausus* regulations has generated a quite considerable migration of students from these Member States towards their smaller neighbours,[137] where, conveniently, the language of instruction is the same. Accordingly, both Belgium and Austria have tried to limit access of foreign EU students to certain specific medical degrees by requiring applicants to be included in the *numerus clausus* in their own Member State[138] and setting explicit quotas for the number of foreign students allowed to enter certain

could have been adopted by the Union. See, for that argument, S. Garben, *EU Higher Education Law: The Bologna Process and Harmonization by Stealth* (Kluwer 2011).

134 Case 293/83 *Gravier* [1985] ECR 593 para 24.

135 Emphases added.

136 Case C-73/08 *Bressol* [2010] ECR I-2735 para 79.

137 Austria indicated that it received up to five times as many foreign as home students in certain degrees, whereas in Belgium foreign students in veterinary degrees amounted to 86%. See C-147/03 *Commission* v *Austria* [2005] ECR I-5969 para 64 and section B12.1 of the referring court's ruling. Cour Constitutionelle, l'Arrêt n° 12/2008 du 14 février 2008, Numéros du rôle: 4034 et 4093.

138 The Belgian case is not particularly relevant since the Belgian government failed to submit justifications for its legislation. See Case C-65/03 *Commission* v *Belgium* [2004] ECR I-6427.

specified degrees.[139] The purpose of these limits was both to stabilize the financing of higher education and to ensure that sufficient medical personnel were trained that would remain on the territory of the state after the degree (the assumption being that German and French students would return to their home state upon completion of their degree). Both measures were challenged by the Commission,[140] which suspended the infringement procedures for five years in 2007 (for political reasons).[141] The suspension, however, did not halt the quota systems from being challenged before the Court. Only months after the armistice, the Belgian Constitutional Court referred a challenge led by Bressol and 59 other students and employees to Luxembourg.

The Court, in *Bressol*, appreciates that the demand to accommodate foreign students should not lead to Member States being unable to provide tertiary education (due to financial effects)[142] or decent healthcare (due to a shortage of doctors).[143] Accordingly, it argues that where it can be empirically demonstrated that the whole system of financing of education is jeopardized[144] by allowing unrestricted access to 'foreign' students, or that such access *directly* leads to the absence of sufficient medical personal within the territory of the Member State concerned,[145] Member States are

[139] Articles 4 and 7 of the Decree of the French Community of 16 June 2006 which regulates the number of students in certain programmes in the first two years of undergraduate studies in higher education (*Moniteur belge* of 6 July 2006, p. 34055). D. Damjanovic, 'Reserved Areas of the Member States and the ECJ: The Case of Higher Education', in B. de Witte and H. Miklitz (eds.), *The European Court of Justice and the Autonomy of the Member States* (Antwerp: Intersentia, 2012) 157.

[140] RAPID Press Release, Free movement of students: the Commission sends letters of formal notice to Austria and Belgium, 24 January 2007, Reference: IP/07/76.

[141] RAPID Press Release, Access to higher education: the Commission suspends its infringement cases against Austria and Belgium, 28 November 2007, Reference: IP/07/1788. While officially intended to allow the Member States to supply more detailed and accurate empirical evidence on the necessity of their restrictive policy, it has been argued that the suspension is the result of the political pressure exercised by Austria in the negotiations of the Lisbon Treaty. See also S. Garben, 'The Belgian/Austrian Education Saga' (2008) Harvard European Law Working Paper 2008/1, 9.

[142] See also C-147/03 *Commission* v *Austria* [2005] ECR I-5969 para 64 and section B12.1 of the referring court's ruling.

[143] Up to 78–86% in certain courses, according to referring court. See also C-147/03 *Commission* v *Austria* [2005] ECR I-5969 para 64 and section B12.1 of the referring court's ruling; and Garben 'The Belgian/Austrian Education Saga', 11.

[144] *Commission* v *Austria* paras 65–7. In *Bressol* this was not a relevant argument, as the financing of higher education in the French Community of Belgium takes place through a 'closed envelope' system, whereby the numbers of students have no impact on the allocation of funds. *Bressol* para 50.

[145] *Bressol* paras 72–3.

allowed to limit the number of foreign students admitted on equal terms as 'home' students. The Court thus imposes a very high empirical threshold before the demands of aspirational solidarity can be classified as having unreasonable consequences for the national welfare state.[146] The Court's approach is generally convincing, as is the imposition of very high empirical thresholds before financial or public health considerations can limit the demands of aspirational solidarity.[147] As AG Jacobs and AG Sharpston clarify, financial contribution by the host state is, after all, implicit both in the logic of regulatory movement and in the non-divisible nature of the public good,[148] and arguments on the basis of the protection of public health are generally premised on the mere presumption that students would return to their home state upon graduation,[149] as well as being logically incoherent.[150] Such concerns cannot limit the student's aspirational right to pursue a 'good life' through transnational access to universities.

The Court's approach is, however, *not* convincing in so far as it fails to discuss the arguably strongest claim by Belgium and Austria, namely that the demand of equal access undercuts the normative policy aim of ensuring free and democratic access to higher education.[151] A coherent interpretation of aspirational solidarity would, as argued above, find its limit in exactly these circumstances: it has consequences for the capacity of a Member State to protect normative commitments entered into by immobile citizens. Both

[146] In *Bressol*, the Court demands that the national court establish the maximum possible number of foreign students to be admitted, and that the causal link between non-resident students and shortage of personnel be clearly established before a quota system is declared compatible with Union law: *Bressol* paras 72–3.

[147] Such empirical requirements follow from the nature of the limits to aspirational solidarity as being consequentialist, that is, dependent on its *effect* on immobile citizens. Sharpston helpfully carried out an empirical assessment in a later education case, to emphasize how we should understand proportionality in aspirational solidarity. See Opinion of AG Sharpston in Case C-542/09 *Commission* v *Netherlands* EU:C:2012: 346 paras 117ff.

[148] See Opinion of AG Sharpston in *Bressol* paras 92–4; Opinion of AG Jacobs in *Commission* v *Austria* paras 42–4.

[149] Opinion of AG Sharpston in *Bressol* paras 115 and 119.

[150] According to the figures mentioned in *Bressol*, between 200 and 250 veterinarians a year used to enrol in the course. Supposedly this number matches the need for veterinarians in Belgium. The influx of non-resident students has increased the numbers of students (over the six years of the course) from 1,233 to 2,343 between 1996 and 2003. Surely the fact that it trains 750 students per year instead of 250 students per year contributes to solving this lack of medical personnel?

[151] C-147/03 *Commission* v *Austria* [2005] ECR I-5969 para 64 and Section B12.1 of the referring court's ruling.

AG Jacobs and AG Sharpston have picked this point up in their argumentation, and have both argued in favour of a more formal and mechanical logic of equal treatment, whereby any educational policy aim must be attained in a non-discriminatory manner, regardless of its effect on immobile citizens. AG Jacobs thus accepts that the demands of aspirational solidarity could skew national redistributive choices: 'clearly, the adoption of less discriminatory measures [governing access to Austrian universities] would require changes to the current system of unrestricted public access'.[152] Equally, AG Sharpston argues that student surplus may be an inherent consequence of the choice to have an open system of higher education, and that it cannot be remedied by discriminatory measures.[153] After all, Sharpston argues,

> if student numbers are a problem, they are not more or less problematic depending on where the extra students come from. The problem is an excess of student numbers per se, not an excess of non-resident student numbers. It seems, rather, that the intention of the Decree was to preserve unrestricted access to higher education for Belgians, while making it more difficult for those foreign students (coming mainly from France) for whom the higher education system in the French Community constitutes a natural alternative to access that system.[154]

It is true that in a course on Russian literature or political theory, a student surplus can only be problematic for the excess of student numbers per se, and can be solved by employing more teachers or expanding the number of students per class. Yet in medical studies, where the number of available places is finite, a student surplus *is* more or less problematic depending on where the students come from. Especially in medical studies, after all, infrastructural constraints exist in the provision of training. As aptly put by the Belgian constitutional court, it is 'not easy to provide for more childbirths and live animals to be tended to'.[155] Only so many students have a chance to receive practical experience each year, an experience that is evidently central in a student's training as a doctor or veterinarian. By allowing equal access for foreign students, Belgian students enter into competition for the available places, which could (and did) lead to such students being excluded from their chosen programme.[156] A more nuanced interpretation of aspirational

[152] Opinion of AG Jacobs in *Commission* v *Austria* para 53.

[153] Opinion of AG Sharpston in *Bressol* paras 100–13.

[154] Opinion of AG Sharpston in *Bressol* para 104.

[155] See also C-147/03 *Commission* v *Austria* [2005] ECR I-5969 para 64 and section B12.1 of the referring court's ruling.

[156] In fact, for a number of years Belgium held a competition for the available spaces. In 2005, of the 795 applicants only 192 possessed a secondary school degree from the territory

solidarity would entail that in areas where training capacities are intrinsically limited (only so many babies are born and sick animals need care) and where a Member State is trying to sustain a system of open access for all its nationals (as opposed to a system of *numerus clausus*), the obligations on the basis of aspirational solidarity can be limited to protect the Member State's capacity to allow its citizens to live a 'good life' in accordance with national commitments of justice. Aspirational solidarity does *not*, after all, require Member States to adapt their normative redistributive choices, which is exactly what would have happened:

> An admission policy that signals to students who graduated from a high school that they are welcome cuts deeply into the lives of adolescents since they are given leave to grow up and to enjoy their youth without having to worry too much about their scholastic performance (...) Young people can explore life without internalising the notorious nerdish obsession with how they perform in the eyes of their superiors. In fact, overcoming such a slavish concern is part of what it means to become an adult. Moreover, young people do not experience grades as determining their peer-group standing and, beyond that, their value as members of society. This type of egalitarianism makes people *more free* than a comparatively more 'competitive' system because the educational system forgets (and hence *forgives*) what they have done in the past.[157]

The question whether this substantive argument is valid is neither here nor there at this point. The concern that Somek correctly expresses is that it is hardly satisfactory to solve a clash between justice norms on the national level ('free access for all Austrian residents') and on the transnational level ('equal access for all Union citizens') by demanding unconditional deferral of the former to the latter, and thereby negating the distributive and normative choices made on the national level. Rather, the nature of the limits to aspirational solidarity is consequentialist: citizens without economic or social ties to the host state society can access such entitlements if their access is not to the detriment of access for citizens that *do* have such ties. While the Court mentions—in passing—that fully equal treatment might threaten the 'homogeneity' of the Belgian educational system,[158] it does not follow

of Wallonia, while only 34 of the 250 successful candidates did so, partly due to a preparatory course that French students undertake but Belgian students do not. See Garben, 'The Belgian/Austrian Education Saga', 11.

[157] A. Somek, 'Solidarity Decomposed: Being and Time in European Citizenship' (2007) 32 ELRev 817. Emphasis in orginal.

[158] *Bressol* para 53.

that concern to its logical conclusion. In *Bressol*, indeed, the Court brushes past any normative concerns about the sustainability of the Belgian policy of 'open and democratic access'. This is perhaps unsurprising given the strong aspirational nature of tertiary education and the tendency of the Court to employ a mechanical logic of equality in matters of cross-border access, but highlights that the Court has not yet grasped the precise nature of aspirational solidarity and its implicit theoretical differentiation between the rights of residents and non-residents, something that the Union legislator might have to correct as it did in the area of healthcare.[159]

5.5 Conclusion

Unlike market and communitarian solidarity, aspirational solidarity is not absolute and unconditional. While it reflects the promise that Member States will not limit the aspirations, choices, and capacity of their citizens to live a 'good life'—whatever that means to the individual citizen—it finds a limit where such choices have an impact on the sustainability of *communal* commitments of justice. As such, EU law forces Member States to re-examine the way in which, and reasons for which, they limit access to employment market, welfare resources, and public goods. At the same time, the limits to aspirational solidarity need to be carefully monitored by the Court if EU law is to enhance, rather than decrease, the capacity of *all* citizens to pursue the 'good life'.

[159] See Article 4 (3) of Directive 2011/24. AG Sharpston has already invited the EU legislator to allocate the costs of funding students more structurally between host and home state. See Opinion of AG Sharpston in *Bressol* paras 151–4.

Conclusion

This book is devoted to an analysis and rationalization of how the European Union can be understood from the perspective of justice. It suggests that the EU *can* significantly contribute to the pursuit of justice. The unique tiered institutional and normative structure of the EU allows for a more complete exploration of what justice is, means, and requires. At the same time, this tiered model of justice is inherently unstable—as it is not backed up by a sufficiently sophisticated political process that can mediate in case of 'conflicts of justice'. In order to contribute to the pursuit of justice in a meaningful manner, then, EU institutions must be very sensitive both to the *existence* and to the *limits* of the different forms of transnational solidarity that have emerged in the EU.

Disentangling the Pursuit of Justice from the Nation State

EU law has successfully managed to disentangle the pursuit of justice from the structures of the nation state. In doing so, it suggests that a tiered institutional and normative framework that takes account both of the nation state and the European Union is better able to fulfil what justice requires. Such a framework is able, after all, not only to reflect collective conceptions of 'the good' (on the national level), but also simultaneously to allow for the individual's pursuit of his or her individual conception of 'the good'. European Union law's structural commitment to extricating the development of justice from the confines of the nation state can be explained in both institutional and normative terms.

In institutional terms, EU law's focus on extricating the pursuit of justice from the nation state serves to demonstrate the added value of the integration process. As Breton has highlighted, the stability of a composite legal and political order crucially depends on (the perception that) both its national and its supranational institutions participate in the generation of the preconditions for the individual to be able to live a 'good life'.[1] The Union's legitimacy, in other words, is to a large extent tied up with its capacity to offer to the individual possibilities that its Member States cannot, and to secure objectives that its Member States struggle to secure. In consequence, EU law is mainly concerned with offering the individual the possibility of pursuing his or her idea of 'the good' beyond the nation state. This is, of course, primarily reflected in the free movement provisions. Whether for reasons of love, work, weather, education, or family; whether aimed at understanding a new language, culture, or cuisine, or discovering a new type of social life; whether for the adventure or for specific aspirations; EU law offers each citizen the capacity to move to the place that best represents his or her particular idea of the 'good life', in a way that Member States cannot.

In normative terms, EU law's focus on extricating the pursuit of justice from the nation state serves to reflect the associative ties that have emerged between citizens *across* and *beyond* national borders. As this book emphasizes, justice is an associative commitment: it is born and sustained by the interaction between particular groups of citizens. Commitments of solidarity, in consequence, exist between citizens that stand in a particular relationship with each other. This might take place within nation states, but also takes place beyond and between nation states. While the sophisticated institutional structure of the nation state is perfectly set up to reflect and articulate internal commitments of justice, it cannot conceptualize the commitments of justice that follow from the relationships between citizens across borders. European Union law fills this normative vacuum. It ensures that the associative connections between citizens across borders are incorporated within the pursuit of justice on the national level by way of the three different ideas of transnational solidarity.

The concept of transnational solidarity serves to 'translate' the associative connections between citizens across borders—which may come in

[1] R. Breton, 'Identification in Transnational Political Communities', in K. Knop, S. Ostryn, R. Simeon, and K. Dwinton (eds.), *Rethinking Federalism: Citizens, Markets, and Governments in a Changing World* (New Brunswick: UBC, 1995) 42.

economic, social, or political forms—into specific rights and entitlements. This book has conceptualized three different types of associative connection that have emerged in the course of the integration process. The first type of solidarity that exists in the EU was defined as 'market solidarity'. Market solidarity tells us something about the way in which transnational economic interactions reshape our commitments of justice. It suggests that economic engagement alone (rather than residence or nationality) constitutes a motive for sharing resources between citizens. The second type of solidarity that has emerged in the EU can best be understood as 'communitarian solidarity'. This solidarity describes the commitments of justice that are implicit in the social, quotidian interaction between citizens in a particular society. It suggests that mere co-presence of individuals (rather than nationality or economic engagement) constitutes a motive for sharing resources with fellow citizens. At the same time, as was discussed, the rights and obligations that are derived from co-presence are staggered: a Greek citizen who has just arrived in Bordeaux has fewer claims to welfare benefits than an Irish citizen who has lived there for 20 years. The third transnational solidarity that is implicit in the integration project has been described as 'aspirational solidarity'. This type of solidarity tells us something about the commitments of justice that follow from the Member States' shared political project. In this sense, it suggests that simply being subject to EU law (rather than nationality, co-presence, or economic engagement) constitutes a motive for citizens to share resources. This third type of solidarity, for evident reasons, is very thin and open to contestation. As discussed above, then, it is a conditional type of solidarity, in so far as it finds its limit where it undermines thicker commitments of justice.[2]

These three ways in which EU law 'translates' the associative commitments between citizens across borders into norms of justice are deeply embedded in EU law. Both the Union legislator and the Court intuitively and implicitly articulate these norms. In doing so, they give substance to the Union's commitment to justice and demonstrate why the Union can (perhaps should) play that role: it can exhaust what justice is, means, and requires in a more complete and coherent manner than Member States can when acting on their own.

[2] J. Waldron, 'Special Ties and Natural Duties' (1993) 22 Philosophy and Public Affairs 3.

The Limits of Tiered Justice in the EU

The way in which the EU contributes to the pursuit of justice is, at the same time, inherently unstable.[3] EU law must be extremely sensitive to its own limits—which are both institutional and normative—at the risk of destabilizing rather than furthering the pursuit of justice in Europe. These limitations have not always been observed by the Union's institutions. This has led to the emergence of a powerful narrative in EU studies, which suggests that the EU is committed to a particularly impoverished vision of the 'good life' that is insensitive to, and even hollows out, the different national conceptions of justice. Evidently, such criticism undermines both the legitimacy and stability of the Union's engagement in the pursuit of justice.

The first limitation that the EU faces in its pursuit of justice can be described in institutional terms. The EU does not dispose of the institutional sophistication required in order legitimately to articulate an autonomous conception of supranational justice. It lacks a robust political process, and crucial social and political structures for cleavage management and centre formation. In consequence, the EU cannot engage in the definition of supranational ideas of equality, fairness, or distributive justice in a legitimate way. In simple terms, its current institutional set-up cannot make sense of such crucial questions of justice. Instead, the Union's idea of justice is *relational*: it depends on the existence (or not) of associative ties between citizens—which tell us something about whether (or not) to extend domestic visions of equality, fairness, or distributive justice to include certain categories of non-nationals.

The Union legislator is sensitive to this institutional limit. The majority of labour law directives, or the more recently adopted Patient's Rights Directive, for example, do not elaborate new supranational conceptions of equality, fairness, or distributive justice. Instead, they explicitly serve to insulate domestic articulations of these values while at the same time incorporating the demands of transnational solidarity.[4] The Court struggles much more to remain sensitive to the Union's institutional limits in the pursuit of justice. To some extent, this follows from the awkward institutional role of the Court. As the reader will have noticed, most 'conflicts of justice' that have emerged in the course of the integration process have been mediated by the

[3] D. Chalmers, 'Gauging the Cumbersomeness of EU Law' (2009) 2 LEQS 3.

[4] See sections 3.3. and 5.4.

Court without the backing of a sophisticated political structure. Questions of justice, however (in balancing between the rights of labour and capital, or in deciding on the minimum healthcare options to be available for all citizens), are deeply political and politicized questions. Only a mediation process that is structured through political institutions can legitimately make sense of them. In consequence, the occasional desire of the Court to answer such political questions itself (rather than deferring to domestic answers) is deeply problematic. First, the absence of a strong political system on the European level makes the Court more sensitive to functional than to normative understandings of justice.[5] The Court's interpretation of equality in the workplace,[6] of the objective and nature of higher education,[7] and of the appropriate balance between 'labour' and 'capital' on the internal market[8] have all been heavily criticized on this account. Fundamentally, this critique suggests that answering questions of justice in the absence of a sufficiently sophisticated political structure that can legitimize the answer leads to significant instances of *injustice*. Second, the incomplete institutional structure of the EU makes the Court's substantive answers as to what justice requires particularly sticky. Changing, say, the balance between labour and capital on the internal market in the aftermath of the Court's rulings in *Viking* and *Laval* requires unanimous agreement between the Member States (as well as the consent of national parliaments). Justice, however, is a living thing. It must be able to accommodate changing visions of the 'good life', of the limits of state responsibility, the claims made by social and political movements or historic events. Entrenching a specific answer to the question of justice rather than deferring to the (national) political process, then, risks depoliticizing (and thereby delegitimizing) the question of justice, as well as its answers.[9]

The second element that makes the Union's engagement in the pursuit of justice inherently unstable is not institutional but normative. Justice is, as discussed throughout this book, a relational concept. The transnational solidarities indeed serve to 'translate' a specific contextual relationship into specific rights and obligations of justice. In doing so, it is very sensitive to

[5] M. P. Maduro, 'European Constitutionalism and Three Models of Social Europe', in M. Hesselink, *The Politics of a European Civil Code* (Alphen aan den Rijn: Kluwer, 2006) 127.

[6] See A. Somek, *Engeneering Equality* (Oxford: OUP, 2011).

[7] *Giersch* suggests a deeply instrumental view: higher education serves to make useful market participants. See Case C-20/12 *Giersch* EU:C:2013:411.

[8] See section 3.3.

[9] See, on the risks of depoliticization, F. De Witte, 'EU Law, Politics and the Social Question' (2013) 14 GLJ 591.

changes in context. It ensures—in simple terms—that a Latvian national who has only just arrived in Madrid has fewer claims to welfare benefits than his or her Belgian neighbour who has worked in Madrid for 20 years. This contextual approach guarantees that the development of justice in the EU remains sensitive to its own limits and does not stretch domestic commitments of solidarity too far. Including migrants into welfare schemes regardless of their specific engagement with the host polity, after all, would impose 'unreasonable burdens' on the welfare state of that polity. The Court has not always understood the need carefully to contextualize its demands of free movement and non-discrimination. On the one hand it does not always pay sufficient attention to the nature and social function of the welfare benefit that it discusses—leading to misunderstandings about the type of commitment that a migrant must show before being granted access. Cases such as *Laval*, *Geven*, and *Bressol*[10] have been criticized on this account. On the other hand, it sometimes pays too much attention to the individual's connections to the host state polity. In cases such as *Prete* or *Prinz*, the Court clearly suggests that the assessment of the scope and limits of transnational solidarity is dependent on a careful contextualization of the claim of migrants in the light of their specific economic, social, cultural, linguistic, and geographical connections to the host state. In these cases, however, the Court risks overshooting the mark. It is one thing, after all, to say that an economic, social, cultural, linguistic, or geographical connection is necessary before an individual can access welfare benefits in the host state; but it is an altogether different thing to suggest (as the Court seems to do) that *any* of these connections—on their own—are sufficient to do so. Again, the risk here is that EU law creates instances of injustice, in the sense of extending access to migrants who cannot demonstrate the required specific connection to the host state (or, conversely, limits access for migrants who can in fact demonstrate the required specific connection to that state). The Court should contextualize relational commitments more explicitly and precisely. If the engagement of the EU in the pursuit of justice is to further rather than inhibit its attainment, after all, the Union institutions need to be sensitive to the limits of their possible contribution—in both institutional and normative terms.

[10] Case C-341/05 *Laval* [2005] ECR I-11767; Case C-213/05 *Geven* [2007] ECR I-6347; and Case C-73/08 *Bressol* [2010] ECR I-2735. See sections 3.3, 3.2, and 5.4, respectively.

Separating the Nation from the State

This book has argued that the European Union can help to explore more fully what justice is, means, and requires, as long as it remains sensitive to its own limitations in the process. In doing so, the EU successfully manages to transcend the basic paradox of justice. That paradox, as discussed in the Introduction, involves the fact that while claims of justice are universal, their implementation is necessarily limited to the spatial context within which its institutions operate: the nation state. The complex political structures required in order to make sense of contradictory and overlapping conceptions of the 'good life' that citizens may have, as well as the moral resources that are required in order to sustain redistributive practices, can be found only on the national level. Even the EU, being the most advanced and sophisticated institutional setting beyond the state, comes nowhere near reproducing these structures. At the same time, the EU has managed to create a legal edifice whereby national institutions take account of the commitments of justice that have emerged on the level beyond the state—and more specifically those commitments of justice that follow from cross-border associations between citizens—be it in economic, social, or political terms. It can be argued that in doing so the EU does not come much closer to transcending the paradox of justice—in the sense that the universal nature of claims of justice does not now find its limit at the borders of the state but at the borders of the EU. At the same time it appears that there is not much particularly European about the type of justice defended in this book. Yes, it is based on far-reaching and long-term commitments of economic, social, and political cooperation between nation states that might be difficult to imagine beyond Europe. But this book suggests that the pursuit of justice beyond the state primarily centres on the associative ties between citizens that follow from such commitments, not a particularly European conception of 'the good'.

There is nevertheless one particularity about the development of justice as described in this book. It makes—far below the surface—one fundamental point: the ethnic idea of the nation is deeply problematic. The reason why EU law problematizes the ethnic idea of the nation state is because of its potential to oppress the individual and because of its capacity to create significant instances of injustice, that is, severely limit the capacity for human flourishing and happiness. Properly understood, this seems to reflect two concerns. First, the ethnic idea of the nation state stands in the way of a meaningful pursuit of justice by obscuring the source of our commitment to justice. Understanding justice as a relational commitment suggests, after all, that it is *not* primarily dependent on nationality (and the strong ethno-cultural similarities between citizens that it presupposes) but rather on specific instances of participation, co-presence, and mutual interaction between individuals. The motive for sharing resources with 'others' in order to alleviate their needs or to realize their aspirations is not their nationality, but their co-presence in a physical environment, their engagement in material or symbolic exchanges, and the interdependencies that follow from such exchanges. Nationality might serve as an indicator of a certain degree of social integration in a particular state, but, in EU law, cannot automatically entitle an individual to a range of social entitlements.[11] This relegation of the concept of nationality from its role as a status and a bundle of rights to a role as a proxy for social integration serves to highlight what the *real* sources of our commitments to justice are.

The second reason why EU law problematizes the nation state in the pursuit of justice is that the nation state is not particularly good at allowing for self-determination of citizens—in the sense of offering citizens the freedom to decide with which specific groups, communities, or individuals to build meaningful relationships of co-presence or mutual engagement. The nation state—with its petrified political systems, cleavages, group structures, and modes of communication—is not sufficiently sensitive to the individual's understanding of the world and his or her 'self'. While the relentless decrease of barriers to movement, communication, information, and choice has created increasingly pluralist and complex societies, allowing citizens endless new frameworks for self-identification, socialization, co-presence, and mutual engagement, the method of the nation state still primarily understands the citizen as a *national*. Citizens may indeed identify with their fellow nationals and wish to articulate the commitments of justice that follow from this identification, but they may also feel the same identification with citizens with whom they share a city, a taste in music or food, a sexual orientation, language, aesthetic, favourite pub or sport, a profession or religion, internet forum, or cycle route. To put it as simply as possible, EU law suggests that in pluralist, complex societies with endless possibilities of communication and mobility, the individual's choices may be a better indicator of their self-understanding than their nationality. As self-understanding

[11] See Opinion of AG Sharpston in Joined Cases C-523/11 and C-585/11 *Prinz and Seeberger* EU:C:2013:524 para 98.

and modes of socialization become more complex and pluralist, then, so the centrality of the political process in defining what justice requires, with its conception of identity as being related to ethnicity and nationality alone, becomes more problematic. Sen explains:

> a person belongs to many different groups (related to gender, class, language group, profession, nationality, community, race, religion and so on), and to see them merely as a member of just one particular group would be a major denial of each person to decide how exactly to see himself or herself. The increasing tendency towards seeing people in terms of one dominant 'identity' (...) is not only an imposition of an external and arbitrary priority, but also the denial of an important liberty of a person who can decide on their respective loyalties to different groups.[12]

This insight from social choice theory, which stresses the importance of allowing individuals to rank available realizations of their lives in reference to their *own* priorities, suggests that transnational solidarity can be understood as an emancipatory device. It emancipates the individual from the narrative of the nation state, not only by allowing citizens to move to Berlin, Athens, Florence, or Malmö in pursuit of their dreams—be they related to work, love, fun, food, weather, culture, or family—but also by carving out space for new forms of associative commitments to be articulated, whether within or between Member States. The different types of transnational solidarity, then, structurally liberate the individual from the oppression of 'the political' and 'the national', and force—much like the integration process as such—the rationalization of the public power accorded to the nation state. As this book suggests, a nuanced and tiered understanding of justice, which builds on the institutional structures of the *state* while emancipating the individual and his choices from the *nation*, offers the beguiling spectre of a Union that more fully satisfies what justice is, means, and requires than its Member States possibly could.

[12] A. Sen, *The Idea of Justice* (Basingstoke: Penguin, 2010) 246–7.

REFERENCES

Alkire, S., *Valuing Freedoms: Sen's Capability Approach and Poverty Reduction* (Oxford: OUP, 2002).

Apps, K., 'Damages Claims against Trade Unions after *Viking* and *Laval*' (2009) 34 ELRev 141.

Ashiagbor, D., *The European Employment Strategy: Labour Market Regulation and New Governance* (Oxford: OUP, 2005).

Ashiagbor, D., 'Collective Labour Rights and the European Social Model' (2009) 3 Law & Ethics of Human Rights 222.

Ashiagbor, D., 'Unravelling the Embedded Liberal Bargain: Labour and Social Welfare Law in the Context of EU Market Integration' (2013) 19 ELJ 307.

Azoulai, L., 'The Court of Justice and the Social Market Economy: The Emergence of an Ideal and the Conditions for its Realisation' (2008) 45 CML Rev 1340.

Bacharach, S., and Lawler, E., *Bargaining: Power, Tactics and Outcomes* (San Francisco: Jossey-Bass, 1981).

Bachman, P., 'Social Needs, Development, Territories and Full Employment Based on Solidarity', in R. Salais and R. Villeneuve (eds.), *Europe and the Politics of Capabilities* (Cambridge: CUP, 2004).

Balibar, E., *We, The People of Europe* (Princeton, NJ: Princeton University Press, 2004).

Barnard, C., 'The Changing Scope of the Fundamental Principle of Equality?' (2001) 46 McGill Law Journal 955.

Barnard, C., 'EU Citizenship and the Principle of Solidarity', in M. Dougan and E. Spaventa (eds.), *Social Welfare and EU Law* (Oxford: Hart, 2005).

Barnard, C., 'The UK and Posted Workers: The Effect of *Commission* v *Luxembourg* on the Territorial Application of British Labour Law' (2009) 38 ILJ 126.

Barnard, C., 'EU Social Policy: From Employment Law to Labour Market Reform', in P. Craig and G. De Búrca (eds.), *The Evolution of EU Law* (Oxford: OUP, 2011).

Barnard, C., and Deakin, S., 'Market Access and Regulatory Competition', in C. Barnard and J. Scott (eds.), *The Law of the Single Market: Unpacking the Premises* (Oxford: Hart, 2002).

Bartolini, S., 'Old and New Peripheries in the Process of European Territorial Integration', in C. Ansell and G. Di Palma (eds.), *Restructuring Territoriality* (Cambridge: CUP, 2004).

Bartolini, S., *Restructuring Europe* (Oxford: OUP, 2007).

Bauböck, R., 'Why European Citizenship?' (2007) 8 Theoretical Inquiries into Law 471.

Bauböck, R., 'The Three Levels of Citizenship within the European Union' (2014) 15 GLJ 751.

Beck, U., 'The European Crisis in the Context of Cosmopolitanism' (2012) 43 New Literary History 659.

Bellamy, R., 'The Liberty of the Post-Moderns: Market and Civic Freedom within the EU' (2009) 1 LEQS.

Bellamy, R., and Castiglione, D., 'Three Models of Democracy, Political Community and Representation in the EU' (2013) 20 JEPP 217.

Benhabib, S., *Rights of Others* (Cambridge: CUP, 2004).

Benhabib, S., *Another Cosmopolitanism* (Oxford: OUP, 2006).

Bercusson, B., *European Labour Law* (Cambridge: CUP, 2009).

Berlin, I., 'Two Concepts of Liberty', in H. Hardy (ed.), *Isaiah Berlin: Incorporating Four Essays on Liberty* (Oxford: OUP, 2002).

Bernard, N., 'Between a Rock and a Soft Place: Internal Market Vs. Open Coordination', in M. Dougan and E. Spaventa (eds.), *EU Social Welfare Law* (Oxford: Hart, 2005).

Bernitz, U., and Reich, N., 'Case Note on Case A 268/04, The Labour Court, Judgment No. 89/09, *Laval*' (2011) 48 CML Rev 611.

Blauberger, M., 'With Luxembourg in Mind...the Remaking of National Policies in the Face of ECJ Jurisprudence' (2012) 19 JEPP 109.

Breton, R., 'Identification in Transnational Political Communities', in K. Knop, S. Ostryn, R. Simeon, and K. Dwinton (eds.), *Rethinking Federalism: Citizens, Markets, and Governments in a Changing World* (Vancouver: University of British Columbia Press, 1995).

Browne, J., Deakin, S., and Wilkinson, F., 'Capabilities, Social Rights and European Market Integration', in R. Salais and R. Villeneuve (eds.), *Europe and the Politics of Capabilities* (Cambridge: CUP, 2004).

Brunkhorst, H., *Solidarity: From Civic Friendship to a Global Legal Community* (Cambrige, Mass.: MIT, 2005).

Buchanan, J., 'Social Choice, Democracy and Free Markets' (1954) 62 Journal of Political Economy 114.

Buchanan, J., 'Federalism and Individual Sovereignty' (1996) 15 Cato Journal 266.

Cabral, P., 'The Internal Market and the Right to Cross-Border Healthcare' (2004) 29 ELRev 677.

Calhoun C., *Nations Matter: Culture, History and the Cosmopolitan Dream* (New York: Routledge, 2007).

Chalmers, D., 'Gauging the Cumbersomeness of EU Law' (2009) 2 LEQS.

Chalmers, D., 'The European Redistributive State and a European Law of Struggle' (2012) 18 ELJ 667.

Chalmers, D., 'Democratic Self-Government in Europe: Domestic Solutions to the EU Legitimacy Crisis' (Policy Network Paper 2013).

Chalmers, D., 'European Restatements of Sovereignty' (2013) LSE Law WP 14.

Chalmers, D., and Booth, S., 'A European Labour Market with National Welfare Systems: A Proposal for a New Citizenship and Integration Directive' (2014) Open Europe Policy Brief.

Cohen, J., and Sabel, C., 'Global Democracy?' (2005) 37 NYU Journal of International Law and Politics 763.

Collins, H., *The European Civil Code: The Way Forward* (Cambridge: CUP, 2008).

Copeland, P., and Ter Haar, B., 'The (In)Effectiveness of the European Employment Strategy' (2013) 23 Journal of European Social Policy 21.

Damjanovic, D., 'Reserved Areas of the Member States and the ECJ: The Case of Higher Education', in B. De Witte and H. Miklitz (eds.), *The European Court of Justice and the Autonomy of the Member States* (Antwerp: Intersentia, 2012).

Damjanovic, D., 'The EU Market Rules as Social Market Rules: Why the EU Can Be a Social Market Economy' (2013) 50 CML Rev 1685.

Damjanovic, D., and de Witte, B., 'Welfare Integration through EU Law: The Overall Picture in the Light of the Lisbon Treaty', in U. Neergaard, R. Nielsen, and L. Roseberry (eds.), *Integrating Welfare Functions into EU Law* (Copenhagen: DJOF, 2009).

Dann, P., 'European Parliament and Executive Federalism: Approaching a Parliament in a Semi-Parliamentary Democracy' (2003) 9 ELJ 558.

Davies, P., 'Market Integration and Social Policy in the Court of Justice' (1995) 24 ILJ 49.

Davies, P., 'Posted Workers: Single Market or Protection of National Labour Law Systems?' (1997) 34 CML Rev 571.

Davies, P., 'Case Note on Case C-346/06 *Ruffert*' (2008) 37 ILJ 293.

Dawson, M., and De Witte, F., 'Constitutional Balance in the EU after the Euro-crisis' (2013) 76 MLR 817.

Dawson, M., and De Witte, F., 'From Balance to Conflict: A New Constitution for Europe' (2015) 20 ELJ (forthcoming).

Dawson, M., and De Witte, F., 'Self-Determination in the Constitutional Future of the EU' (2015) 20 ELJ (forthcoming).

Deakin, S., 'Labour Law as Market Regulation: The Economic Foundations of European Social Policy', in P. Davies, A. Lyon-Caen, S. Sciarra, and S. Simitis (eds.), *European Community Labour Law: Principles and Perspectives* (Oxford: Clarendon, 1996).

Deakin, S., 'The Capability Concept and the Evolution of European Social Policy', in M. Dougan and E. Spaventa (eds.), *Social Welfare and EU Law* (Oxford: Hart, 2005).

Deakin, S., 'Legal Diversity and Regulatory Competition: Which Model for Europe?' (2006) 12 ELJ 448.

Deakin, S., 'Regulatory Competition after *Laval*' (2008) 10 CYELS 581.

Deakin, S., 'Reflexive Harmonisation and European Company Law' (2009) 15 ELJ 224.

Deakin, S., and Wilkinson, F., 'Rights vs. Efficiency? The Economic Case for Transnational Labour Standards' (1994) 23 ILJ 296.

De Groot, G. R., 'Towards a European Nationality Law', in H. Schneider (ed.), *Migration, Integration and Citizenship: A Challenge for Europe's Future* (Maastricht: Forum Maastricht, 2005), i.

Delanty, G., *Citizenship in a Global Age: Society, Culture, Politics* (Milton Keynes: Open University Press, 2000).

Delanty, G., *Formations of European Modernity* (London: Palgrave Macmillan, 2013).

Dewhurst, E., 'Intergenerational Balance, Mandatory Retirement and Age Discrimination in Europe: How Can the ECJ Better Support the National Courts in Finding a Balance between the Generations?' (2013) 50 CML Rev 1343.

De Witte, B., 'Non-Market Values in Internal Market Legislation', in N. Nic Shuibhne (ed.), *Regulating the Internal Market* (Cheltenham: Edward Elgar, 2006).

De Witte, F., 'The Ends of EU Citizenship and the Means of Non-Discrimination' (2011) 18 MJ 86.

De Witte, F., 'EU Law, Politics and the Social Question' (2013) 14 GLJ 591.

De Witte, F., 'Sex, Drugs and EU Law: The Recognition of Moral and Ethical Diversity in EU Law' (2013) 50 CML Rev 1545.

De Witte, F., 'Union Citizenship and Constrained Democracy', in A. P. Van der Mei and M. De Visser (eds.), *Twenty Years Treaty on European Union: Reflections from Maastricht* (Antwerp: Intersentia, 2013).

De Witte, F., 'Who Funds the Mobile Student? Shedding Some Light on the Normative Assumptions Underlying EU Free Movement Law: *Commission* v *Netherlands*' (2013) 50 CML Rev 203.

Dougan, M., 'The Court Helps Those Who Help Themselves...The Legal Status of Migrant Work-seekers under Community Law in the Light of the *Collins* Judgment' (2005) 1 European Journal of Social Security 15.

Dougan, M., 'Fees, Grants, Loans, and Dole Cheques: Who Covers the Costs of Migrant Education within the EU?' (2005) 42 CML Rev 954.

Dougan, M., 'The Constitutional Dimension of the Case Law on Union Citizenship' (2006) 31 ELRev 613.

Dougan, M., and Spaventa, E., '"Wish you weren't here...": New Models of Social Solidarity in the European Union', in M. Dougan and E. Spaventa (eds.), *Social Welfare and EU Law* (Oxford: Hart, 2005).

Durkheim, E., *The Division of Labour in Society* (Bqsingstoke: Palgrave. 1984).

Dustmann, C., and Frattini, T., 'The Fiscal Effects of Immigration to the UK' (2014) 124 Economic Journal 563.

Eleftheriadis, P., 'Citizenship and Obligation', in J. Dickson and P. Eleftheriadis (eds.), *Philosophical Foundations of European Union Law* (Oxford: OUP, 2012).

Esping-Andersen, G., *The Three Worlds of Welfare Capitalism* (Cambridge: CUP, 1990).

Fabbrini, F., and Granat, K., 'Yellow Card but No Foul: The Role of National Parliaments under the Subsidiarity Protocol and the Commission Proposal for an EU Regulation of the Right to Strike' (2013) 50 CML Rev 115.

Faist. T., 'Social Citizenship in the European Union: Nested Membership' (2001) 39 JCMS 51.

Falk, A., and Fischbacher, U., 'A Theory of Reciprocity' (2001) CESifo WP No. 457.

Favell, A., *Eurostars and Eurocities* (Oxford: Blackwell, 2008).

Favell, A., and Recchi, E., 'Social Mobility and Spatial Mobility', in A. Favell and V. Guirandon, *Sociology of the European Union* (Basingstoke: Palgrave, 2011).

Ferrera, M., *The Boundaries of Welfare* (Oxford: OUP, 2005).

Ferrera, M., 'The JCMS Annual Lecture: National Welfare States and European Integration: In Search of a "Virtuous Nesting"' (2009) 47 JCMS 223.

Fligstein, N., *Euro-Clash: The EU, European Identity, and the Future of Europe* (Oxford: OUP, 2010).

Follesdal, A., 'Union Citizenship: Unpacking the Beast of Burden' (2001) 20 Law and Philosophy 326.

Follesdal, A., and Hix S, 'Why is there a Democratic Deficit in the EU: A Reply to Moravcsik' (2006) 44 JCMS 533.

Garben, S., 'The Belgian/Austrian Education Saga' (2008) Harvard European Law Working Paper 2008/1.

Garben, S., *EU Higher Education Law: The Bologna Process and Harmonization by Stealth* (Alphen den Rijn: Kluwer, 2011).

Giubboni, S., *Social Rights and Market Freedom in the European Constitution: A Labour Law Perspective* (Cambridge: CUP, 2006).

Giubboni, S., 'Free Movement of Persons and European Solidarity' (2007) 13 ELRev 361.

Giubboni, S., 'European Citizenship and Social Rights in Time of Crisis' (2014) 15 GLJ 935.

Glyn, A., *Capitalism Unleashed: Finance, Globalization and Welfare* (Oxford: OUP, 2007).

Golynker, O., 'Student Loans: The European Concept of Social Justice According to *Bidar*' (2006) 31 ELRev 394.

Golynker, O., 'Case Note on *Förster*' (2009) 46 CML Rev 2033.

Green, T. H., *The Political Theory of T. H. Green: Selected Writings* (New York: Appleton-Century-Crofts, 1964).

Greer, S., and Sokol, T., 'Rules for Rights: European Law, Health Care and Social Citizenship' (2014) 20 ELJ 79.

Griffin, J., *On Human Rights* (Oxford: OUP, 2008).

Grimm, D., 'Does Europe Need a Constitution?' (1995) 1 ELJ 293.

Gutman, A., 'Democratic Citizenship', in J. Cohen (ed.), *For Love of Country: Debating the Limits of Patriotism* (Boston, Mass.: Beacon, 1996).

Habermas, J., 'Struggles for Recognition in the Democratic Constitutional State', in A. Gutmann (ed.), *Multiculturalism: Examining the Politics of Recognition* (Princeton, NJ: Princeton University Press, 1994).

Habermas, J., *The Inclusion of the Other* (Cambridge, Mass.: MIT, 1998).

Habermas, J., *The Crisis of the European Union* (Malden, Mass.: Polity, 2012).

Habermas, J., 'The Crisis of the European Union in the Light of a Constitutionalization of International Law' (2012) 23 EJIL 338.

Habermas, J., 'Democracy, Solidarity and the European Crisis', Lecture delivered on 26 April 2013 in Leuven.

Halberstam, D., 'The Bride of Messina: Constitutionalism and Democracy in Europe' (2005) 30 ELRev 777.

Halberstam, M., *Totalitarianism and the Modern Conception of Politics* (New Haven, Conn.: Yale University Press, 1999).

Hartley, T., 'Equal Treatment in Education', in N. Green, T. Hartley, and J. Usher (eds.), *The Legal Foundations of the Single European Market* (Oxford: OUP, 1991).

Hatzopoulos, V., and Do, T. U., 'The Case Law of the ECJ Concerning the Free Provision of Services: 2000–2005' (2006) 43 CML Rev 972.

Held, D., 'Between the State and Civil Society: Citizenship', in G. Andrews (ed.), *Citizenship* (London: Lawrence & Wishart, 1991).

Held, D., and McGrew, A., *The Global Transformation Reader* (Cambridge: Polity, 2000).

Hemerijck, A., 'The Self-Transformation of the European Social Model(s)', in G. Esping-Andersen (ed.), *Why We Need a Welfare State* (Oxford: OUP, 2002).

Heritier, A., 'Elements of Democratic Legitimation in Europe: An Alternative Perspective' (1999) 6 JEPP 278.

Herzog, R., and Gerken, L., 'Stop the European Court of Justice', Frankfurter Allgemeine Zeitung, 8 September 2008.

Honneth, A., 'Redistribution as Recognition: A Response to Nancy Fraser', in N. Fraser and A. Honneth, *Redistribution or Recognition: A Politico-Philosophical Exchange* (London: Verso, 2003).

Honneth, A., *The I in We: Studies in the Theory of Recognition* (Cambridge: Polity, 2012).

Höpner, M., and Schäfer. A., 'Polanyi in Brussels? Embeddedness and the Three Dimensions of European Economic Integration' (2010) MPIfG Discussion Paper 10/8.

Höpner, M., and Schäfer, A., 'Embeddedness and Regional Integration: Waiting for Polanyi in a Hayekian Setting' (2012) 66 International Organisations 429.

Hyman, R., *Industrial Relations: A Marxist Introduction* (Basingstoke: Macmillan, 1975).

Joerges, C., 'European Law as Conflict of Laws', in C. Joerges and J. Neyer (eds.), *Deliberative Supranationalism Revisited* (2006) 20 EUI Working Paper.

Joppke, C., 'Transformation of Citizenship: Status, Rights, Identity' (2007) 11 Citizenship Studies 38.

Judt, T., *Ill Fares the Land* (New York: Penguin, 2010).

Kahn-Freud, O., 'Labour Law', in M. Ginsberg (ed.), *Law and Opinion in England in the 20th Century* (London: Stevens, 1959).

Kilpatrick, C., 'Laval's Regulatory Conundrum: Collective Standard-Setting and the Court's New Approach to Posted Workers' (2009) 34 ELRev 850.

Kingreen, T., 'Fundamental Freedoms', in A. Von Bogdandy and J. Bast (eds.), *Principles of European Constitutional Law* (Oxford: Hart, 2008).

Klymica, W., 'Liberal Nationalism and Cosmopolitan Justice', in S. Benhabib, *Another Cosmopolitanism* (Oxford: OUP, 2005).

Kochenov, D., 'The Right to Have What Rights? EU Citizenship in Need of Clarification' (2013) 19 ELJ 502.

Kostakopoulou, D., 'European Union Citizenship: Writing the Future' (2007) 13 ELJ 630.

Koutrakos, P., 'Healthcare as an Economic Service under EC Law', in M. Dougan and E. Spaventa (eds.), *Social Welfare and EU Law* (Oxford: Hart, 2005).

Kristeva, J., *Nations without Nationalism* (New York: Columbia University Press, 1993).

Kumm, M., 'Constitutionalising Subsidiarity in Integrated Markets: The Case of Tobacco Regulation in the European Union' (2006) 12 ELJ 513.

Kumm, M., 'The Idea of Socratic Contestation and the Right to Justification: The Point of Rights-Based Proportionality Review' (2010) 4 Law & Ethics of Human Rights 157.

Lafargue, P., *The Right to be Lazy, and Other Studies* (Chicago: Kerr, 1907).

Lenaerts, K., and Foubert, P., 'Social Rights in the Case-Law of the ECJ' (2001) 28 LIEI 267.

Lovett, F., and Pettit, P., 'Neorepublicanism, a Normative and Institutional Research Program' (2009) 12 Annual Review of Political Science 11.

Lord, C., 'The Democratic Legitimacy of Codecision' (2013) 20 JEPP 1056.

Lord, C., and Pollak, J., 'Unequal but Democratic? Equality According to Karlsruhe' (2013) 20 JEPP 190.

Luhmann, N., *Political Theory in the Welfare State* (Berlin: de Gruyter, 1990).

Lukes, S., 'Invasions of the Market', in M. Miller (ed.), *Worlds of Capitalism* (London: Routledge, 2005).

Maduro, M. P., 'Reforming the Market or the State? Article 30 and the European Constitution' (1997) 3 ELJ 62.

Maduro, M. P., *We, the Court* (Oxford: Hart, 1998).

Maduro, M. P., 'European Constitutionalism and Three Models of Social Europe', in M. Hesselink (ed.), *The Politics of a European Civil Code* (Alphen aan den Rijn: Kluwer, 2006).

Maduro, M. P., 'A New Governance for the European Union and the Euro: Democracy and Justice' (2012) RSCAS Policy Paper 2012/11.

Majone, G., *Rethinking the Union of Europe Post-Crisis* (Cambridge: CUP, 2014).

Mancini, G., 'Labour Law and Community Law' (1985) 20 The Irish Jurist 1.

Marshall, T. H., *Citizenship and Social Class* (London: Pluto, 1992).

Mayerfield, J., *Suffering and Moral Responsibility* (Oxford: OUP, 1999).

Menéndez, A., 'The Existential Crisis of the European Union' (2013) 14 GLJ 453.

Miller, D., *On Nationality* (Oxford: OUP, 1997).

Miller, D., *Citizenship and National Identity* (Cambridge: Polity, 2000).

Muir, E., 'Enhancing the Effects of Community Law on National Employment Policies: The *Mangold* Case' (2006) 31 ELRev 886.

Muir, E., *EU Regulation of Access to Labour Markets* (Alphe aan den Rijn: Kluwer, 2012).

Mulhall, S., and Swift, A., *Liberals and Communitarians* (Oxford: Blackwell, 2007).

Müller, J. W., *Contesting Democracy* (New Haven, Conn.: Yale University Press, 2011).

Müller, J. W., 'Beyond Militant Democracy' (2012) 73 NLR 44.

Murphy, C., 'An Effective Right to Cross-Border Healthcare? On Patients, Primacy and Procedural Autonomy: Comment on *Elchinov*' (2011) 36 ELRev 555.

Nagel, T., 'What is it Like to be a Bat?' (1974) 83 The Philosophical Review 441.

Nagel, T., 'The Problem of Global Justice' (2005) 33 Philosophy & Public Affairs 115.

Newdick, C., 'Citizenship, Free Movement and Healthcare: Cementing Individual Rights by Corroding Social Solidarity' (2006) 43 CML Rev 1645.

Newdick, C., 'The European Court of Justice, Transnational Healthcare, and Social Citizenship—Accidental Death of a Concept?' (2009) 26 Wisconsin International Law Journal 844.

Neyer, J., *The Justification of Europe: A Political Theory of Supranational Integration* (Oxford: OUP, 2012).

Nicol, D., *The Constitutional Protection of Capitalism* (Oxford: Hart, 2010).

Nussbaum, M., 'Political Liberalism and Respect: A Response to Linda Barclay' (2003) 4 Nordic Journal of Philosophy 42.

O'Brien, C., 'Real Links, Abstract Rights and False Alarms: The Relationship between the ECJ's "Real Link" Case Law and National Solidarity' (2008) 33 ELRev 653.

O'Brien, C., 'Case Note on *Teixeira* and *Ibrahim*' (2011) 47 CML Rev 203.

Offe, C., 'Whose Good is the Common Good?' (2012) 38 Philosophy and Social Criticism 680.

Offe, C., 'The European Model of "Social" Capitalism: Can it Survive European Integration?', in M. Miller (ed.) *Worlds of Capitalism* (London: Routledge, 2005).

O'Leary, S., 'Developing an Ever Closer Union Between the Peoples of Europe?' (2008) Edinburgh Mitchell Working Papers 6/2008.

O'Leary, S., 'The Curious Case of Frontier Workers and Study Finance: Giersch' (2014) 51 CML Rev 601.

Orlandini, G., 'Right to Strike, Transnational Collective Action and European Law: Time to Move On?' (2007) 8 Jean Monnet Working Paper.

Parker, O., *Cosmopolitan Government in Europe* (Abingdon: Routledge, 2013).

Pattie, C., Seyd, P., and Whitely, P., *Citizenship in Britain: Values, Participation and Democracy* (Cambridge: CUP, 2004).

Pechar, H., and Andres, L., 'Higher-Education Policies and Welfare Regimes: International Comparative Perspectives' (2011) 24 Higher Education Policy 25.

Peck, B., 'Compulsory Schooling in Europe' (1995) 76 Phi Delta Kappan 616.
Peers, S., 'Equal Treatment of Atypical Workers: A New Frontier for EU Law?' (2013) 32 Yearbook of European Law 30.
Pennings, F., 'Inclusion and Exclusion of Persons and Benefits in the New Co-ordination Regulation', in M. Dougan and E. Spaventa (eds.), *Social Welfare and EU Law* (Oxford: Hart, 2005).
Pennings, F., *European Social Security Law* (Cambridge: Intersentia, 2010).
Pescatore, P., 'The Doctrine of Direct Effect: An Infant Disease of Community Law' (1983) 8 ELRev 158.
Piore, M., 'Labor Standards and Business Strategies', in S. Hersenberg and J. Perez-Lopez (eds.), *Labor Standards and Development in the Global Economy* (Washington, DC: US Department of Labor, 1990).
Piris, J. C., *The Future of Europe: Towards a 2-Speed EU?* (Cambridge: CUP, 2012).
Polanyi, K., *The Great Transformation* (Boston, Mass.: Beacon, 2002).
Rawls, J., *A Theory of Justice* (Oxford: OUP, 1971).
Reich, N., 'Free Movement v. Social Rights in an Enlarged Union—The Laval and Viking Cases before the ECJ' (2008) 9 GLJ 141.
Rennuy, N., 'The Emergence of a Parallel System of Social Security Coordination' (2013) 50 CML Rev 1234.
Risse, T., *A Community of Europeans? Transnational Identities and Public Spheres* (New York: Cornell University Press, 2010).
Rodrik, D., *The Globalisation Paradox—Democracy and the Future of the World Economy* (New York: W. Norton, 2011).
Rosanvallon, P., *The Society of Equals* (Cambridge, Mass.: Harvard University Press, 2013).
Ruger, J., *Health and Social Justice* (Oxford: OUP, 2009).
Sandel, M., *Liberalism and the Limits of Justice* (Cambridge: CUP, 1998).
Sangiovanni, A., 'Global Justice, Reciprocity and the State' (2007) 35 Philosophy & Public Affairs 19.
Sangiovanni, A., 'Justice and the Priority of Politics to Morality' (2008) 16 Journal of Political Philosophy 137.
Sangiovanni, A., 'Solidarity in the European Union' (2013) 33 OJLS 220.
Sayde, A., 'One Law, Two Competitions: An Enquiry into the Contradictions of Free Movement Law' (2011) 13 CYELS 370.
Sayde, A., *Abuse of EU Law and Regulation of the Internal Market* (Oxford: Hart, 2014).
Schäfer, A., and Streeck, W., *Politics in the Age of Austerity* (Cambridge: Polity, 2013).
Scharpf, F., *Governing in Europe: Effective and Democratic* (Oxford: OUP, 1999).
Scharpf, F., 'Legitimacy in the Multi-Level European Polity', in M. Loughlin and P. Dobner (eds.), *The Twilight of Constitutionalism* (Oxford: OUP, 2010).
Scharpf, F., 'The Asymmetry of European Integration, or: Why the EU Cannot be a "Social Market Economy"' (2010) 8 Socioeconomic Review 218.
Scharpf, F., 'Monetary Union, Fiscal Crisis and the Preemption of Democracy' (2011) 36 LEQS.

Scharpf, F., 'Political Legitimacy in a Non-optimal Currency Area', in O. Cramme and S. Hobolt (eds.), *Democratic Politics in a European Union under Stress* (Oxford: OUP, 2014).

Schepel, H., 'Constitutionalising the Market, Marketising the Constitution, and to Tell the Difference: On the Horizontal Application of the Free Movement Provisions in EU Law' (2012) 18 ELJ 177.

Schiek, D., 'Age Discrimination before the ECJ—Conceptual and Theoretical Issues' (2011) 48 CML Rev 777.

Schmidt, S., 'When Efficiency Results in Redistribution: The Conflict over the Single Services Market' (2009) 32 West European Politics 855.

Schnapper, D., *Community of Citizens: On the Modern Idea of Nationality* (New Brunswick: Transaction, 1995).

Schumpeter, J., *Capitalism, Socialism and Democracy* (London: Routledge, 2010).

Sellars, J., *Stoicism* (Chesham: Acumen, 2006).

Sen, A., *The Idea of Justice* (Cambridge, Mass.: Harvard University Press, 2009; Basingstoke: Penguin, 2010).

Sen, A., 'Plural Utility' (1981) 81 Proceedings of the Aristotelian Society 193.

Sen, A., *Rationality and Freedom* (Cambridge, Mass.: Harvard University Press, 2002).

Shutte, A., 'Politics and the Ethics of *Ubuntu*', in M. F. Murove (ed.), *African Ethics: An Anthology of Comparative and Applied Ethics* (Scottsville: Kwazulu-Natal Press, 2009).

Simitis, S., and Lyon-Caen, A., 'Community Labour Law: A Critical Introduction to its History', in P. Davies, A. Lyon-Caen, S. Sciarra, and S. Simitis (eds.), *European Community Labour Law: Principles and Perspectives* (Oxford: Clarendon, 1996).

Shanks, M., 'The Social Policy of the European Communities' (1977) 14 CML Rev 375.

Smith, A. D., *The Ethnic Origin of States* (Oxford: Blackwell, 1988).

Smith, Adam, *An Inquiry into the Nature and Causes of the Wealth of Nations* [1776] (Oxford: Clarendon, 1976).

Snell, J., 'The Internal Market and the Philosophies of Market Integration', in C. Barnard and S. Peers, *European Union Law* (Oxford: OUP, 2014).

Somek, A., 'Solidarity Decomposed: Being and Time in European Citizenship' (2007) 32 ELRev 807.

Somek, A., *Engineering Equality* (Oxford: OUP, 2011).

Somek, A., 'The Social Question in Transnational Context' (2011) LEQS 39.

Somek, A., 'The Darling Dogma of Bourgeois Europeanists' (2014) 19 ELJ 688.

Stjernø, S., *Solidarity in Europe: the History of an Idea* (Cambridge: CUP, 2005).

Streeck, W., 'Citizenship Under Regime Competition: The Case of the "European Works Councils"', (1997) 5 EIoP No. 3.

Streeck, W., 'The Crises of Democratic Capitalism' (2011) 71 NLR 26.

Streeck, W., 'Taking Capitalism Seriously: Towards an Institutionalist Approach to Contemporary Political Economy' (2011) 9 Socioeconomic Review 158.

Streeck, W., 'How Will Capitalism End?' (2014) 87 NLR 40.

Suk, J., 'From Anti Discrimination to Equality: Stereotypes and the Life Cycle in the United States and Europe' (2011) 60 American Journal of Comparative Law 75.

Tan, K. C., *Justice without Borders* (Cambridge: CUP, 2004).

Terzi, L., 'The Capability to be Educated', in M. Walker and E. Unterhalter (eds.), *Amartya Sen's Capability Approach and Social Justice in Education* (Basingstoke: Palgrave, 2007).

Thomas, E., 'Who Belongs?: Competing Conceptions of Political Membership' (2002) 5 European Journal of Social Theory 329.

Tilly, C., *Democracy* (Cambridge: CUP, 2007).

Toebes, B., 'The Right to Health as a Human Right in International Law', in A. Eide, C. Krause, and A. Rosas (eds.), *Economic, Cultural and Social Rights* (The Hague: Kluwer, 2001).

Unger, R., *The Left Alternative* (London: Verso, 2009).

Van der Mei, A. P., *Free Movement of Persons within the European Community* (Oxford: Hart, 2003).

Voltaire, *Candide, ou L'Optimisme* (New York: Penguin, 2006).

Von Hayek, F., *The Constitution of Liberty* (Chicago: University of Chicago Press, 1978).

Waldron, J., 'Special Ties and Natural Duties' (1993) 22 Philosophy and Public Affairs 3.

Waldron, J., 'Cosmopolitan Norms', in S. Benhabib, *Another Cosmopolitanism* (Oxford: OUP, 2006).

Webb, S., and Webb, B., *Industrial Democracy* [1897] (Basingstoke: Palgrave Macmillan, 2003).

Webb, S., and Webb, B., *Labour Law and Freedom* (London: Lawrence & Wishart, 1995).

Weiler, J. H. H., 'Van Gend en Loos: The Individual as Subject and Object and the Dilemma of European Legitimacy' (2014) 12 ICON 94.

Weiler, J. H. H., and Lockhart, N., '"Taking Rights Seriously" Seriously: The European Court of Justice and its Fundamental Rights Jurisprudence' (1995) 32 CML Rev 604.

Willemse, N., and De Boer, P., 'Three Worlds of Educational Welfare State? A Comparative Study of Higher Education Across Welfare States' (2012) 22 Journal of European Social Policy 115.

Wilkinson, M., 'The Specter of Authoritarian Liberalism: Reflections on the Constitutional Crisis of the European Union' (2013) 14 GLJ 527.

Williams, A., *The Ethos of Europe* (Cambridge: CUP, 2010).

Wilthagen, T., and Tros, F., 'The Concept of "Flexicurity": A New Approach to Regulating Employment and Labour Markets' (2004) 10 European Review of Labour and Research 215.

Wright, M., and Reeskens, T., 'Of What Cloth are the Ties that Bind? National Identity and Support for the Welfare State across 29 European Countries' (2013) 20 JEPP 1443.

Žižek, S., 'Eastern Europe's Republic of Gilead', in C. Mouffe (ed.), *Dimensions of Radical Democracy: Pluralism, Citizenship, Community* (London: Verso, 1992).

INDEX

The manufacturer's authorised representative in the EU for product safety is Oxford University Press España S.A. of el Parque Empresarial San Fernando de Henares, Avenida de Castilla, 2 – 28830 Madrid (www.oup.es/en or product.safety@oup.com). OUP España S.A. also acts as importer into Spain of products made by the manufacturer.

www.ingramcontent.com/pod-product-compliance
Lightning Source LLC
LaVergne TN
LVHW011756200926
848484LV00003B/723
* 9 7 8 0 1 9 8 7 2 4 3 4 6 *